DUNROAMIN

HARROW WEALD.
BENGARTH DRIVE (off Whitefriars Drive).

HARROW & WEALDSTONE STATION.

(Bakerloo & L.M.S.)
12 minutes.

L. G. O. C. Omnibus passes Estate.

MORTGAGE TERMS:

FREEHOLD £875.

A Mortgage of £828 can be obtained.

LEASEHOLD £740.

A Mortgage of £691 4s will be granted.

One of Several Designs.

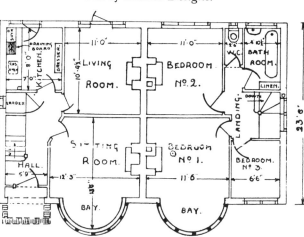

Garage.

Most houses have space for garage.

Builders will erect at very low cost.

Plots vary from 80 ft. to 140 ft.

Built on slope, in exceptionally high position.

PRICES [*ALL SEMI-DETACHED*]:
LEASEHOLD £740.   FREEHOLD £875.
ALL LEASES 99 YEARS AT £7 10s. PER ANNUM.

No Road Charges.

DUNROAMIN

The Suburban Semi and its Enemies

Paul Oliver · Ian Davis · Ian Bentley

Barrie & Jenkins

London Melbourne Sydney Auckland Johannesburg

This book is dedicated to the 76,112 builders
who created the four million houses of pre-War
Dunroamin

Barrie & Jenkins Ltd

An imprint of the Hutchinson Publishing Group

17–21 Conway Street, London W1P 6HL

Hutchinson Group (Australia) Pty Ltd
30–32 Cremorne Street, Richmond South, Victoria 3121
PO Box 151, Broadway, New South Wales 2007

Hutchinson Group (NZ) Ltd
32–34 View Road, PO Box 40–086, Glenfield, Auckland 10

Hutchinson Group (SA) (Pty) Ltd
PO Box 337, Bergvlei 2012, South Africa

First published 1981
© Paul Oliver, Ian Bentley, Ian Davis 1981

Filmset in Perpetua by
Willmer Brothers Limited, Birkenhead, Merseyside

Printed in Great Britain by the Anchor Press
and bound by Wm Brendon & Son
both of Tiptree, Essex

British Library Cataloguing in Publication Data
Oliver, Paul
    Dunroamin.
    1. Great Britain–Suburbs and environment–History
    I. Davis, Ian   II. Bentley, Ian
    306.7′4′0941   HN386
ISBN 0 09 145930 3

FRONTISPIECE
From 'A Brochure of the Well-Built Freehold and Leasehold Houses
erected at Harrow Weald and Wembley by Mr Arthur Thornborough',
c. 1930. (*The Grange Museum, Brent Library Service*)

CONTENTS

ACKNOWLEDGEMENTS

This book arose from a series of lectures under the title *Semi-Detached* given by the authors to students in the Department of Architecture, Oxford Polytechnic in the Spring Term, 1979. Graham Paul Smith of the Department staff was actively engaged in the programme and the ensuing work, and we are indebted to him for his extensive photographic coverage of the subject, including many photographs in this book. The lectures were augmented by seminars, field studies and student work. Some of the new material obtained has been included here, and we wish to express our thanks to Daniel Forshaw, Colin George, Kevin Hemmings, Paul Johnson and David Pickles, students on the course who have assisted us. We are also grateful for the advice and comments of a number of our colleagues, including Laura Cohn and David Whitham, while emphasising that the opinions expressed here are our own.

Several academics have been generous with their time, advice, and the opportunity to make use of their files and libraries and we particularly wish to thank Dr Valentine Cunningham, Dean of Corpus Christi College, Oxford, Dr John Goldthorpe, Official Fellow, Nuffield College, and Dennis Sharp of the Architectural Association in this connection. We have also had valuable assistance from the staff of the Library and Slide Library of the Architectural Association, the staff of the Oxford City Library, Local History Collection, the Local Studies Librarian, Uxbridge Library, and staff of the BBC Hulton Picture Library.

Much of the work involved interviews with past and present residents of Dunroamin, the majority of whom would prefer to remain anonymous; to them our warmest thanks and hopes that we have not misrepresented their world in the Twenties and Thirties. Special thanks are due, however, to Brenda and Tony Innes, William and Elsie Johnson and Mrs D. I. Oliver, who have helped in many ways.

To our wives Iva, Judy and Val, we owe a special debt of gratitude for their patience and forbearance during the past couple of years. Iva Bentley and Val Oliver helped with the typing of the manuscript and to them, and to Jean Smith and Joy Cipriano, our thanks for their work – often under pressure.

Finally we wish to thank the many publishers, copyright-holders and owners of illustrative material who have generously permitted their use here.

INTRODUCTION

Paul Oliver

DUNROAMIN – a declaration to the world that a family has settled in the home of its choice; an innocent exposure of poor taste and puerile humour; or the epitome of middle-class bourgeois complacency?

DUNROAMIN – a real place, or no place; a suburban home, or a symbol of Suburbia? The name may be seen on a plate on the wall of any house in any suburb, and how we respond to it is a reflection of our values.

This book is about values; more specifically, it is about the conflict of values of those who choose to live in the English suburbs and of those who work in the professional and educational milieu of architecture and planning.

About half of the population of Britain lives in the suburbs. Of these the largest proportion lives in houses which are semi-detached, three-bedroomed dwellings, though many dwell in terraces of two- and three-bedroomed villas, in bungalows and in detached houses. But the suburbs are more than the aggregations of houses and bungalows; they comprise complexes of roads, shopping centres, public utilities from post-offices to church halls, cul-de-sacs and crescents, arterial roads and avenues. They add up to a substantial proportion of the entire built environment of Britain.

A building phenomenon of such an extent, and with so great an impact on the built forms of the country, should have, one might suppose, a profound effect upon the nature of architectural and planning education. But it is certain that the study of the suburban environment has played no significant part in such education. The conspicuousness of the suburbs is only exceeded by the conspicuous neglect which they have suffered from architectural press and practice; a neglect that is considerable but not total; references to the suburbs do occur in architectural writings, but the positions that are taken are markedly at variance with those expressed within the suburbs themselves.

It can be argued that there is no reason why a designer should be interested in the semi in the suburb; it is not his responsibility to be involved with 'bad' building but to create good architecture. As suburban semis are neither architect-designed nor made respectable/acceptable by tradition, they are, almost by definition, bad buildings. And, as the agglomeration of semi-detached houses leads inevitably to soul-destroying monotony, there is no justification for the planner to be concerned with them; in fact, his profession was established, in part, to oppose suburban growth. Such a point of view would find adherents among the majority of architects and planners, not only in Britain but in nations throughout the world whose industrial, commercial and communications growth has encouraged large middle-class populations to live within reach of the major city centres.

It is tempting, and certainly easier, to consider all suburbs as essentially similar, varying only in size and shape, location and topography, and only different perhaps in details of buildings, or the mix of detached and semi-detached houses, bungalows or chalets. Taken overall, they might be regarded as being much the same in kind and character, inhabited by people of a single class with similar tastes and modest aspirations. But is a generalised picture of the suburbs an accurate one?

Suburbs may be identified as having certain common characteristics and may be crudely classified into broad types. This David Thorns has done, sketching a typology of eight categories which correspond to working-class and middle-class divisions and which are, in both classes, characterised as planned residential, unplanned residential, planned industrial and unplanned industrial.[1] Though these groupings, and the sub-divisions that might be developed from them, may assist in defining common features they do not come close to the specifics of identity in any one suburb. To this the answer may be that there is little sense of identity in the suburb; certainly one of the most frequent epithets is 'soul-destroying anonymity', or a version of it: 'Anywheresville/Nowheresville'.[2]

Until high-rise slabs of apartment accommodation and 'towers within the park' were developed by mid-twentieth century architects and planners, suburbs were typified by low-rise, low-density developments which spread out from the cities along communication routes to penetrate deeply, and eventually to obliterate the rural environs. Their growth was accelerated by industrialisation in the nineteenth century, and further encouraged by centralisation of administration and commerce in the capital and major cities of the industrialised world. Many factors influenced their shape, size and form which were environmental, as well as man-made and man-engendered, so that the largest suburbs are not necessarily around the highest concentrations of industrial and commercial endeavour. To many, the five thousand square miles of Los Angeles epitomise the endlessly expanding suburbanised city. With suburbs spreading to the horizons Brisbane claims to be the largest city in the world under a single municipal authority, but its houses bear no resemblance to those of Birmingham. They are as far removed from those of an English suburb as they are from those around Paris, or any other of a few score European cities, even if parallels for individual buildings can generally be found.

Yet we identify all these areas as suburbs. The plot sizes tend to be fairly uniform: often six or up to a dozen to the acre among those owned by the average wage-earner; the houses perhaps standing alone in a half, or even an acre of ground in the suburbs of the more affluent. Industries are seldom seen among them; golf courses are often closer at hand than are factories. But there are corner shops serving the neighbourhood and big stores can be reached by private or public transport in the downtown areas. Progressively, the opening of malls and precincts and large, drive-in shopping centres to serve the weekly needs of the suburbs are to be found throughout the United States and Canada, often in Australia, and with increasing frequency in Europe, including England.

English suburbs though, are different in many subtle, not easily describable ways, and in some ways that are distinguishing and obvious. Of the latter, quite the most significant is the prevalence of the three-bedroomed, semi-detached house. The 'suburban semi' is a cliché which summons up a mental picture of rows of red-roofed, rough-cast pairs of houses, each with its bay windows, its porched entrance, its 'third bedroom' above. It recalls images of small front gardens and bigger rear ones, side garages and garden gates, in endless succession. To D. H. Lawrence the houses were 'horrid little red mantraps'; to W. H. Auden and Christopher Isherwood at the height of the 1930s building boom they were 'Isolated from each other like cases of fever'.[3] A large proportion of the suburbs was built in the decade before the outbreak of the Second World War, and it is these, unsung and unpraised, but by no means unloved, which we have collectively designated as Dunroamin. But before the peculiarities and the values of Dunroamin can be discussed, it is necessary first to review briefly the growth of the English suburb.

It is the sheer scale of suburban growth in the first half of this century that makes it susceptible to generalisations, with suburbs spreading over hectares of former farmland to the dismay of planners and observers. The factors that influenced their spread were not wholly related to the movement of populations from rural areas to the city: the clearance of slums, the re-location of the inhabitants of inferior workers' homes and the development of new, more spacious estates further from the city centres, and the drift to South-East England from areas in economic decline, combined to redistribute the population and

Ripe for Development – Hillingdon's fields await the building of
superior houses 'close to Met. Station' (London Borough of Hillingdon)

The advancing suburbs. Building supplies being delivered by horse and
cart to a new site at Ruislip, c. 1930 (from Dennis F. Edwards, *Metro Memories*)

enlarge the compass of the cities without significantly adding to the overall population. So Manchester's two million population in 1900 grew by only 9 per cent in the following decade, principally through natural increase. There were only eleven thousand more people by 1921, scarcely sixty thousand more ten years later when the population stood at 2,427,000. In the ensuing score of years, the period of greatest suburban expansion overall, it actually decreased while in T. W. Freeman's analysis of the 1951 census report the number of occupied houses grew by 22 per cent from 600,000 to 738,400. Within Manchester city itself over the same twenty-year period the 700,000 inhabitants had fallen by some 36,000, though the city buildings now covered twice the area.[4] Similar statistics may be produced to illustrate the suburban growth of cities and towns throughout England and Wales.[5]

Though the growth of the suburbs was steadily increasing throughout the first decades of the century, it was considerably accelerated in the Twenties and after the Depression. By far the greatest numerical increases occurred in Greater London, which added to its 7,250,000 population of 1911, two million people in the subsequent twenty years. A fifth of the population of England and Wales now lived in Greater London and more than a quarter of all urban dwellers in the country were located in this one area. While the population of central London slightly declined the suburbs spread dramatically, with the outer ring of the city growing from three million to nearly four in the Twenties. Encouraged by the policies of the London Passenger Transport Board, the suburban railway lines extended ever more deeply into the country. Fastest growing was the Metropolitan Line, for which there were plans for a link with the Midlands, though its eventual limit was Aylesbury in Hertfordshire. Expansion of the Underground system 'over-ground' further consolidated the new suburbs. In West London many areas increased rapidly in the ten years before 1931, Hendon doubling by over 100 per cent to 115,000. Hayes increased its population one and a half times, Wembley trebled, while Kingsbury increased from a small community of some two thousand people to eight times its former size.[6] In the following decade the rates of growth were even greater.

Some 150,000 houses were being built on average each year during the Twenties, of which, in England, a quarter were built by local authorities. During the following ten years the graph rose steeply, reaching some 200,000 new houses per annum even in the worst years of the Depression and rising by 1936 to a peak just short of 350,000.[7] Until the outbreak of the Second World War the rate was well in excess of 300,000 a year, a figure not attained again until the Sixties. Though the precise figures vary, between 4,170,000 and 4,300,000 houses were built between the wars, of which some 2,700,000 were built in the Thirties. They comprised over a third of total housing stock in Britain.

Who were the migrants to the new suburbs, and what were their occupations? It must be remembered that by 1931 there were 51 towns in Britain with over 100,000 people, and the range of occupations was broad; the Census identified some 30,000 separate modes of employment. While many of the new suburban families had moved out from the central cities and their breadwinners were still employed in the same jobs, large numbers moved from the rural areas and other regions. Over 56 per cent of the population of Middlesex, where the expansion of Greater London was particularly marked, were born outside the county. Neighbours in adjacent roads in a typical Middlesex suburb, North Harrow, in the late 1930s, by way of example, included: insurance agent, railway clerk, builder, accountant, solicitor, commercial traveller, hairdresser, Marine sergeant, stockbroker, bank teller, theatre box-office manager, LMS railway inspector, schoolteacher, post-office clerk, and several 'civil servants', or people with 'jobs in the City'.

Such a list is arbitrary but probably representative. It is illustrative of the predominance of middle middle-class, white-collar occupations among the wage-earners in the suburb. In 1931 over one and a half million people were employed in transport and communications, and almost as many in commerce; finance and insurance together accounted for more than a fifth of the entire work force. Great increases had taken place in banking and insurance during the Thirties, while the expansion of the suburbs generated employment in the transport industries, in the moving of goods, the selling and distribution of commodities of all kinds. At a time when agricultural workers were earning around thirty shillings a week and the average weekly wage in the nation as a whole was £2.15s.0d, Dunroamin's wage-earners were doing quite well: from £3 to £6 a week. It was enough to pay off the mortgage, save up to buy a car and take the family for a fortnight's holiday in Bognor even if it left few margins for other luxuries.

Not by any means were all Dunroamin's wage-earners working in the city centre; the suburbs required new facilities and services from the Post Office Telephones to the water companies. New shops were opening in the Jubilee shopping parades and every business in those pre-computer days required clerical staff. So too did the industries that had sprung up with electrification and improved rail services. Factories producing household appliances and everything for the automobile industry from sparking plugs to headlamps needed office workers. New arrivals in Dunroamin were usually in their late twenties or early thirties and their young families filled the new schools, giving employment to a growing army of teachers. They, like the nurses, were largely women, but in

Labour intensive building on a suburban housing estate; Becontree, 1924
(twelve men appear in the photograph) (BBC Hulton Picture Library)

Suburban low densities saved lives and property during the war. 1000-lb
bombs, V1s and V2s caused destruction, but adjacent houses gave the lie to
assertions of 'jerry-building'. Ruislip Manor, 1944 (Chaloner Collection,
London Borough of Hillingdon)

Dunroamin few women were out at work, the great majority preferring to stay at home to bring up their families.

Apart from accommodation, the scale of what was soon termed the 'housing boom' had other beneficial effects, with the rate of employment in the building industries and decorating trades rising to double that of other industries. And there were many spin-offs in increased employment in other servicing industries associated with building. Thus the boom substantially contributed to Britain's post-Depression recovery.[8] It also had the effect of reducing urban over-crowding, improving conditions of health and accommodation within the city. At the end of the First World War there were over 600,000 families without houses; within twenty years there was as large an excess of houses over families – an astonishing rate of recovery. Many of the surplus houses were now situated in areas where there were problems of unemployment; the suburbs on the other hand, were developing along communication routes which brought the breadwinners directly to their places of employment. According to Marian Bowley, local authorities built over a million houses in the two decades, while private enterprise, mainly in the form of small building firms, built nearly three million.[9] Of these about one in seven was built by private enterprise with government subsidy.

Housing figures rapidly become numbing and it is easy to forget that the house and the home are one to the occupying family; that the home is the focus of the family unit, the setting for eating and sleeping and loving and caring, for growing up and for retiring in. Statistics, nevertheless, are ammunition for Dunroamin's opponents, useful as supporting evidence to the maps that illustrate the extent of suburban sprawl and the layout of extensive developments built by speculative builders. Geographers' and planners' graphic conventions convey nothing of the quality of space or place; only at the most superficial level does the cartographer's map correspond with the mental one. Such maps are paralleled by the aerial photographs that so often accompany the brief discussions of the suburbs in the literature of architecture or planning, many of which have been taken to indicate the extent and the monotony of the housing forms, the fragmentation of the housing plans and the neglect of town-planning principles. At such elevations individual dwellings are reduced to ciphers, and rein-forcement is given to the arguments advanced by detractors of the suburb, observing with detachment the phenomena they describe. The view is not from the bay window or the rear garden but from the bomb bay and the rear gunner's seat. It was a view that thousands of men from the suburbs would experience in reality for the first time when they joined the armed services with the outbreak of war.

Edgware from the air in 1926. Some suburban developments have
been laid out in the fields near the village (Aerofilms Ltd)

Edgware in 1948. The site of the former photograph is to be found at
the road intersection, centre right. See also illustration following page
29 (Aerofilms Ltd)

Whether they were in the transports bringing the troops to the front line, whether they were women serving on home bases, civilians engaged in essential services or merely of an age before or beyond call-up, the people of Dunroamin were liable to hear and read the critical disapproval by the pundits of the very environments that they were fighting to defend. The values that helped to motivate and inspire the suburban dwellers, as they discarded mufti and donned military serge and worsteds, were not the values that inspired the architects and planners who had seen the suburbs expand. The many publications of the Forties which planned for 'a new Britain' after the war persistently emphasised the damage done by 'suburban sprawl'. It is some testimony to the security that the suburbs had engendered that this did not lead to schizophrenic attitudes to their home districts, though it must have promoted ambivalent ones.

There was no doubt in the minds of the writers that the suburb, uncontrolled and unplanned (by planners, that is), was an evil which had destroyed the amenities of the countryside, damaged the integrity of the city, and had created an environment lacking in human warmth or dignity. Writings by planners during and after the Second World War in particular, were united in their demand for planning controls and regulations, and had no hesitation in declaring that 'we must' exercise restrictions on development. Architects advocated new solutions to mass housing which would not be as damaging to the environment as the semis that had been built in millions between the wars. Their view had been conveyed to a large audience by Anthony Bertram, whose Pelican *Design*, published in 1938, was based on his popular series of radio talks, *Design in Everyday Things*.[10] He deplored the 'indiscriminate sprawling of our towns through ring after ring of shoddy suburb, to ribbon development and the commercial exploitation of our countryside'. But there was 'an alternative': the block of flats. Aware of public resistance to them he wrote:

> Many people think of modern flats as the old pre-war tenements, gloomy, stuffy, mechanical horrors . . . but the best flats being built today are a thousand miles from that. To begin with, many are not merely blocks of flats. They are villages, as it were, with some dwellings on the top of others. The most striking example in England, perhaps, is Quarry Hill, a block now being built in Leeds.[11]

Strongly influenced by the extensive housing blocks built in Vienna a decade before, R. A. H. Livett's Leeds scheme took five years to build and, to many socialist architects, was a symbol of the new city that would supplant the suburbs. Maxwell Fry, in 1941, gave it his unqualified approval, praising the 'new flats, laid out spaciously', which were to house a thousand families on the

23-acre site, where old housing had been demolished 'at one sweep'. [12] This was the model for post-war housing and an example of the bold measures that would have to be taken to ensure its development.

Many architects and planners contributed to the demands for a new housing policy in the post-war years which would not repeat the mistakes of the past, or the evil of unrestrained suburban sprawl. Endlessly and emphatically repeated, these appeals were heard by the sympathetic ears of the Attlee government. Over a million houses had been damaged in London alone, but the scale of destruction was even greater where smaller cities had been bombed: in Portsmouth 65,000 of the total housing stock of 70,000 were destroyed or damaged; in Hull, with some 93,000 houses, only 6,000 were unharmed. [13] Close on half a million houses were destroyed by enemy action, or beyond repair. 'This country needs 4,000,000 houses immediately', declared the pseudonymous Hugh Anthony in 1945; [14] it was to take about eighteen years to reach that figure. In the five years prior to the outbreak of hostilities private enterprise housing produced three times the number of units that were built under local authority auspices. Now the proportion was almost exactly reversed: a little over 126,000 houses were built by private enterprise in accordance with the severe restrictions imposed on the building industry. In the five years after the war some 432,000 houses were built under government, and local-government direction. [15]

New Town development corporations followed Garden City lines in the application of planning and architectural principles, but the dream of a modern world with cities of high rise apartment blocks as envisaged by Le Corbusier still glowed in the imaginations of progressive architects and planners: the 'City of Tomorrow' could be a reality today. Unashamedly modelled on Le Corbusier's Ville Radieuse and Unité d'Habitation, the slab blocks of the LCC estate at Roehampton for instance were part of a vast and celebrated scheme which provided housing for close on 10,000 people. One of the team that designed the slab blocks, the late William Howell, admitted that 'we went to Roehampton thinking we had a certain mission: we felt this would turn the tide back from the suburban dream . . . a return to the excitement of the city . . . . This is what we must do; we don't want to rush out and live in horrid little suburbs and semi-detached houses.' [16] Asked why they hated the suburban dream so much, Howell explained:

> because we felt that it discarded the positive things from the city and got very little in exchange. We saw this in terms of the fact that we wouldn't want to go and live there because everything from the bright lights to the art galleries, the continental restaurants,

Quarry Hill Flats, Leeds: originally designed to have 938 flats and
social facilities. Erected 1934–39; demolished 1979 (Leeds City
Council)

Oak and Eldon Gardens, Birkenhead. Demolished with the use of
controlled explosives, November 1979 (*Building Design*)

in short 'life', the thing one goes to the city for – it didn't seem to be happening out in the suburbs. [17]

Whatever it may have been as an architectural gesture, the experiment was a social failure. From the neglect of the ground level spaces and the congestion of unanticipated motor vehicles to the lack of casual encounters, the Roehampton blocks had many problems. But to the international architectural community this answer to the suburbs was a focus of attention and admiration. [18]

By the early Sixties most urban authorities had accepted high-rise developments as the solution for housing needs. They were ready to apply the minimum standards of the 1961 Parker Morris Report as a virtual design tool rather than as a guide to necessary levels of space provision and heating. Extensive schemes were being built, or were on the drawing board, like Park Hill and, subsequently, Hyde Park, Sheffield, which were developed on the scale prepared by Quarry Hill.

The collapse of a corner of the Ronan Point flats in 1968 dramatically and tragically signalled the failure of the industrialised, formula-designed building on which so many authorities had depended. But it was not until the Seventies that some architects at any rate were forced to admit that the high-rise blocks had been socially disastrous. In the United States the lesson had been painfully learned in St Louis, where Yamasaki's award-winning housing scheme for disadvantaged blacks had generated so many problems that the city authorised the blowing up with explosives of the entire project. [19] Since then, several blocks in Britain have suffered the same fate, like Oak Gardens and Eldon Gardens in Birkenhead on Merseyside, and, with bitter irony, the brave pioneering development of Quarry Hill itself; the self-same model of a bright future which was to provide the 'cheerful, healthy conditions, which only proper planning can ensure'. [20]

High-rise was not the only form of post-war housing to gain local-authority or government support: local authorities also promoted low-rise, compact housing estates, often in the form of terraces. Ministry of Housing loans subsidised such developments by housing associations. The application of industrialised systems was pervasive in this area too, with 40 per cent of all local authority building being of this type by 1969, and some three hundred rival systems competing for contracts. [21] Speculative builders learned that simplified designs 'without frills' won the approval of local authorities, and they discovered too, that the severe shortfall in housing meant that people on housing waiting lists needed a home too much to afford to be choosy.

Though some architects endeavoured to relieve the colourless appearance of terrace rows, with low-pitched roofs and chimney stacks eliminated, their efforts often achieved little. Standardisation won out against individuality. Planners and local-authority architects have, in the past couple of decades, enjoyed unprecedented power, specifying the colour of doors, in some cases even of curtains, in the interests of 'the total composition'. House-owners were, and are, effectively inhibited from expressing their individualism in such schemes, even the front gardens having been dispensed with and communal grass areas adopted in many housing estates. Modern Movement architects were successful, in the post-war years, in affecting housing policies for the reconstruction of the cities and the development of the New Towns. But their efforts at social engineering through architecture neither saved the tower blocks nor provided an antidote to the 'New Town blues'.

And Dunroamin?

The war brought an end, not to the suburbs but to the building of the kind of suburbs that Dunroamin represented. In spite of the invective against the 'sprawl' which planners so deplored, Dunroamin was not demolished, either by Hitler or by the planners. Its low-density housing proved an effective defence against the bombs of the Luftwaffe and the V2s, and there would have been little support for destroying what Germany failed to do, even in the name of Post War Britain. Yet the way of life which Dunroamin had so ideally accommodated had gone with the war; the suburbs of the early Fifties may have been somewhat similar to their pre-war counterparts but, with the advance of the next decade, dramatic social changes, higher wages, mass media and increasing personal mobility through the motorcar, the suburbs changed. In this context it would not be surprising to have seen reflected in the physical nature of Dunroamin the upheaval that had taken place in society. If Dunroamin had avoided degenerating into slums before the advent of the war, afterwards, perhaps, it might have declined rapidly. If it were as socially sterile, as culturally impoverished, as self-deceptive, as much a prison and potential slum as pundit and satirist agreed, it would have been far from unreasonable to anticipate total social collapse. And if the buildings were so tasteless and uneconomic, so jerry-built and poorly designed for appropriate living in the Thirties, there would seem to be little hope for their survival in the Sixties, or the Eighties.

But Dunroamin, though not rebuilt in its own image, survived in its original form – survived, and flourished. While the corridors and lifts of tower blocks were vandalised; while foyers and staircases were spaces to be feared; while mothers were divided from their children by several floors or obliged to pen their infants for fear of their falling from high balconies; while litter and broken windows, stoved-in doors, peeling paint and falling plaster proclaimed the physical decay of buildings and environments that had barely lasted a score of years; while the despairing aerosol graffiti proclaimed anger, frustration and boredom – Dunroamin continued to provide homes and neighbourhoods which displayed, in no significant degree, any of these signs of failure.

In part this reflects the fact that suburban semis were largely privately owned, and almost wholly so after the passing of the Rent Acts. Tower-block flats were rented and did not inspire the protective instincts that are expressed in pride of ownership. But there were other factors, such as the poor conditions for supervision or the lack of provision of 'defensible space', that were directly related to the physical form of tower blocks. To cultivate and to maintain his own garden, to define his own territory, and to open his front door are ambitions that can be achieved by almost any houseowner, but these simple and basic requirements remained unsatisfied in thousands of flats.

It is all the more surprising, in view of the evident success of the suburbs built between the wars to provide a satisfactory, and satisfying, home environment for so many millions of people over so long a period, that they have been so summarily dismissed. Post-war housing in all its forms has had innumerable advocates, but Dunroamin has had few writers in the architectural, or even the sociological field, who have had a good word in its favour. One of the few was J. M. Richards, whose *Castles on the Ground* was written during the war and published soon after. [22] 'The book was scorned by my contemporaries, as either an irrelevant eccentricity or a betrayal of the forward-looking ideals of the Modern Movement, to which the suburbs were supposed to be the absolute antithesis', he recalled in 1980. [23]

Through the 1970s the inadequacies of the Modern Movement received growing attention. An 'International Style', which had its foundations in the writings of Le Corbusier, the teachings of the Bauhaus and the profound influence of expatriate continental designers in Britain and the United States, it was seen to have had many weaknesses after half a century of theory and practice. The wholesale application of functionalist principles has led to many social problems and created clashes of style where Modern Movement buildings have been inappropriate to their context. The 'Post-Modernist' debate that has marked the passing of the Modern Movement as an apparently consistent theory of architecture, has cautiously inspired approaches to architecture based on revised concepts. [24] In many cases these are no more than the concepts of the Modern Movement expressed in a new formalism. More significant has been a new eclecticism which draws liberally, though tentatively, on the forms, styles and sometimes the theories, of the past or of contemporary exotic cultures. Another tendency has been towards a neo-vernacular style, which derives its forms from a tradition developed outside the framework of a formalised architecture. And there are others.

These tendencies, though drawing inspiration from a wider span than hitherto in the past sixty years, are not reinforced by a consistent theory. The shock-wave that is being felt through architectural practice and education as the successes and failures of the Modern Movement are being examined, makes this a particularly important time for a reconsideration of the suburb.

In our view, developed in this book, the values that have shaped attitudes to the suburb are themselves due for scrutiny. While it is not claimed that an appraisal of the suburbs would of itself create a consistent theory for a developing architecture, it is our contention that such an evaluation would be important in the shaping of one. Part of the problem of the Modern Movement was the separation of its architects and planners from community values. Through their total adherence to a single ideology, much was rejected which now merits re-examination. This is particularly so where the suburbs are concerned, for the success of their buildings and their stability as communities, while not demonstrable in every case, is still sufficiently widespread to demand serious attention.

Whereas recent writing on the suburbs has been directed to their study as an historical phenomenon, our intentions are different. We perceive the problems of recognising and understanding the suburbs as the result of opposing values. Those values whereby the architecture of the Modern Movement, and the adoption of its theories, was eventually to shape post-war housing policy, were fundamentally different in kind from those which shaped Dunroamin. We believe that it is important to endeavour to understand what the values of the architectural establishment were, and why the suburbs were seen as such a threat to them; to know more of the values of the builders and developers who gave the suburbs their shape. It is necessary to ascertain what values the intending house purchasers sought in the buildings they bought, and to discover, insofar as this is possible, the standards by which they lived that made the suburban house so appropriate a dwelling. We have found that much of this material is already irreclaimable and that, with each passing year, the distance between the present and the vital years in which Dunroamin was shaped makes recall more difficult.

Semi-detached houses have been the subject of frequent criticism of Dunroamin's design and details. Considering them fundamental to Dunroamin's character we have paid them particular attention. Comparison of housing built by private enterprise and the contemporary council estates has revealed significant ways in which the householders of Dunroamin's semis were able to exercise choice in details and to use them as vehicles for expression of individual taste. These planes of choice we have considered in terms of the imagery which the owners have built into them, and have suggested ways in which the symbolism of both the external elements and the internal furnishing of the home were expressive of the values of the suburban family.

In presenting this appraisal of opposing values and the pre-war English suburbs it is not our intention to deny that many of them are vast and unrelieved, or that there are many that are dull and lacking in stimulation. Not all suburban areas are of equal merit, nor are they all equally successful in supporting a sense of community and belonging. Alienation occurs and loneliness is a problem; the uniformity of some speculative housing developments has inhibited individual expression. It would be foolish to disregard the fact that in many of the suburbs planning defects have been glaring; the streets of Dunroamin are sometimes long and monotonous, others may be unnecessarily narrow, tortuous or confined. Ribbon developments and unplanned, loose and minimally controlled speculative housing have led to suburban forms that have been meandering, wasteful, uninspired.

Nevertheless, we contend that many suburbs deserve respect and repay careful examination. We do not suggest that this discussion is representative of the suburbs as a whole, nor even of the Thirties' suburbs of Dunroamin. No claim is made that the examples chosen are typical all over England. If the monotony and 'same-ness' that makes one suburb indistinguishable from another (which has been the substance of many criticisms of Dunroamin) has any basis in fact, the examples given should typify all other suburbs. But if, as we believe, each suburb has its own identity, no single work can hope to be representative. In compiling this book we have drawn on suburbs of which, by virtue of upbringing, residence or continued contact, we have first-hand experience — suburbs which happen to be in North-West London and in Oxford.

It seems likely that the vociferous critics of Dunroamin had no personal experience of the suburbs, had not lived in them, and drew their conclusions from the railway carriage window on the way to their rural retreats. 'The trouble is,' said Gertrude Stein about Oakland, 'when you get "there", there's no "there" there.' Her aphorism was witty, but was it true? It was the view from the city centre. To go 'there', to the suburb, required an effort of will and an unfamiliar excursion.

This book, then, is by way of an excursion to Dunroamin, made with the intention of discovering the relationship of its values to its built form. It is focused on the period between the wars, when these suburbs grew, and when they were occupied by a new generation of middle-class householders. This was the period when the Modern Movement made its initial impact on a select but vociferous body of architects in Britain, whose values were far removed from those of the Dunroaminers.

The following chapters discuss different facets of the conflicts of values between architects, planners, builders and developers, local authorities and the residents of the new suburbs. They are therefore concurrent in content, rather than historically sequential, seeking to show how these values were expresssed. For example, in Chapter 1 Ian Davis examines the ideological and aesthetic basis of Modern Movement opposition to the suburbs, but in Chapter 2 Ian Bentley identifies other motivations for this hostility. Or again, in Chapter 6 Ian Bentley shows how the processes of choice and adaptation were made possible by the forms and fittings of the inter-war semi-detached house, whereas Chapters 7 and 8 are concerned with how these elements became vehicles for the expression of Dunroamin's values.

For us, this excursion has been an educative experience. And we believe the lessons to be learned from it could have significant implications for the practice of architecture in the future.

ONE OF THE GREATEST EVILS...

Dunroamin and the Modern Movement

Ian Davis

ON my first day in a school of architecture I handed my tutor the usual form indicating name, age and home address: Hillside Drive, Edgware, Middlesex. He read my form and gave me a probing stare, followed by: 'I take it that you live in one of Edgware's semi-detached houses?' My affirmative prompted the observation that I should make early plans to move to a more civilised address, such as Camden Town. Later the same morning the First Year were gathered together for an initial briefing on the course and Modern Architecture in general. We were strongly recommended to find out about a Swiss architect called Le Corbusier, 'the greatest living architect in the world'. We were advised to read his books and visit his buildings as soon as possible. Thus, before our first coffee break, the process of indoctrination was well under way. Architecture in 1953 was to do with great events that happened in Marseilles (or for that matter Camden Town), but very definitely not in Edgware, Middlesex.

The suburbs had been a thread of continuity that tied together the very different locations of Barrow-in-Furness, Leeds, Ashford in Middlesex, and Edgware where my childhood had been spent. The landscape of back garden, house, front garden, pavement, grass verge, street, shopping parade and public park had been received without any judgment. It was neither good, bad, nor indifferent; merely the normal way of life. My neutrality was not shared by my parents, relatives and neighbours, all of whom seemed well satisfied with both homes and their settings.

Therefore, there was a persistent dilemma in those early months of my architectural course as to who was correct – home or tutor? My tutor's views were echoed by other staff and, perhaps more significantly, by fellow students. Their attitudes ranged from affectionate disdain to outright contempt. I recall thinking hard before inviting any friends home to such a place as Edgware. Inevitably, as a result of exposure to such criticism and group pressure, my initial questionings were soon swept aside. The credos of Modern Architecture assumed a control of my mind and drawing board which lasted for all of fifteen years. This blinkered attitude had significant consequences on my appreciation of any architectural expression that failed · to conform to the prevailing functionalism of the Fifties. One victim was Victorian architecture; but more serious casualties were the 'other traditions' which ran in parallel with pioneer modern architecture: Edwin Lutyens, Neo-Georgian, the streamlined Odeon cinemas and suburban semis, all of which were unworthy of mention. These non-conforming expressions had certain common characteristics: soft forms, ornamental features and associational and symbolic references, paraphernalia which were considered as aberrations of the emerging architecture. Informing and colouring such attitudes there was, I gradually discovered, a large and generally hostile literature. The suburb provoked radio programmes, magazine articles and references in novels by some of Britain's leading writers. The 'suburban semi' was an easy target for cartoonists and it did not escape the attention of poets. Architects and planners wrote articles and books, an occasional politician felt constrained to speak on the topic, and the suburb came under attack by those who would now be termed 'environmentalists'.

In the inter-war period writings proliferated by various groups or individuals who felt an urgent need to voice their concern at what was taking place. Criticism was concerned with the occupants of Suburbia and with their values, and it extended from national or regional developments to the thickness of a bogus timber beam. A single critical article could move with extraordinary ease from aesthetic issues to economic factors, to social criticism and to aspects which relate to the effect of such developments on the physical environment of town, road and countryside. The greatest volume of writing is contained within the period 1920–39 which coincides with the main period of suburban growth. Post-war interest has been a more leisurely pursuit, lacking the urgent imperatives that drove earlier writers to protest. Recent writing has flowed in the wake of nostalgic concern for the Twenties and Thirties. Much of the literature in both the pre- and post-war eras is superficial in quality and at times wildly inaccurate. But it was as important as more substantial material in shaping attitudes.

The literature is a battlefield where antagonists of the suburb strike aggressive postures. Targets vary: sometimes the city is under attack as the cause of suburban ills; sometimes the suburb is criticised on the grounds that it fails to live up to urban traditions. The battles recur; there are close similarities between the debates of the Twenties and Thirties and those concerned with the growth of Victorian suburbs in the late nineteenth century. Literary defence of the suburb in the period between the wars is hard to find; the little writing which regards the suburb favourably is of recent origin.

Much of the literature about the semi-detached house or the suburbs pre-dates the building era of Dunroamin, a consequence of the writers' experience in Victorian or Edwardian suburbs. One of the principal concerns of writers throughout the nineteenth century was the town or city and its many failures, which were helping to create the suburban explosion. Greed was diagnosed as the basic cause of the city's degradation by William Morris in 1888 when he wrote of the profit motive, the root cause of the polluted landscape and overcrowded towns. [1]

Hatred of the town was one of the principal drives behind the Garden City Movement. Its main spokesman, Ebenezer Howard, argued that the patterns of wealth in Britain were the cause of the squalor in the towns, but that such vested interests could not stand in the way of change. He believed that the city would have to make way for a new solution, and in proposing a change he saw that it was in conflict with the 'crowded, ill-ventilated, unplanned, unwieldy, unhealthy cities', which were barriers to the introduction of 'scientific methods'. Ebenezer Howard proposed to unite town and country, not in a suburban sprawl, but in a new Garden City. Out of this 'joyous union', he wrote, 'will spring a new life, a new civilisation'. [2] Within five years of writing his book the first Garden City, Letchworth, had been built. For the new town M. H. Baillie Scott devised simple, three-bedroomed cottages and semi-detached houses which were to become prototypes for the typical suburban house. These projects were the result of continuous experimentation with the problems of the small house. In an article written in 1895, he described the need for more care in the design of such buildings:

> We should spend more thought on our homes rather than more money . . .. The English people pride themselves not a little on their love of home, a word which indeed hardly has an equivalent in other languages; but how can we dignify with such a title the cheerless dwellings in which so many of us live. [3]

Baillie Scott's achievement was the instinctive recognition of domestic needs. Throughout his prolific career he retained an understanding of the essential distinction between a house and a home, and it was this quality which enabled his architecture to become a natural bridge between the Arts and Crafts tradition and the suburban building boom. But to Baillie Scott the popular taste that was embodied in the small house put up by speculators or local builders was a continual frustration. In 1918 he replied to the suggestion put by Alfred Simon

Suburban Edgware. To the left of the Ritz Cinema (now ABC)
'Suntrap' estate – Herbert Welch's Rectory Gardens. To the right

London Transport
poster of 1908,
advertising the
'Delightful Prospects'
of suburban life in
Golders Green (London
Transport)

-ton-built half-timbered housing; behind the Ritz (1932) the first
)-Georgian shopping parade built 1925 (F. and J. Hare)

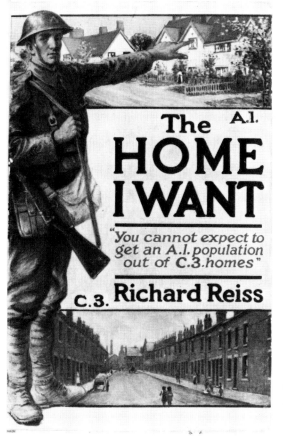

The A.1.
HOME
I WANT
"You cannot expect to
get an A.I. population
out of C.3. homes"
C.3. Richard Reiss

'Homes for Heroes'.
Army health standards
applied to housing,
from C3 City slums to
A1 suburban semis,
1918 (Bodleian Library)

that good design was wasted on the lower classes. [4] He deplored 'the depraved tastes of the poor' in both their homes and other possessions. Such degenerate taste, however, also characterised the middle classes, 'whose conception of the ideal house centres on a bay window adorned with lace curtains, and fences . . . say with a cast iron railing picked out in blue or gold'. [5]

In the years after the Great War, however, the polite debate in the pages of learned journals was far removed from the realities of the housing issues facing Britain. In 1918 Lloyd George's slogan, 'Homes fit for Heroes', was the starter's gun for two decades of rapid house building. During this period an average of 17,590 houses were completed each month (as compared with about 9,000 per month being built in 1980), and the boom was only halted by the outbreak of the Second World War. In the years after the Armistice it was suggested there was a close link between social goals and house building. The king himself had declared: 'An adequate solution of the housing question is the foundation of all social progress'. Lord Long spoke of the 'black crime' that would be perpetrated on the returning troops if they were not housed 'decently and rapidly . . . to let them come back from the horrible waterlogged trenches to something little better than a pig-sty here would indeed be criminal on the part of ourselves, and would be a negation of all that has been said during the war'. [6] For many returning soldiers and their families, Lord Long's fears were not justified. The new housing estates, for all their defects in construction, were immeasurably superior to the back-to-back dingy terraces or the tenement blocks where so many of the new owner occupiers had lived as children. In subsequent years, when critics were so hostile towards the suburbs, they rarely recognised the social achievement of housing so many, so rapidly.

The acute shortage of homes just after the war concerned W. R. Lethaby who lectured in 1920 on the housing crisis and what he regarded as an even greater problem, the lack of a 'fine tradition of living in houses'. All excrescences of style, which he described as 'trivial, sketchy, picturesqueness' must be rejected. 'Frankness is the great thing: disguises and subterfuge are always repulsive in building. Bungling, pretence and compromise are the enemies to be feared.' Lethaby suggested solid values as the basis for house design: 'Whenever we concentrate on some directing datum, some reality like health, serviceableness or even perfect cheapness, true style will certainly arise as an expression of this and the other human qualities embodied.' [7]

One man who would have nodded in agreement at Lethaby's Athenaeum lecture was W. R. Davidge who shared Lethaby's concern for 'healthy homes' and who noted the problems facing home buyers as they searched fruitlessly for decent homes. He wrote in 1921 that: 'The joys of house-hunting have with all of us at some time or another been reduced to disillusionment and disappointment in the house that is found'. Davidge lamented the limited choice that was available to buyers, and reflected on the housing situation: 'In the central areas the last thirty years have seen a steadily growing tendency to concentration in tall block dwellings or palatial hotels or flats, while simultaneously in all the suburbs there has been a steadily creeping paralysis of two-storey villadom, mile after mile of brick and mortar, slowly eating up the countryside'. But he believed that the suburb had advantages over the town on health grounds. He recognised that housing blocks within cities were only necessary in the exceptional conditions where workers had to work in the inner city, and suggested that, 'even in these cases it may well be argued that cheaper rents and healthier conditions in the suburbs more than outweigh the slight saving of time effected by living in a crowded tenement'.[8] This was a reference to what was to become a perennial concern of critics, and a source of enthusiastic copy for house salesmen, 'the health risk of the city and the solution: the suburb'. Perhaps the widespread incidence of TB and other respiratory conditions fuelled this concern. Another possibility is that the new estates were to be largely occupied by ex-servicemen who had bitter experience of trench and gas warfare and who were thus easy targets for the healthier alternative to the town. In the last year of the war 41 per cent of conscripts had been graded medically unfit for military service, and Crossley Davies took up the health issue in 1923. He criticised the new suburban homes for their many defects: the absence of a scullery, 'tiring and perilous stairs', a bathroom door that could not be opened since it collided with a washbasin, electric-light fittings but no power points, and the lack of central heating, dressers and built-in wardrobes. 'This sort of thing will not do', he admonished.[9]

Crossley Davies could see only the physical anatomy of the suburban semi; he failed to perceive that there was another dimension to the popularity of these homes. In the same year A. Clarke wrote in *The Story of Blackpool*: 'We must always keep in mind that Blackpool . . . is not just a place of bricks and mortar. There are dream-builders as well as brick-builders, and dream-builders really lay the foundations for the brick-builders.'[10] This recognition, that there were deeper issues in the aspiration of families for their homes than strict physical criteria, was totally lost on most architects and writers. Few were able to grasp the significance of the dreams, associational imagery (the objects and decorations with which people surround themselves because of their associations) or the symbols of the suburb. These mysteries were the secret province of estate agents, builders and purchasers. Historical association, images of security or fulfilment, are the very essence of the suburb – its street names, its homes and details as well as the ornaments in its front gardens. But to the Welsh architect

33

Clough Williams-Ellis the result of this mixture was 'most hilarious'. He and his wife paid a visit to Oxford in 1924 observing that: 'A visit to almost any centre of non-collegiate intellectual activity will certainly make the enthusiast realise that as yet architectural sensibility plays a very small part in the lives of people of universally praised culture.' The evidence for such a judgment was to be found in

> Boar's Hill, near Oxford, for instance, which was, and indeed is, a Mount Helicon. There we may see poets and philosophers innocently housed in the jerrybuilder's most hilarious efforts. Variegated shrubs, highly varnished rustic summer-houses, conservatories, fancy bargeboards and cast-iron ridging, and all the paraphernalia of a suburban lay-out here make a little Peckham. But the intellectual flower of the century has noticed nothing. [11]

Clough and Amabel Williams-Ellis wrote this description in their first book, *The Pleasures of Architecture*. The curious conundrum of such writing, and this book in particular, is the contradiction between their rather rigid view of what architecture should be and what Williams-Ellis subsequently built. His description of Boar's Hill could easily be mistaken for part of the fantasy creation of Portmeirion, which he commenced building just two years after his Oxford visit.

One writer was sufficiently perceptive to see vices and virtues simultaneously. J. B. Priestley wrote in 1927 of the dilemma posed by the new suburbs, 'where a desire for beauty wars with our common sympathy. A few more of these houses and this place will no longer charm the eye; a great many more of them and it will be hideous.' But against such objections, his humanity recognised that 'a number of people will have the chance of living decently and in comfort', and that 'people should come first . . . their chunks of happiness or misery are more important than certain delicate satisfactions of our own.' Thus social priorities reluctantly triumph over aesthetics: 'We should be content to make the whole country hideous if we know for certain that by doing so we could also make all the people in it moderately happy.' [12] Of all the writers and critics of the suburbs between the wars perhaps Priestley was uniquely sensitive to the social context in which the new estates were being built, even if such concern was voiced in a paternalistic tone.

Concern was growing in the late Twenties over the threat to the environment and in 1928 Clough Williams-Ellis returned to the fray with a major critique of the 'spate of mean building all over the country that is shrivelling the Old England'. Both house design and house occupants were at fault: 'mean and perkey little houses that surely none but mean and perkey little souls should

Contempt of the suburbs expressed in the officially condoned vandalism of Electricity Board sites for pylons; early 1930s (John Topham Picture Library)

'Suburban Synthesis' (*left*), and a 'Civilised Version' (*right*), by Clough and Amabel Williams-Ellis, 1924 (from C. and A. Williams-Ellis, *The Pleasures of Architecture*, 1924)

inhabit with satisfaction'. This patronising attack underlines the entire thrust of the book: a cry against the rape of the environment, it frequently turns into a rampage against the values and taste of the lower orders and against builders as 'vindictive monsters'. Despite its limitations, however, it remains a significant manifesto of environmental protest, written many years before most architects and planners could see the scale of the threat to the English landscape. [13] Williams-Ellis genuinely feared that suburban development would eventually destroy the countryside; in fact he was more concerned with the preservation of Old England than with an evolving architecture. His attitude was characteristic of criticism prior to 1930, which weighed suburban developments against the 'sanity' of the Georgian terrace, the Garden City or the suburbs of Letchworth, Welwyn and Hampstead.

In the following decade criticism shifted focus as the suburbs were attacked against the standard of modern housing prototypes. In spite of the influence of European Modernism in the other arts in Britain, modern architecture had made no impact in Britain in the Twenties. There was, therefore, a clear distinction between the criticisms levelled at suburban houses, life and values in the Twenties and the standpoints taken in the Thirties in relation to Modern Architecture. Moreover, the debate was confined to specialist journals, or addressed to the public through books of relatively small circulation. The position was soon to change, with the belated influence of the Modern Movement in architecture and the coincident developments in popular media.

A handful of English architects in 1930 were very enthusiastic about the 'new architecture' described in Frederick Etchells' 1927 translation of Le Corbusier's *Vers Une Architecture*. [14] Le Corbusier had emerged in the 1920s as one of the leaders of the Modern Movement and his book presented, through polemics and illustrations, a picture of a new and rational architecture. Ocean liners, American factories and grain silos, the race track on the top of the Fiat factory, combined to create a 'precise' imagery of the new era. His ideas, including his views on housing, permeated the thinking of young architects. These had become apparent when in 1926 he described a radically new housing project he had designed for the suburbs of Pessac, a small town near Bordeaux. 'This is an example', he wrote, with characteristic confidence, 'of modern town planning, in which historical mementoes, such as the Swiss chalet and the Alsatian "dovecote" have been left behind in the museum of the past'. Such associations had to be dispensed with, since 'a mind stripped of romantic trammels tries to resolve a problem that has been precisely formulated. . ..' [15] Interest in these developments was initially confined to 'those in the know' in Britain, but very rapidly it was to reach a wider audience. Between April and June 1933 the BBC broadcast a series of eleven programmes on the theme of *Design in Modern Life*. This was the first occasion when the subject of Modern Architecture was discussed on the radio, and thus it was significant in taking the subject out of the confines of the specialist press to a radio audience and the readers of *The Listener*, where all the discussions were published. [16]

The sixth discussion was held between Geoffrey Boumphrey and Wells Coates in May 1933. Boumphrey was an engineer and writer with a deep commitment to Modern Architecture. He was one of the early members of the MARS (Modern Architectural Research) Group which was inaugurated in the same year. Wells Coates was to become its first chairman. He was a Canadian engineer who had established himself as one of the pioneer architects of the Modern Movement in England. This discussion was on 'Modern Dwellings for Modern Needs'. Boumphrey began by questioning why the public clutched to past traditions of architecture, 'Tudor or some other "period"', while at the same time they are very careful indeed not to be behind the times in the matter of clothes. Coates added that clothes were essentially transitory but housing was an expensive investment that would last:

> The right thing for an Englishman is, of course, to have a castle all to himself – or at least what they call in the advertisements a 'baronial hall' – to give him the feeling of stability, security and individuality. It is amazing how many discomforts he will put up with to secure this.

Although Coates could grasp the underlying reasons for 'Tudor baronial halls', he failed to see the reason why architects should recognise status or security as vital determinants when designing houses. They proceed to discuss the development of suburbs and the erosion of the countryside by 'ill-planned, jerry-built housing schemes'. Such housing failed to suit what they described as 'current conditions of life'. This expression referred to Coates' vision of less permanent houses which would be smaller, in response to smaller families and cost factors, and to the new mobility achieved by the motor car resulting in families spending less time at home. (Car ownership, which had been 32,000 in 1907, rose to 109,000 in 1919 and to 2,000,000 by 1939.) Finally he saw the need for homes to be 'restful and convenient' to suit a servantless society; and showing a total disregard for the basic need of people to surround themselves with *their* objects and possessions, he prescribed that all 'cumbersome articles such as loose furniture' must be removed from the house since these were not

Semi-detached castle at Kingsbury, Middlesex,
by E. M. Trowbridge, 1927 (Ian Davis)

'part of the structure of the dwellings'. So houses were to be built devoid of their essential trappings and, when photographed, devoid of people. His arguments centred on the waste of land from such developments, and the superfluous labour of each housewife doing her own cooking and washing: '. . . the next step in the design of dwelling units must be the block or group of dwellings with every centralised service which the sharing of costs makes economically possible. . . .'

The discussion resulted in total unanimity. Both speakers shared the conviction that the values of 'stability, security and individuality', so manifest in the suburban developments taking place around them, were of little consequence. The arguments were all underpinned with confidence in a functional ideal, and in a concept of progress or rapid change from one way of living, viewed as primitive, to another, seen as inevitable.

Just two months after this radio broadcast, Coates and Boumphrey travelled to Marseilles to participate in the fourth meeting of the International Congress of Modern Architecture (CIAM). In August 1933 the Congress deliberated on a boat sailing between Marseilles and Athens. The passengers included some extraordinary talent: José Luis Sert, Siegfried Giedion, Cornelius van Esteren, Fernand Léger, Laszlo Moholy-Nagy and Alvar Aalto. The British contingent was confined to members of the MARS Group and included Ernö Goldfinger, F. R. S. Yorke, J. Morton Shand, Wells Coates and Geoffrey Boumphrey.

Without a doubt, the dominating figure was Le Corbusier who exercised his authority and influence in the intense discussions on the broad theme of the future of the Urban Environment. No less than 95 declarations emerged, and amongst them were several particularly virulent attacks on the suburb: 'The suburb is the symbol of waste and, at the same time, for the risky venture, it is a kind of scum churning against the walls of the city' (Observation Number 20). Those who sought to deal with the suburban problems by building Garden Cities were admonished:

> There are those who seek to turn those disordered suburbs in which the time-distance function poses an ominous and unanswerable question, into garden-cities. Theirs is an illusory paradise, an irrational solution. The suburb is an urbanistic folly, scattered across the entire globe and carried to its extreme consequences in America. It constitutes one of the greatest evils of the century.

The abuse continued, describing the 'bleak ugliness of the suburb', 'a squalid antechamber of the city', 'a reproach to the city it surrounds'. The observations then made three specific criticisms: the suburb clogs the traffic on approach roads to the town or city; when seen from the air it 'reveals disorder and incoherence'; and for the railroad traveller 'excited by the thought of the city, it is a painful disillusion'. [17]

Most of the criticism contained in the Athens Charter had been expressed elsewhere in the previous decade; what was new was the vehemence of criticism. The totally unsubstantiated invective is reminiscent of the prose style of *Mein Kampf*, which had been published a few years earlier. Perhaps this was no coincidence, since four years after this congress, Anthony Bertram wrote in praise of CIAM's leader, Le Corbusier, and his writings. 'All Europe', he asserted, 'has felt his influence. He is not only an intensely original and clear sighted architect, but also by far the most effective propagandist of the new architecture'; then the supreme compliment: 'His books are the *Mein Kampf* of the movement.' [18]

Why should the building of these suburban estates have generated such abuse? It might appear that the authors were conducting a vendetta against suburban society, but clearly this is not so, since the list of CIAM delegates includes some men with deep social commitment. Perhaps their small voice was submerged by the onslaught of Le Corbusier's rhetoric or they may have genuinely subscribed to the findings, as their association with the charter would indicate. [19] One possible explanation for the invective may have been that some of the architects present (notably Le Corbusier) had suffered the systematic rejection of their bold projects by the administrators of the time, characterised in France as 'petit-bourgeois' or in England 'suburbanites', who, with smug satisfaction, inhabited the little houses of the suburbs.

The isolation of the Congress members on board the Steamship *Patris II* in the Mediterranean is symbolic of their remoteness from the values of a very large proportion of the population of Europe. The delegates' most extreme abuse was not directed towards the idea of the suburb or its more obvious failures; rather it was against the occupants, whose tastes and values had been enshrined in housing which aptly reflected their needs and aspirations.

The Athens Charter was not made public for a decade when it was clandestinely published in Paris at the height of the Nazi occupation, with an anonymous author. However, the second edition came out in 1957 under the authorship of Le Corbusier. When the charter is compared with Corbusier's major planning study *La Ville Radieuse* of 1933 (the same year as the CIAM voyage) there emerge some predictably strong similarities in his attitude towards the suburb. He describes the various ills of suburban life in a highly unlikely conversation with his secretary who arrives late for work owing to overcrowded commuter trains; the dialogue is pure French soap-opera: she is bored to death, has few relatives in the suburbs, there are no people of her age to meet. In any event, after a week of long hours in Paris with travel on overcrowded trains there is little inclination for a Sunday walk: 'The suburbs aren't much fun to walk in. It's not like the real country', she sighs. Le Corbusier concludes the account with a similar cry of despair: 'The Martyrdom of Suburbanites. And something else again, the terrible solitude in the crowd of that vast urban agglomeration.' [20]

In 1935, two years after their influential series *Design in Modern Life*, the BBC broadcast the first programme to consider seriously the suburban building explosion: *Suburbs or Satellites*. [21] Those who listened to this debate, or read the transcript in *The Listener*, were treated to the most significant presentation within the popular media that occurred between the wars on the pros and cons of the suburbs. The spirited discussion made such an impression on one of its participants, Geoffrey Boumphrey, that five years later he quoted from his side of the argument with some embellishments in his book *Town and Country Tomorrow*. [22]

Many of the objections already discussed in this chapter were repeated in this debate between Geoffrey Boumphrey of the MARS Group and John Cadbury of Bournville Garden Suburb. However, there were fresh arguments as well as some defence not previously expressed. New criticisms were made on the effect of the suburb on the town or city: the impact on commuter travel and on social planning issues.

Boumphrey's main attack was centred on the compromising effect of the suburbs on the city, where his loyalties obviously rested. 'We have surrounded our towns', he declared, 'with an inefficient fringe of suburbs'. The price tag was 'millions of pounds a year lost by clogging the traffic, and thousands of lives lost in rural accidents due to increased road travel'. The town child who needed the country most had been denied access to it by the suburban wedge. Further, 'We've dirtied still more the air he breathes'. He suggested that the suburbs posed a major threat to adjacent towns or cities as their expansion resulted in the merging of towns which had previously retained their identity. The major difficulties occurred in large towns; small towns could absorb suburban growth more readily. A small town in his definition was somewhere where you could cycle home from work at lunchtime.

At the conclusion of the discussion Boumphrey suggested, in apparent ignorance of the economic forces which shaped the suburbs, that resources must be redeployed to the neglected city:

> The mad building of suburbs must be stopped – before it strangles the towns themselves. If half the energy and money poured into the suburbs in the last 17 years had been spent on the towns inside them, the country would be a better place, and the towns more fit to live in.

The anonymous 'witnesses' who participated in the debate were unanimous in their hostility to the 'worst of suburban life', the time spent in travelling to and from work. 'It wastes the one thing a man cannot replace – life itself.' Yet Cadbury applauded the tube-train for its virtues: 'quick, not noisy and does not cause any traffic problems – the best method of cheap travel yet invented'. His was a lonely voice; the others shared the distaste expressed by Le Corbusier's secretary for overcrowded trains, regarded as a health hazard and a waste of money, energy and leisure time just when mechanisation was beginning to reduce the long working day.

In reaction against the performance of suburbs already completed, there were some very specific criticisms of the design of houses and layouts. 'Repetitive houses should not be built', declared Cadbury (with a sidelong swing in the direction of ribbon developments) without regard for the natural features of the site, the orientation of rooms, privacy and a social balance. This could only be achieved, he reasoned, with a slower rate of building which would result in a greater variety of house types and a wider spectrum of social groups to occupy them.

There was further criticism of the lack of adequate suburban amenities. The effect of the low-density planning of houses at the unquestioned ratio of twelve to the acre (in contrast to the thirty to the acre of inner city terraces) was that all distances were magnified and amenities dispersed. 'Shops should be in reasonable reach of the houses, in several groups, rather than in one centre a long way off.' One witness made specific patronising criticisms. The suburbs were damaging young workers who were 'arriving home too late and tired to adequately prepare for their jobs'. They were also fragmenting relationships: 'They're making friends at their work when there is no parental control over their choice.'

Praise for the suburb came exclusively from Cadbury, who applauded the achievement of building rapidly 40,000 homes in Birmingham for nearly a quarter of a million people. He also admired the way the suburb brought the country into the towns: 'I do not call it a waste of land to give a man his own house and garden, where he can feel that it is his own to do with as he wishes, and where at least he can have more than enough fresh air around him.' This prompted the others to agree that private gardens were the best and most popular feature of suburban life.

In Cadbury's defence of the suburb there was a strong aspiration towards an ideal yet to be realised in any general scale. Perhaps his image of the suburb was that of a satellite town on the lines of Bournville. However, he did grasp, without being paternalistic, the possibility of individual freedom and fulfilment within the suburban environment. 'My suburb', he speculated, 'will be a place

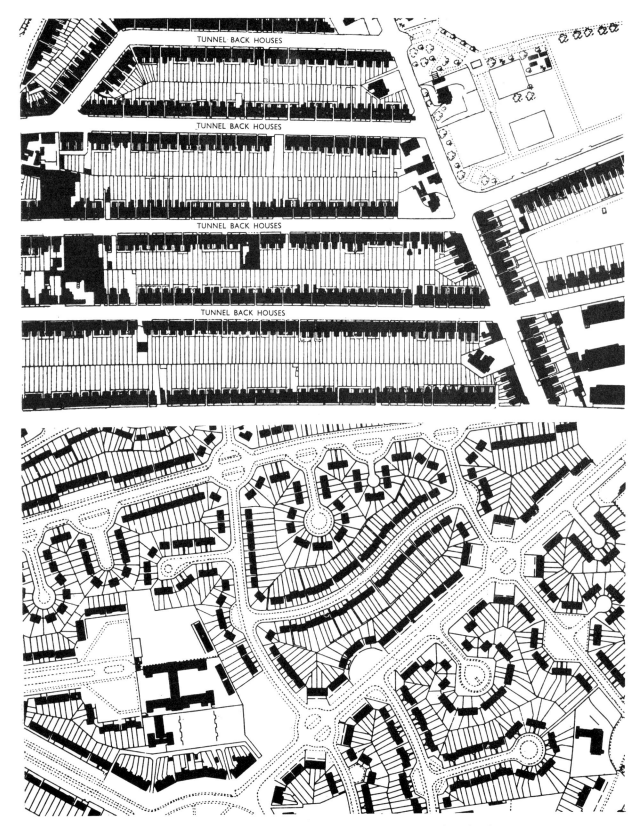

TUNNEL BACK HOUSES

TUNNEL BACK HOUSES

TUNNEL BACK HOUSES

TUNNEL BACK HOUSES

Comparison of high density inner city housing (*top*) with suburban development
at 12 houses to the acre (from *When We Build Again*, 1940)

Osbert Lancaster's 'By-Pass Variegated' suburban estate from
Osbert Lancaster, *A Cartoon History of Architecture* (John Murray)

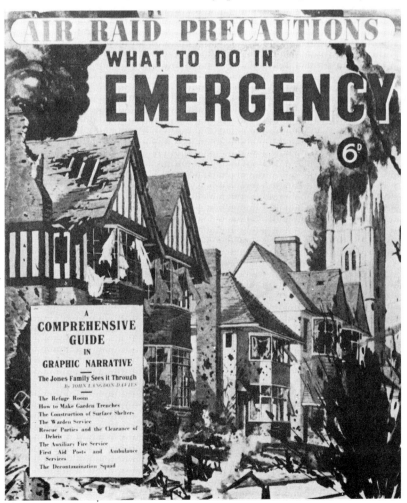

Officialdom belatedly recognises the semi-detached house, but not
without an oblique comment: 'The Jones Family Sees it Through' in
'Graphic Narrative' (from *What To Do In An Emergency*, 1939)

worth living in, and I do not mean just sleeping in either—a place where you can spend your evenings and free time profitably to yourself and others, without the need of going away for all your pleasures.'

Harold Bradshaw, Secretary of the Royal Fine Arts Commission, writing in 1939, along with most architects writing in the decade, placed great confidence in planning controls to resolve the problems of shoddy house layouts. Optimistically, he believed that if only architects designed houses they would possess: 'A beauty which the monotonous planning of the speculative builder, in spite of his efforts to create variety by such means as false gables, sham half-timbering, pebble-dash walls and assorted shapes in bay windows, cannot hope to achieve.'[23]

Stanley Ramsay, writing in 1939, grudgingly admitted that there was some achievement behind the statistics of building societies, as lending had risen from £66 million in 1914 to £700 million in 1939. But, he reasoned, any progress had been bought at a high price. 'It is the opinion of those who are best qualified to judge', he declared, 'that there has been very little "Jerry-building" in these post war houses, but there has unfortunately been a great deal of "Jerry-designing".' The passing reference to those 'best qualified to judge' should not go unnoticed. Clearly, they included the architect Stanley Ramsay. The occupants of the houses, all 18 million or so of them, were assumed to be incapable of recognising bad design or construction when they saw it or, perhaps more significantly, when they emptied their bank accounts to put down deposits to pay for it.

However, Ramsay, in all seriousness, saw a possible virtue in such shoddy construction: 'We could look forward to their having a very short life, and although this might be hard on the individual purchasers, it might in the long run be a good thing for the country.'[24] Even more extraordinary were the tongue-in-cheek aspirations of Osbert Lancaster and John Betjeman towards a far speedier solution to demolish the suburbs. Lancaster wrote:

> It is sad to reflect that so much ingenuity should have been wasted on streets and estates which will eventually become the slums of the future. That is, if a fearful and more sudden fate does not obliterate them prematurely, an eventuality that does much to reconcile one to the prospect of aerial bombardment.[25]

Betjeman, writing in 1937, regarded the Luftwaffe threat in similar terms:

> Come friendly bombs, and fall on Slough;
> It isn't fit for humans now—

The bomb-aimers were then given specific targets—factories, houses and suburban conformity.[26] By 1938 the bombs had yet to fall and Betjeman turned his attention West from Slough to Oxford. He wrote in a similar manner to Clough Williams-Ellis who, fourteen years previously, had despaired of another Oxford suburb, Boar's Hill:

> And now we come to Cumnor Hill. What an approach to a city of learning! What learned architecture! Here the half timbered villa holds its own boldly beside the bogus-modern, here the bay windows and stained glass front door survey the niggling rock garden and arid crazy paving.

Betjeman ruminated on what the scholar gypsy (who roamed these slopes in Matthew Arnold's poem written in 1853, *The Scholar Gypsy*) would make of such a sight:

> Those slopes . . . are now dotted with residences raised piecemeal and looking like so many slices of cake. The scholar gypsy must wash his bronzed face in birdbaths and sleep under the shade of stone toadstools if he is still to roam the slopes of Cumnor Hill.[27]

Some five years earlier in 1933 Betjeman wrote *Ghastly Good Taste*, a personal history of architecture. At the very end of the book he contrasted the ability of British designers with suburban 'deadness', in a description of the

> housewife's dream, the labour-saving kitchen, that throbbing heart of efficiency in the midst of the dead 'period' decoration of every villa in lovely Mill Hill, Hendon Heights, healthy Edgware, bracing Bootle, beechy Bucks, charming Surrey or moderate Morden.[28]

This dismissal of suburban taste by Betjeman was to be replaced subsequently by an affectionate recognition of certain values within the suburb. But this change in attitude was to take all of twenty years, by which time he was writing with romantic nostalgia about a world that no longer existed. It was partly this motivation that prompted J. M. Richards to write in 1946 *The Castles on the Ground: The Anatomy of Suburbia* whilst serving in the armed forces in the Middle East.[29] Another stance taken by books written during the war was inspired by utopian zeal. 'The folly of the last century must go . . . with its chaos, slums and dirt', wrote Ralph Tubbs (later he was to become the architect of the Dome of Discovery in the 1951 Festival of Britain) in 1942 in a handy Pelican paperback widely distributed to British troops. He picked up the CIAM judgment on the suburbs, 'one of the greatest evils . . .' and continued: 'so also the crimes of

47

our own century, the mock-Tudor suburbs, the ribbon development and the imitation Classic'. [30]

Thomas Sharp, a popular advocate of the new profession of Town Planning, had written a series of important planning studies in the late 1930s, all of which attacked the suburb with a vengeance. In 1940, he developed his basic argument that the entire concept of the suburb stood on three premises. It was an escape from reality, it was individualistic and it was, at root, selfish. He believed that people were 'sick of the wretched towns they have to live in' and that inevitably they 'escape' to Suburbia. He likened the escape to that of an 'unorganised band of prisoners breaking gaol with no very definite plans for what lies before them', and he questioned whether the suburbs were in reality any escape, any genuine improvement on the evacuated town. The solution, he believed, was to stay in the towns and become concerned with 'redeeming them from their degradation of the last century by adjusting, adapting, exploiting them to our changed conditions'. Sharp's concept of urban renewal was highly prophetic since it was to take all of thirty years for this to become public policy. He went on to reprimand the residents of the suburbs for behaviour that he considered to be 'selfish and anti-social' in that each person 'who goes to the suburbs seeking the edge of the countryside pushes the countryside away from somebody else and he in turn suffers from having it pushed away from him'. The whole process was an elusive quest: 'the inhabitants of suburbia continually thwart themselves and each other, and the more they strive to embrace the object of their desire the more it escapes them; the more they try to make the best of both worlds the more they make the worst'. [31]

The arguments against suburban sprawl were influential and in 1938 Parliament passed the 'Green-Belt Act' which required the towns and cities of England to apply brakes on future expansion. Suburban growth did eliminate vast tracts of countryside previously accessible to town-dwellers, but whether the underprivileged urban poor ever had the spare time or money to enjoy it seems highly unlikely. The suburbs had devoured land at a rate of 70,000 acres per annum, and much of this was prime agricultural land set in ideal locations close to urban markets. However, not all the land was lost in terms of agriculture. Gardens were highly productive of fruit and vegetables both before the war and during the 'Dig for Victory' wartime campaigns for home produce.

In taking stock of the onslaught against Dunroamin and the puny defence in its favour, it is apparent that the numerous items singled out for attention fall into three broad categories which move from the general to the highly specific. First, there is the attack on the very idea of suburban living, and this spills over into criticism of the values of the occupants. Second, the planning of estates is strongly opposed; and finally, the detailed design and construction of houses is criticised.

At the root of the attack on suburban living there is the strong presupposition that a collective expression of housing (for example a Georgian terrace, or apartments by Le Corbusier) is somehow preferable to the individualistic expression of a single house. The reasons for the view were often related to the lower land consumption of flats over houses, but underlying this logic the style of suburban 'boxes' was probably the real issue. Such an attitude was part of the ethos of the Modern Movement, and when analysed tends to consist of little more than prejudice in lieu of any serious concern to understand the needs and aspirations of the new house-owners. These included: a desire to live as close as possible to work; a house that provided and expressed individuality and status; a labour-saving house; an escape from the cramped, dirty and unhealthy city; an actual or symbolic need to be close to the country; the need for a garden; and, probably the highest priority of all, security of tenure with its consequent opportunities for the exercise of personal choice.

The suburb was already regarded as a threat to the survival of both the town and country, and in their opposition critics made snide (and inevitably unproven) accusations that suburban families were selfishly running away from life's realities, with their 'innate snobbery', 'blatant vulgarities', and 'primitive instincts'. [32]

Secondly, the estates were attacked on numerous grounds: their monotonous sprawl; their lack of privacy and basic amenities; their generation of traffic jams – the list is extensive. Some of these objections repeat their predecessors' *ad nauseum* without any recognition of newly emerging facts. For example, critics continued to argue that excessive traffic to and from the city was one of the main failures of the suburbs. Despite the rapid growth in the 1930s of large factories for consumer goods *within* the suburbs, there was not a glimmer of recognition that for numerous house-owners their suburban home was near to their place of work. In 1935 the *Daily Telegraph* reported that 209 new factories had been opened in the London area out of a national total for the year of 478. And there was no awareness of the consequent cross-suburban traffic as evidenced for example by the building of the London North Circular Road in the mid Thirties.

Thirdly, the design of the houses was opposed on several counts; but most of these failures, it was suggested, could have been rectified if only architects had designed the houses, rather than villainous speculators or builders. The 'jerrybuilding' was a further source of criticism.

Many of the critics of the suburban building boom were men with a strong loyalty to the basic concepts of the emerging New Architecture. One of its fundamental tenets was concern that architecture should meet the deepest social needs of society and particularly in the provision of good housing. It remains a mystery that *none* of the leaders of the New Architecture in Europe or England displayed any recognition whatsoever of the achievement of providing over four million homes in the space of just 22 years; homes that despite their many faults were infinitely superior as living environments to the overcrowded urban housing that had preceded them. Architects, committed to the Modern Movement, followed the lead of CIAM or Le Corbusier's rhetoric from Europe, or at a domestic level that of Wells Coates and the inflexible position taken by the MARS Group towards anything other than doctrinaire Modern Architecture. One strange paradox of Coates' position was that the layout of, for example, his 'Sunspan' housing was similar to that of any typical row of semi-detached houses. What he and his contemporaries in the Modern Movement seem to have disliked so strongly was the *style* of the houses rather than their basic configuration.

Another possible explanation for the failure of these architects to see anything positive in the housing boom is that the social commitment of these pioneers was skin deep; or, taking a more charitable view, that the suburbs were so alien to their values that they never even considered the possibility that the housing revolution of which they dreamed was actually occurring all around them, even if it was a rather different one from their aspirations.

At a more pragmatic level, the main reason for the relentless hostility could have been that architects and planners were impotent as the growth of the suburbs continued remorselessly, largely without their designs and certainly despite all their criticism. Since this self-appointed élite could not stop the houses being built they were left to abuse the developers, builders and occupiers – a process that released their frustrations and retained their essential distance from the vast mass of humanity beneath them.

Turning to the other side of the architectural coin, a major question remains unanswered: why was there so little support for the suburbs from the architects who, during the Twenties and Thirties, continued to work within the Arts and Crafts tradition inherited from Baillie Scott, Voysey and Lutyens? Some of the architects loyal to this movement actually designed suburban housing estates, so perhaps the issue was that if *architects* designed semi-detached houses in the suburbs all was well; the problems started with 'non-professional designers'. On the surface it would appear that architects working in the Arts and Crafts idiom would have found much to enjoy in the better built suburban houses which grew out of a tradition with rich historical associations.

CIAM Congress in session aboard SS *Patris II*, 1933. Participants shown include Siegfried Giedion and (*right*) Le Corbusier (photo: Laszló Moholy-Nagy, from *Le Charte d'Athènes*, 1943)

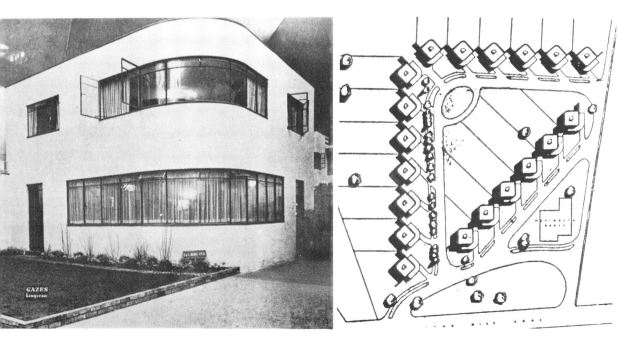

'Sunspan' housing of 1934 by Wells Coates and Pleydell-Bouverie; modern in style, yet planned in a traditional suburban lay-out (from M. and C. Quennell, *A History of Everyday Things in England*)

1815

1885

1925

1938

Modern architecture marks, in Lionel Brett's words, the 'Return of the Prodigal Son' after a 123-year absence (from Lionel Brett, *The Things We See*, 1947)

Undoubtedly the prevailing attitude of contemporary critics was that the suburban house was more a degenerate offspring of the Arts and Crafts tradition than any continuation of the movement. J. M. Richards wrote of this in 1938 (just six years before his wartime conversion to the suburbs):

> Real originality was shown by such as Ernest Newton, Dunbar Smith, Baillie Scott and Guy Dawber. But the influence of these and of Bedford Park is seen at its worst in the caricature Tudor styles of the ordinary speculative suburban villa, which persists today as the legacy of the romantic movement of the end of the nineteenth century. [33]

Praise for the suburb was confined to four issues: the achievement in building so many homes, improvements in health standards, the homely associations of housing, and the opportunity for personal fulfilment in the new suburbs.

The final word in the clash between the ideals of the Modern Movement and Dunroamin may be heard in the lonely voice of John Gloag, who in 1945 reflected:

> The Modern Movement does not yet speak English. It has so far been regarded, though not acknowledged, as a fashion. Those who have practised it, have sometimes forgotten that they are architects and have become social reformers, intent on telling their countrymen how they should live, instead of providing them with the best background for living in their own way. [34]

The analogy, made at the outset of this chapter, of the literature to a battlefield proves to be false; it was nothing less than a massacre. Praise, sympathy, understanding, support or even acceptance of the semi-detached house in the suburbs, or for that matter the values and lifestyle of their occupants, from architects or planners is virtually non-existent. Leaving aside the handful of solitary supporters mentioned above, the assertion that suburbs were *not* 'one of the greatest evils of the century' did not come from writers; the real defence came in the half-timbered façades, bricks, pebble-dash and mortar of the great building explosion that continued unabated throughout two decades of Dunroamin, and its continued success to the present.

=2=

ARCADIA BECOMES DUNROAMIN
Suburban Growth and the Roots of Opposition

Ian Bentley

THE powerful tradition of anti-suburban feeling inherited by architects has played an important rôle in toppling the speculative semi from its inter-war position as the middle-class housing norm to a state of relative decline since the 1960s. Understanding this decline depends on understanding *why* architects and planners despised the suburban dream. An explanation must start in the late eighteenth century, when the modern suburb emerged as a distinctive pattern of development, as a response to the living conditions of the early industrial town.

During the latter part of the eighteenth century the enclosure movement, and developments in farm technology, reduced agricultural employment. Production increased, but the labour force declined. Many people thrown out of work by these changes could not stay in the countryside: there were no alternative jobs, and rural housing was systematically demolished so that they could not stay to become a drain on parish resources. Industrialists began to increase employment opportunities for these people in the new factory towns. Since factories employed many workers, they clustered near existing work-forces. Long, inflexible working hours were exhausting; to shorten the walk to work, therefore, housing clustered at high densities round the factories.

Low wages and high food costs restricted the housing rents which workers could pay. This exacerbated the environmental problems of high-density living by ensuring that housing standards were poor. Even worse, the inhabitants of this cheap, crowded housing were without urban living skills. First-generation rural immigrants were used to the countryside's ability to absorb, uncomplainingly, all their effluent and waste. Dense urban environments could not perform in the same forgiving way; dangerous levels of air and water pollution became common. By the 1840s, epidemic cholera was inseparable from urban life.

Even in old settlements, *new* housing often produced the most threatening living conditions. Thoughtful design was no guarantee of improvement, for early attempts to handle health problems often made them worse, as when water-borne sewage polluted drinking water. This paradoxical situation was widely broadcast, through improved communications media like local newspapers. Hitherto, in most people's minds, urban pollution had been associated with old and decrepit areas. To find it now rampant in the most modern housing was something new and frightening. Age and decay of the housing stock could no longer be blamed: it seemed that the city *itself* must be the source of danger.

The city was seen as damaging to more than physical health, as sensitive observers reported the psychological stresses of urban life. In 1840, for example, Dickens wrote of people 'feeling amidst the crowd a solitude which has no parallel but in the thirst of the ship-wrecked mariner, who . . . looking on the water which hems him in on every side, has not one drop to cool his burning tongue.'[1]

Not surprisingly, given the physical and psychological stresses of lower-class urban life, cities became the focus of political unrest, culminating with the Chartists of the 1830s and 40s. In turn, this unrest increased middle-class fear of the city; by the 1840s deep-rooted, anti-city values were already part of middle-class culture. However, the middle class benefited greatly from the process of industrialisation, which was now inseparably and irrevocably linked with urbanisation. Middle-class people wanted to escape the city, but to continue enjoying the benefits of industrialisation they had to accept the city as their work-place and as the source of their wealth.

This dilemma was resolved in the suburbs: low-density, middle-class housing areas at the city's periphery. From suburbs the breadwinner commuted to work in the dense central areas which still housed work-places and workers. The *suburb*, as its name implied, was still intimately connected into the urban system. Given that there was no radical alternative to cities which would not have swept away the source of middle-class wealth, it was the best escape available. The concept of the suburb took root very quickly, because it addressed every level of human need. At a physiological level, it avoided the health hazards of the inner city. In terms of safety, it offered escape from political unrest and from the psychological stresses which such unrest engendered. Its open layout boosted the suburban householder's esteem by association with the prestige of the landed gentry and, at least for the breadwinner, it gave more opportunities for self-development through the increased range of options and experiences which it added to the daily contact with inner-city life.

Once in the suburbs, the middle-class family had little contact with the lower orders, partly because of the physical relationship between the suburb and the rest of the city. Observing Manchester during the 1840s, Friedrich Engels noticed that middle-class people

> can take the shortest route [from their homes] through the middle of all the labouring districts to their places of business, without ever seeing that they are in the midst of the grimy misery that lurks to the right and the left. For the thoroughfares leading . . . in all directions out of the city are lined, on both sides, with an almost unbroken series of shops . . . [which] conceal . . . the misery and grime which form the complement of their wealth. [2]

Engels was not alone in remarking on what he called 'this hypocritical plan': in 1842 William Cooke-Taylor, again referring to Manchester, noted that: 'The isolation of classes in England has gone far to divide it into nations as distinct as the Normans and Saxons.' [3]

Within the suburb itself, servants and tradespeople were unavoidably present; but the design of suburban houses reduced inter-class contact to a minimum. Tradespeople used side entrances screened by hedges. When not on duty, servants were restricted to basements and attics. Gradually, through unfamiliarity, the working classes came to seem strange, alien beings; the mob, uncouth and uncultured, to be shunned whenever possible. In turn, as this view became widespread, it increased the pressures for a middle-class exodus from the increasingly working-class city; so the suburban idea became strongly self-perpetuating.

But there was another reason for the vigour of the suburban idea: it had the power to reconcile the meaning of the built environment with the naturalistic philosophy implicit in middle-class values. This philosophy reflected the early development of industrialisation, which was extremely competitive: success or failure justified by the concept of the 'survival of the fittest'. This justification received a theoretical boost with Charles Darwin's *Origin of Species* (1859); but Darwin was only stating more explicitly ideas which had long been a part of industrial practice. [4] Concepts such as *competition* and *progress*, which were central to the development of early industrial capitalism, were not seen as man-made inventions. They were seen as *natural*, as part of the God-given order of things.

It was the system's apparent naturalness which gave it legitimacy, enabling people of average humanity to accept with equanimity the sufferings of others, even to accept with resignation their own misfortunes. But it was hard to reconcile this naturalistic view of social and economic life with the all too evidently artificial, man-made character of its manifestation in the city, which acted as an uncomfortable reminder of the man-made character of social and economic institutions. Much of the strength of the suburb concept stemmed from its ability to blur this reminder by physically embedding the man-made world in the natural one; so that natural forces could be seen to play as large a rôle in the built environment as they were supposed to do in social and economic affairs.

The suburb was therefore designed with gardens and plants of a scale large enough to hold their own with the buildings, which were relatively small, separate single-family houses. In addition, its location on the edge of the town enabled the suburb to be linked closely with the open countryside. By thus treating nature as a general matrix into which individually designed and developed houses were inserted, a new urban pattern – apparently owing its visual order to 'nature' rather than to architecture – was created from the disparate efforts of the large number of small-scale, relatively unco-ordinated development agencies of the period. This new pattern of development can be seen as a physical analogy of the naturalistic, yet individualistic world view which underlay the process of industrialisation itself. A reconciliation between ideal and physical worlds had been achieved.

Architects did not object to these early suburbs. Indeed, the most fashionable designers were involved in their layout: George Dance's abortive 1775 scheme at Camberwell, and John Nash's later Park Village West are two examples. But this type of suburb was only for the well-to-do. Large gardens underpinned its 'Arcadian' imagery; and expenses were further raised, in the larger towns, by travel costs. Before public transport, suburban living in the large town required an expensive horse and carriage.

The change from earlier traditions of urban housing towards the new Arcadian pattern can be traced, for example, in the suburbs of North Oxford. Park Town, the first substantial development, was designed by S. L. Seckham and completed in 1855. Old-fashioned in layout, it looked back to Georgian prototypes, with terraced crescents and public gardens: an urban development in a suburban location, rather than a true suburb.

Developing from the 1860s, however, the adjacent Norham Manor Estate followed the Arcadian pattern. Large front gardens encouraged lush greenery, now past its prime, but still masking the buildings from many viewpoints. Though the planting took generations to mature, the original architects' drawings often show it fully grown, at a scale sufficient to compete with the architecture. The graphic image emphasises – even exaggerates – the stress on the natural over the man-made from which the arcadian image drew its strength.

By the last quarter of the century, however, Arcadia was no longer the

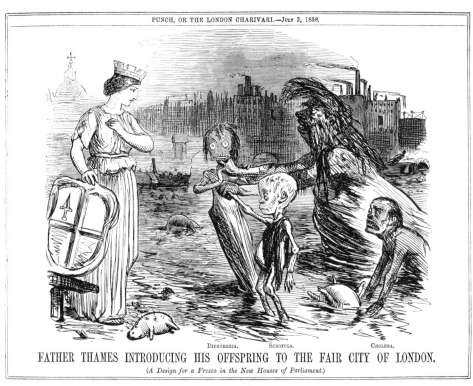

DIPHTHERIA.   SCROFULA.   CHOLERA.

FATHER THAMES INTRODUCING HIS OFFSPRING TO THE FAIR CITY OF LONDON.
(A Design for a Fresco in the New Houses of Parliament.)

Punch, 3 July 1858

Design drawing by the architect William Wilkinson, showing the conceptual
importance of planting in the planning of Norham Manor, c. 1865

The balance between the Natural and the Man-Made from which the Arcadian suburb drew its strength: Bradmore Road, Norham Manor, Oxford, c. 1865 (Graham Paul Smith)

The doll's-house terraces of Summertown, Oakthorpe Road, Oxford, c. 1895 (Graham Paul Smith)

suburban norm. Improved public transport, starting in London with Shillibeer's 1829 Paris-imported omnibus, and continuing with suburban train and tram systems, opened the suburbs to ever larger numbers of people. With workmen's cheap rail fares widely available by the 1880s, suburban living was no longer exclusive to the middle class.

The suburban expansion largely consisted of rented rather than owner-occupied housing, for many small investors saw housing for rent as a safe and predictable investment in a time of periodic boom and slump. Property had a solid permanence compared with stocks and shares which might suddenly become worthless paper; and suburban housing was the most attractive kind of property for the small investor. It was sought after, as a home, by the man of standing and proven thrift; likely to have considerable respect for property, he would treat the house with care. Possessed of white-collar skills, he was also unlikely to default on rent through unemployment.

The desire to invest in suburban housing brought pressures to widen the market for suburban living. Suburban housing had to be made cheaper – by increasing densities, by reducing house sizes, and by linking dwellings in economical combinations – so they could be let at lower rents. Garden sizes were reduced, and houses became semi-detached, though often still large in area. Finally, with the import of the small terraced house from the inner city in the 1880s and 90s, the cheapest type of suburb came into existence.

Like Arcadia before it, this pattern of change shows clearly in North Oxford. The large detached houses of Norham Manor give way to semi-detached pairs as development moves northwards from the city centre; and finally even these are superseded by the three-bedroomed dolls' house terraces of Summertown.

The market for these cheaper suburbs was further expanded, from about 1880, as increased disposable incomes made suburban living more widely available. During the same period, for most people, life became safer and more secure: welfare legislation began building social and economic safety nets for the poor, whilst the development of an increasingly conservative working-class culture allayed middle-class fears of social unrest.

With basic needs for health, safety and security thus met, aspirations towards prestige and individual development became important to more people. But these new aspirations were made possible by changes – in industry, in trade and in the administration of public affairs – which made jobs, even for middle-class workers, more routine and boring. By the end of the century even the white-collar worker, who had traditionally found satisfaction in work, relied increasingly on the home to fulfil his new aspirations. His attitude was summarised by Charles Pooter, 1890s anti-hero of the Grossmiths' *Diary of a Nobody*:

After my work in the City, I like to be at home. What's the good of a home, if you are never in it? . . .. There is always something to be done: a tin tack here, a Venetian blind to put straight, a fan to nail up, or part of a carpet to nail down—all of which I can do with my pipe in my mouth. [5]

For Ernest Radford, in 1906, even travel in the smoky steam underground was a small price to pay for life in *Our Suburb*: [6]

He leaned upon the narrow wall
That set the limit to his ground,
And marvelled, thinking of it all,
That he such happiness had found.

He had no word for it but bliss;
He smoked his pipe; he thanked his stars;
And, what more wonderful than this?
He blessed the groaning, stinking cars

That made it doubly sweet to win
The respite of the hours apart
From all the broil and sin and din
Of London's damnèd money mart.

The suburbs seemed to offer a favourable setting for satisfying higher-order aspirations. Even when suburban houses were connected in terraces, gables, bays and porches were used to emphasise the individuality of each house, and thus, by implication, of its inhabitants. Small front gardens, open except for low walls or railings, and free from the restrictions of landlord/tenant agreements, enabled the householder to make his personalising mark on the public realm. Finally, the style of the houses—often based on the Norman Shaw-inspired 'Queen Anne'—carried many layers of association and meaning: the individual could appropriate from it his *own* image of home. The architecture of the Queen Anne style, said Moyr Smith in 1883, was loved for many reasons: [7]

One loved her for her homeliness, another for her dignity and picturesque grace; this admired her because she was so domestic and unpretending, that other because she was so rich and so queenly. She was pure English, pure Flemish, pure Italian.... She spoke now in soft bastard Latin, now in French, now in Dutch, and now in pure Anglo-Saxon.

The cheapest of suburbs, then, out-performed the other options available—flats, or the unified terraces of the sub-Georgian tradition—as a setting for the higher-order aspirations. And yet, by the century's end, many influential people had become outspoken critics of such development. From 1903, Thomas Horsfall began reporting the techniques developed to control urban sprawl in various European countries.[8] Horsfall was widely influential amongst architects and others, inspiring no less a person than the Archbishop of Canterbury to contribute as follows to a 1907 House of Lords debate:

> Nothing could be more deplorable either aesthetically or from the point of view of health than the miserable monotonous rows of long, ugly, mean streets which are growing up all around London in a way which is absolutely impossible in the case of many large cities on the Continent.[9]

Similar sentiments were echoed by the professional institutes, partly, no doubt, inspired by snobbery: the usual inclination of those with influence to look down on the 'ugly, mean streets' of their social inferiors. Partly, too, it was a defence of upper middle-class Arcadia, now severed from the open countryside, and hemmed in by the relatively congested suburbs of the *hoi polloi*. But to see this as a cynical defence of privilege against the aspirations of the less well-off would be gross over-simplification. Architects, supporting the arguments against suburban expansion, saw themselves defending environmental quality against the jerry-builder, intent on ruining the countryside with his mindless sprawl.

Architects—not *all* architects, but architects in general terms nonetheless—*had* to promote the environmental interests of powerful social groups, with their vested interests in Arcadia. Ultimately, architects depended on the patronage of the powerful in order to earn their living; but they also needed to believe that in serving the interests of the powerful they were also promoting the wider public good. This belief was made credible by the development of an ideology which made attempts to curb suburban growth seem objectively *right*.

The development of this ideology stemmed from changing attitudes to the city. By the late nineteenth century, a range of systems, from sewers to police forces, had made the city 'safe' in middle-class terms. It could now be seen as something positive: a man-made environment fit to take its place alongside nature-dominated Arcadia. Once it became possible to think in these terms, it also became possible—even inevitable, given the natural desire of the dominant strata to protect their own living environments from the encroachments of those below them in the hierarchy—to analyse the built environment *in terms of* those two apparently fundamental categories. There was the man-made town; and there was nature, or nature-dominated Arcadia. Anything else was a bastard, a half-breed, a woolly-minded compromise. The image of the town as separated from the countryside by a wall or clear 'edge' became one of the most powerful elements in the urban imagery of the late nineteenth century, to be found at one extreme in the urban-form theories of Camillo Sitte [10] and at the other in Kate Greenaway's children's books. [11]

In practice, of course, this would have left the rich living in Arcadia – which they alone could afford – whilst everyone else would have had to make do with the high-density urban environments from which most were doing their best to escape. This was obscured by the apparently objective analysis of the world into the two fundamental terms of Town and Nature, on which the image was founded. The objectivity of this analysis – more apparent than real, for why should *those* particular terms have been chosen, unless to fudge the conclusion in the first place? – enabled designers to equate the interests of the rich and powerful with 'good design'. This was fine for the rich and powerful, and fine for the designer. But it brought about a wide divergence between the values of architects – who saw the cheaper, higher-density suburb as bad – and the values of ordinary people, who still saw it as offering them the best chance of fulfilling their own aspirations.

The gulf between these two sets of values was widened still further by changes in architectural patronage during the last decades of the nineteenth century. In commerce, for example, British business organisations were changing: the individualistic entrepreneur was giving way to the board of directors as the dominant management influence. Looking back on the 1880s and 1890s with a quarter-century of hindsight, the designer C. R. Ashbee recalled that 'business was becoming more and more impersonal. *Mechanical methods, which so far had only been applied to workshop production, were beginning to react upon business organisation.*' [12]

The same period, from about 1880, also saw the strengthening of municipal organisation in towns all over the country: Joseph Chamberlain, for example, began his political career in 1876 by organising the development of Birmingham's new Corporation Street. The age of big business and big government had arrived; and because both were becoming major patrons, their rise had important architectural implications; for while these new patrons were not in themselves opposed to the suburbs, they nevertheless prepared the ground for new architectural ideas which, in the end, proved strongly anti-suburban.

The men who achieved high office, in the new corporate organisations, were different in character from the earlier 'tooth-and-claw' entrepreneurs. The new men valued concepts such as *organisation* and *objectivity* and reduced the emphasis on *competition*, a change reflected in their architectural preferences. In addition, unlike the earlier entrepreneurs, they could not exercise their patronage by personal whim. As the representatives of *corporate* patrons, they had to justify their architectural decisions both to other members of their own organisations, and to the shareholders or voters upon whose support they ultimately depended. This justification was made possible by the development of a special kind of architecture, designed by a special kind of architect. As part of this development, the architect came gradually to change his rôle from artist to professional. With the professorship of Charles Reilly at Liverpool University in 1894, full-time schools of architecture began to offer students the opportunity to learn objective principles of design, and to sit formal examinations as proof that they had reached a competent level of proficiency in their use.

The transformation did not take place without a struggle. Powerful spokesmen for the traditional role – including eminent architects such as Norman Shaw and Philip Webb – opposed the 1891 Registration Bill on the grounds that 'the attempt to make architecture a close profession . . . is opposed to the interests of architecture as a fine art'. [13] This rearguard action on behalf of an 'artistic' view of architecture was, however, bound to fail; for the new approach was highly congenial to the corporate organisations who were becoming increasingly important as architectural patrons. If all professionally qualified architects were demonstrably competent in the use of seemingly *objective* principles of design, then the appointment of any professional architect could be justified as an objective exercise of patronage.

Two conditions had to be met to ensure the effectiveness of this system of professionalism. First, the architectural principles which were taught had to be examinable; and secondly, they had to seem 'objective', in the sense of being based on factors outside the designer's subjectivity. In practice, the only architectural tradition which appeared to satisfy both these conditions was that of the Beaux Arts. Originating in France during the latter part of the eighteenth century, that tradition had developed in response to the needs of state patronage. It had been further developed to meet the needs of a latter-day form of corporate patronage in the commercial buildings of the United States; whence, helped by Professor Reilly's links with American practice, it came to form the teaching basis in the new British university schools. By the First World War, the Americanised Beaux-Arts tradition, known in Britain as the 'Liverpool Manner', had spread so widely through the architectural profession that it was well on the way to monopolising the design of large buildings. [14]

The fundamentalist ideals of clarity, simplicity and consistency, which underlay the Liverpool Manner, were opposed to the eclectic, complex, multivalent character of the speculative builder's 'Queen Anne': the Queen

A typical Edwardian speculative terrace: Nos 46–48 Lonsdale Road, Oxford (1905) by Frank Mountain (Graham Paul Smith)

Speculative housing for the upper middle-class: Nos 1–3 Lathbury Road, Oxford (1905) by Frank Mountain (Graham Paul Smith)

Anne Manner made reference to *many* historical architectures, achieving a rich variety of associations through a complex additive aesthetic, using elements such as bays, porches, gables and dormers to break up the overall building mass.

Once again, the North Oxford suburbs are rich in examples of this kind of design. Houses in Lonsdale Road, Summertown, are typical: designed in 1905 by the local architect Frank Mountain, for the speculative builders Capel and Co., their image forms an instructive contrast to that of more expensive speculative houses nearby, in Lathbury Road. Large four-bedroomed houses, these were designed by the same architect only a few months later, for upper middle-class occupation by the sort of managerial and professional people most likely to approve of the corporate virtues of unity and simplicity.

Mountain, though an uninspired designer, was able to respond to this commission with a credible pastiche of the contemporary architecture of C. F. A. Voysey. Undecorated except for quasi-structural references, with strong unifying lines of ridge, eaves and windows, the design of these houses shows that the debased Queen Anne of Mountain's work at Lonsdale Road was not the mere by-product of an ignorance of other styles. The contrast between the two styles – the complex multivalence of Lonsdale Road versus the consistency of Lathbury – clearly reflects the divergence between middle- and lower-class individualism and the corporate values of the upper middle class.

Though rooted in the soil of corporate patronage, the ideas which supported the Liverpool Manner were seen by their protagonists as *objective*, and therefore beyond mere matters of style. This meant, inevitably, that they were seen as applicable to *all* types of buildings, whether commissioned by corporate patrons or not. Applied to domestic buildings, for example, they encouraged support for modular planning, undecorated white walls and the general sense of unity – underscored by long horizontal roof and window lines – of the late Arts and Crafts architecture of designers like C. F. A. Voysey. To an even greater extent, and for similar reasons, they supported the spread of Neo-Georgian, in whose development Mervyn Macartney was, perhaps, the key figure. An assistant to Norman Shaw, when Shaw was himself working towards a classical mode of design, Macartney became editor of the influential *Architectural Review* in 1905. From 1906 onwards, he ran a regular monthly feature in the magazine, called 'The Practical Exemplar of Architecture'. This gradually made available to architects a comprehensive Neo-Georgian design guide, covering 'any given subject from a chimney stack to a door knob'. [15] Its object, said Macartney, was 'Correctness: it is not intended that the host of adapters should be increased, so much as to ensure that the adaptations should be correct.' [16] The ready availability of this design guide gave added support to the Neo-Georgian movement, which in any case had been gathering momentum from the 1890s in the work of such designers as Leonard Stokes and Ernest Newton. By the outbreak of the First World War even the intransigent Baillie Scott, better known for his splendidly robust approach to Arts and Crafts design, was making Neo-Georgian experiments.

The corporate virtues which Frank Mountain found in Voysey's work could be seen as clearly in Neo-Georgian architecture; and Neo-Georgian—based on clearly articulated principles of design—was more easily taught. If the unity and consistency of Neo-Georgian represented good design, as the schools and the architectural press claimed, then the suburban terrace was badly designed indeed. According to the values of an increasing number of architects, the debased Queen Anne forms of the individual speculative house were bad in themselves. Repeated ad nauseam in the suburban terrace, they were too horrible to be borne: 'a form bad in its inception becomes insupportable when repeated indefinitely', said Lionel Budden, Liverpool's Associate Professor of Architecture, in 1916.[17] But the design could not be improved *merely* by avoiding such repetition:

> The remedy for the evil is not to vary its species—as the promoters of so many speculative estates have thought. It is no mitigation of the offence to make it different in every instance; to substitute bull's-eye casements for frames *à la guillotine*, to ring changes on the discord of stained glass above the front door, to surround one entrance with a *gaucherie* in trellis and another with a lampoon of the Orders.[18]

To avoid such superficialities, the houses should be treated consistently, rather than being made arbitrarily different from one another; Budden therefore favoured standardisation in mass housing. For rather different reasons, his view was supported by Stanley Adshead, at that time Professor of Town Planning at University College, London.

Adshead's reasons for supporting standardisation were part of a widespread wartime concern for national efficiency: 'The standard cottage is an essential appendage of a highly organised social system, and without it we cannot have that which lies at the very root of national efficiency, organisation, and economy'.[19] The reasons for this were clear:

> If the war has proved anything, it has proved that national efficiency in the future will depend almost entirely upon good organisation . . . . Organisation demands the marshalling of individuals having similar interests, and within limits there should follow uniformity in the appearance of their homes.[20]

Picturesque design in an early Ministry of Munitions scheme, the Well Hall estate, Woolwich (1915) by Frank Baines (Graham Paul Smith)

The influential Neo-Georgian alternative for munition workers' housing at Dormanstown, Yorks (1918) by Stanley Adshead, Stanley Ramsay and Patrick Abercrombie

But Adshead was no mere bureaucrat: he was concerned with beauty as much as with national efficiency. He and Budden, with growing numbers of other school-trained designers, wanted an architecture which could stand repetition *without* becoming aesthetically enervating. The answer, they felt sure, lay in Neo-Georgian: 'How perfectly this aim was accomplished in the past is demonstrated by the domestic work of the late Eighteenth Century', [21] said Budden; whilst Adshead's article was illustrated entirely with drawings of Neo-Georgian inspiration.

The mounting support for Neo-Georgian found expression in the design of wartime housing. For obvious reasons, the outbreak of war brought house-building to a virtual halt; but an exception to this, which was to have great influence on the design of post-war suburbs, was the housing built for munitions workers. Some of the great arms factories, such as that at Gretna in Scotland, drew their expanded work forces from far afield; so the number of nearby dwellings was inadequate, and landlords sometimes charged inflated rents for the small amount of housing available. The introduction of rent controls, which was one of the authorities' responses to this state of affairs, was to have far-reaching effects on the development of the suburbs after the war. Of equal importance, because the experience gained from their design was to affect post-war legislation through the 1918 Tudor Walters Report on working-class housing, were the government schemes built from 1915 onwards for the munitions workers at Gretna and elsewhere. [22]

Some early examples of munitions workers' housing—such as the 1915 Well Hall Estate at Woolwich, designed by Frank Baines—were complex and picturesque in design; but later schemes increasingly adopted the Neo-Georgian style. In part the decision to use Neo-Georgian was a response to corporate patronage, and in part it reflected the need for economy. But the closing stages of the war also saw the development of new pressures which, though not themselves concerned with architectural style, nevertheless ultimately supported Neo-Georgian.

By 1918 social unrest in Britain, sending shivers down establishment spines, began to affect official thinking on housing: 'if "unrest" is to be converted into contentment, the provision of good houses may prove one of the most potent agents in that conversion', said the king in 1919. [23] Advanced architectural thinkers saw the Neo-Georgian style as uniquely suitable for the public housing which statements such as the king's implied. Stanley Adshead, for example, had seen his 1916 advocacy of the 'standard cottage' as having a social dimension:

It will not be the home of an individual, of an anarchist; but the home of a member of a certain class of the community, of a communist. . . . The standard cottage is an essential appendage of a highly organised social system. [24]

In addition to producing an aesthetically acceptable form of standardisation, with supposed advantages in terms of promoting a 'highly organised social system', the use of Neo-Georgian made it possible for architects to expresss the idea of community through built form, in ways that would have been difficult to achieve with the picturesque style of such schemes as the Well Hall Estate. The complexities of Baines' design at Well Hall differentiated one dwelling from another; whilst the generally horizontal lines of the bland Neo-Georgian terraces of Gretna or Dormanstown subordinated the individual home to the larger whole, expressing an idea of the good life founded on the concept of the egalitarian community, in which communal interests were more important than those of the individual.

These values were not shared by the speculative builder, catering for a middle-class clientèle whose own vision of the good life was still firmly based on the earlier laissez-faire idea of the primacy of the free individual. The speculative builder therefore vigorously expressed the individuality of each dwelling in the new suburbs which began to expand rapidly after the war.

The new suburbs were universally developed at the relatively low density of twelve houses to the acre, and this ensured the rapid horizontal spread of new suburban areas. Because of the relationship between land prices, building costs and house values, this density was economically rational so far as the developer was concerned; but in any case it was usually enforced by a system of development control which leaned heavily upon the advice of the Tudor Walters Report. Even developers who envisaged economic advantages in higher densities were usually prevented from putting their ideas into practice: 'as a great concession for the worst building land that can be had in any particular area, and as little as can possibly be zoned by the Local Authority, you get . . . the equivalent of 15 houses to the acre', complained W. H. Heath, the builder, in 1936. [25]

The land available for suburban development – greatly increased through factors like better suburban transport – could not *actually* be developed, however, without changes in the system by which housing was funded. The invention of a new system of funding – or, rather, the rediscovery of a very old one – made it possible to use the newly available land, and made Dunroamin practicable.

Before the war, most people had lived in rented houses: it has been estimated that only some 10–15 per cent of all families were owner-occupiers. [26] At the end of the war, however, many factors combined to reduce private investment in housing to rent. The wartime Rent Restriction Acts were due to terminate in 1923; but they set a precedent for government intervention in housing rents which caused investors to feel insecure: rightly, as events were to show. Additional factors such as the high interest rates and building costs of the immediate post-war period discouraged private housing investment, particularly as it was expected that these costs would soon fall. Finally, the government itself initiated a vigorous local-authority house-building programme in 1919, threatening stiff competition for the would-be private investor in the rental market.

Nevertheless, the slump in the British economy, particularly in the period after 1920, made housing – as opposed to houses – seem more attractive than stocks and shares to many investors. So, although private investment in rented houses declined, funds began increasingly to flow into the building societies which had largely financed the development of the pre-war rented suburbs. The societies had to adapt to these changed circumstances or go under: the financing of owner-occupation – which, after all, had been the original function of the early terminating societies of a century before – became once again their major concern. [27]

Several factors combined to make it practicable for the building societies to change direction in this way. First, the incomes of wage-earners – unless they were amongst the 10–20 per cent who were actually unemployed during the Depression – rose substantially: it became steadily easier for prospective home-owners to make the necessary mortgage repayments; whilst government intervention, in the form of tax relief on mortgage interest payments, made it easier still. Later, the building societies themselves further widened the home-ownership market by reducing the cash deposit which they required from intending purchasers.

There were many reasons for the wide appeal of these new opportunities for home ownership. The psychological importance of the home was increased by changes which affected people's working lives. As the Depression began to kill off many smaller firms, and as 'rationalisation' affected the larger survivors, work for most people became increasingly a matter of routine. This was as true for the clerk as for the manual worker; so an instrumental view of work as being merely a means to earn money – a view hitherto associated mostly with working-class attitudes – became increasingly common among members of the middle class. Opportunities for job satisfaction were lacking; whilst the slow growth of pressures towards equal status for women made it more difficult for the middle-class wage-earner – still almost certainly male – to adopt a selfishly consumerist lifestyle centred *outside* the home. The home itself became the only remaining environment in which the 'small man' could retain some measure of control over his own destiny. Indeed, with successive governments apparently powerless to control an economy which seemed to be in the grip of impersonal economic forces, and with the value of political representation thus called into doubt at the most fundamental level, many people saw their homes as the *only* places over which they could exercise control.

The confluence of all these factors brought about an explosion in terms of suburban growth. This, in itself, was enough to arouse opposition from the anti-suburban tradition which had grown up during the decades before the war; but to make matters worse, the detailed design of the new suburbs violated the notions of order, simplicity and consistency which the professional architect had come to understand as 'good design'.

As Ian Davis has shown in Chapter 1, this kind of suburban building was intensely disliked by architects and by architectural critics. Though the declared reasons were largely aesthetic, there were others which affected the profession directly. In the first place the suburbs, with few exceptions, did not provide a source of architectural commissions: at least until the slump of the Thirties, it was corporate patrons who provided the architect with increased job opportunities; and they required a *justifiable* architecture, where characteristics such as a clear formal order, unity and consistency were defined as 'good design'. The clearest expression of these needs was to be found in architecture for the local authorities. 'Typical official architecture is that of the London County Council . . . the Council has taken the safe route of adopting for nearly all its buildings a modified Georgian style', said J. M. Richards in 1940, referring to the inter-war period. [28]

Because of the growth of corporate patronage, there were important economic reasons why the architect *needed* to define 'good design' in terms of order and consistency. Reflecting and reinforcing this need, the schools of architecture trained the young designer to *want* to design in this way: 'speculative builders build in the imitation Tudor cottage style, and architects in the Georgian Revival', said Frederick Gibberd in 1935, claiming that:

> Economic conditions brought about by the war, and the advancement in architectural education through the establishment of schools of architecture, bring about . . . simpler and more academically correct buildings . . . this simplification reaches such an extent that in many buildings all traces of Classic details have disappeared. [29]

This distinction between the style of the architect and that of the speculative builder was echoed many times during the second half of the 1930s. Expressed in

'Ten Cottages in an Unbroken Line', in the Dormanstown scheme, photographed
soon after completion (from Dorman Long Company catalogue, 1924)

A group of inexpensive Village Cottages erected by a Builder.

A group of Cottages erected by the same Builder from the same plans,
but with the collaboration of an Architect.

The distinction drawn between the style of the speculative builder and
the architect's Neo-Georgian (from *House Building 1934–36*)

graphic form, it influenced many of the illustrations in the more serious of the contemporary books on housing. Those in *House Building 1934–36*, for example, show its effects particularly strongly. [30] The distinction was, in fact, over-simplified: some notable architects, such as Oliver Hill, continued to design in both Tudor and Neo-Georgian, in addition to 'Modern', throughout the Twenties and Thirties. [31] Significantly, though, Hill's Tudor buildings were seen as unfashionable by the smart, *Country Life* reading upper middle-class circles of upper management. *Country Life* published only his Neo-Georgian buildings together with a few of his 'Modern' ones. It was left to the middle middle-class *Homes and Gardens* to show his Tudor work.

Speculative suburban houses, like Hill's Tudor buildings, were not seen by architects as either orderly or consistent: functionally identical elements, such as porches and bay windows, were differently expressed on adjoining houses, whilst houses identical in plan and section were designed in arbitrarily different styles. To the architect, therefore, the speculative suburb represented 'bad design'. Since he did not depend on Dunroamin for employment prospects, there was no need for him to come to terms with suburban values in any way: indeed, in the public interest, it seemed to many architects that the 'bad design' which the suburb represented ought to be exposed.

The unanimity with which architects adopted this view left them with a problem: if Dunroamin was so awful, why was it so popular? The most plausible argument claimed that people bought suburban semis by default, for lack of any alternative. '[They] are catered for – and have to take what is provided, with but little choice – by the speculative builder', wrote the architect Gordon Allen, in 1936. [32] It was soon possible to see how this theory stood up to the facts.

By the mid Thirties, the speculative builder could see the approach of market saturation: virtually everyone who could afford a speculative house had already bought one. This realisation had three main effects. First, it encouraged attempts to reduce costs by simplifying the form and construction of the house. Secondly, it encouraged a wider range of dwelling types, designed to attract marginal market groups such as the elderly and the newly married. Finally, it stimulated changes in building society attitudes towards the financing of houses for the less well off.

The desire to reduce building costs aroused the interest of many developers in the experimental 'International Style' houses which began to appear in small numbers, for avant-garde patrons, during the late 1920s and early Thirties. The simplified forms of these buildings seemed potentially cheap to build, so a number of firms offered speculative versions, at the cheap ends of their ranges, from 1932 onwards. The 1934 Ideal Home Exhibition saw a determined effort to promote this kind of house. All the show houses, exhibited by six different firms, and including one by the distinguished designer Wells Coates, owed some allegiance to the International Style, whilst their impact was increased by combining them into a 'Village of Tomorrow'. Despite these efforts, backed by extensive advertising based around the contemporary cult of the sun, and despite low prices, these houses proved extremely difficult to sell. This is not surprising, for by now the Modern Movement was associated, in the minds of many people, with big business and big government.

Since the First World War, the simplified classicism of the Liverpool Manner or of Neo-Georgian had been the best available, in terms of the corporate virtues of simplicity, order and consistency. The Modern Movement – or, at least, the style based on the forms of the Modern Movement – appeared to make these virtues its sole raison d'être, and it was increasingly taken up by corporate patrons from the 1930s onwards. Its consequent associations with work and with bureaucracy were in themselves enough to damn it in the eyes of the Dunroaminer; so the relatively few speculative houses which were built under the influence of the International Style have usually been fairly drastically personalised at some stage in their lives. Significantly enough, the first such houses in England – at Braintree, designed in 1919 by Quennell and Crittall – were themselves commissioned by a corporate patron, the Crittall Metal Window Company, [33] whilst the only considerable group of such houses to retain almost exactly its original form – the employees' housing at Silver End, Essex, designed by Thomas Tait for the same corporate patron in 1927 – was again not built for the speculative market. Recently sold to the local authority, these houses have always been rented rather than owner-occupied.

Ultimately far more important, in terms of their influence on Dunroamin, were new building-society attitudes to house purchase. Previously, the societies had usually required a 20 per cent cash deposit from prospective buyers, but after the mid 1930s it became less important for the buyer to have cash available, as the required deposit was reduced, and sometimes waived altogether. This involved the building societies in higher risks, which they offset by taking a guarantee from the builder to cover expenses should the purchaser default on his payments. 'This system has great advantages as it permits about three times as many people to purchase their houses as would be possible if the purchaser had to pay out of his savings 20 per cent of the value', said John Laing, the noted builder, in 1936. [34]

This dramatic increase in the size of the speculative market, coming at a time of slump when corporate commissions were declining in number, made architects view the speculative builder in a new light. The potential advantages of courting him were spelled out, in an article in the RIBA Journal, by Alwyn Lloyd, architect and sometime president of the National Housing and Town Planning Council:

> Looked at from the architects' point of view, a wide field of useful work would be available, only the fringe of which has been explored, and to the young practitioner, particularly, such an opportunity should make a definite appeal. At a time when, for various reasons, there is a shrinkage in the volume of employment in the various trades and professions, it is significant that in connection with the erection of small houses there are possibilities for much wider technical direction, which are capable of almost indefinite expansion. [35]

After considerable discussion by its Public Relations Committee, the RIBA made several moves to exploit this market for architects' services. Competitions were held to show the contributions which architects could make to the design of speculative housing, whilst considerable reductions were made in the scale of minimum fees which the Institute's members had previously been required to charge for such work. Though there was a legacy of poor relationships between the architect and the speculative builder to be overcome, it is possible that the economic realities of the later 1930s, reflected in the RIBA's changing approach to the speculative builder, might have brought about a creative accommodation between the architect's values and those of Dunroamin. An increasingly powerful current of wartime ideas, however, led to new emphasis on the planned use of the country's resources.

By the time peace was restored in 1945, the wartime techniques of planning, claiming a significant contribution to the victory, appeared to have proved their effectiveness so well that they were carried over into the administration of peacetime affairs. The consequent enthusiasm for planning was strongly anti-Dunroamin, whilst escalating land costs – themselves due in part to the reduction in the supply of developable land brought about by the operations of planning itself – contributed to a rapid rise in house prices. It became more and more difficult, particularly in the rapidly-developing South-East, to market semi-detached houses at prices which could be afforded by the kinds of middle and lower middle-class people who had bought them during the period between the wars. As a pattern for mass housing, Dunroamin was no longer feasible.

A Celebration Of Ambiguity

The Synthesis of Contrasting Values held by Builders and House Purchasers

Ian Davis

Unlike verbose architects or planners, builders in the period between the wars were normally too busy making or losing money to put pen to paper to explain why they built as they did. And house purchasers confined their creative energies to their flowerbeds or putting up plywood pelmets rather than writing about why they chose one house in preference to another. Therefore the source material for an analysis of the values of builders and public comes from detailed observation of the design of houses and estates. Information can also be gleaned from the memories of builders active in the period, sales brochures, newspaper advertisements, Ideal Home Exhibition catalogues as well as from articles in such magazines as *Ideal Home, Metroland, Good Housekeeping* and the *Estates Gazette*.

In the late Thirties when the housing market became saturated, house prices dropped to such an extent that in 1937 a semi-detached house, with a garage and large garden, cost a mere £479. This required a down payment of 11s. 1d. Competition also occurred within building societies and interest rates dropped as low as $4\frac{1}{2}$ per cent in the quest for house purchasers to take out mortgages. One effect of the buyers' market was the intense advertising of major builders and their copy provides an insight into the theme of this chapter, which is concerned with values which were frequently ambiguous. Such values were not taught in schools of design, or broadcast in any BBC discussion to educate the masses, but were rather the attitudes shaped by the experience (or prejudice) of developers, builders and inevitably, of house purchasers. These values are complex: some are explicit, others implicit with social, aesthetic and practical dimensions. Although the texts of advertisements, or sales brochures, directly express the values and attitudes of builders they also reflect the attitudes of buyers with some precision. The questions being continually asked in estate offices would be communicated to builders in formulating the next estate development, or in selecting copy for advertising purposes.

In 1941 Gilbert and Elizabeth Glen McAllister reflected on the sorry state of domestic architecture between the wars and they were very confident where to place the blame: 'The speculative builder', they asserted, 'was responsible for the worst of the housing horrors', giving the public 'a wanton insult to their hardly articulate aspirations'. 'Such builders', the McAllisters maintained, 'held a pitifully low regard of their customers, seeing them as being preoccupied with "nice houses", with "pretty gardens" set in a "better part of town" '; but, they sighed:

> They did not know about architecture: how could they? . . . They thought of it (if at all) as the Victorians did, as something 'applied' to a building – ornament, decoration, gables. And so in the world of the airliner, vacuum cleaners and television they were given the pseudo-Tudor and the 'ye olde', the gimcrack, the ramshackle, the fifth-rate; it was the biggest confidence trick of the age. [1]

What the McAllisters did not realise was that the public being given 'ye olde' in the television age belonged to an enduring English tradition. In 1955 Nikolaus Pevsner gave the BBC Reith Lectures under the curiously eliptical title of *The Englishness of English Art*. One of the national characteristics that he enthusiastically identified, as an expatriate, was the English love of ambiguity. Thus the soaring heights of French Gothic extravaganzas, such as Bourges or Amiens, were 'sensibly' scaled down in their English equivalent to the squat vaults of Salisbury or Lincoln. [2] However, stronger and certainly more plentiful evidence for Pevsner's contention could be found in any suburban drive. Ambiguity was well demonstrated in the vocabulary that was employed: *half* timbered walls of '*semi*-detached' homes for the '*middle*' classes set on *sub*urban estates. The copy of builders and developers was liberally peppered with descriptions of brick *and* rendered construction; advantages of town *and* country.

It was this ambiguity that so irritated the little band of Modernists (including the McAllisters) whose extreme positions had been imported, with the minimum of adaptation, from Berlin or Vienna. They advocated *large* blocks of flats, with *unadorned* surfaces of *unambiguous* volumes of pristine simplicity that would have delighted the eye of Plato. It was an architecture of monastic austerity at a visual level, and socially it was equally austere. In their search for an expression of collective anonymity, designers wanted their buildings to possess the absolute minimum of personal idiosyncrasies. Just after the Second World War Lionel Brett was still perpetuating this doctrine. He advised 'novices' to look for *simplicity* and for the time being 'to treat *smartness, streamline* and *luxury* with suspicion'. [3]

The desire for ambiguity was never catered for directly within house advertisements or sales brochures; it was reflected largely subconsciously with occasional oblique references. But this reticence did not inhibit a message being clearly communicated between house purchasers and builders. Both had a strong distaste of extremism in any shape or form.

The spirit of ambiguity was apparent in five major areas: the desire for strong anchorage with the distant past in the buildings' style, whilst wanting (at least in the bathroom or kitchen) all the latest and progressive ideas in planning or labour-saving appliances; the need for a cosy, warm, inward-looking house with oak beams and brick fireplaces whilst simultaneously wanting an expansive outlook for light, air and sunlight; a concern to express the owner's individuality in his home whilst still recognising that it was a part of a street or community; the ambition to own a house that gave an unmistakable appearance of affluence but at a minimum cost to the purchaser; finally, the wish to live in a practical house, that hinted at modernity. London Transport were shrewd enough to recognise the need to balance nostalgia with new technology when they extolled the sublime pleasures of living in Edgware in their advertisements, following the completion of the Northern Line in 1926:

> Stake your Claim at Edgware. Omar Khay-yam's recipe for turning the wilderness into paradise hardly fits an English climate, but provision has been made at Edgware of an alternative recipe which will convert pleasant, undulating fields into happy homes. The loaf of bread, the jug of wine and a book of verse may be got there cheaply and easily.

Leaving the joys of the simple life they hastened to add that Edgware also provided:

> A shelter which comprises all the latest labour-saving and sanitary convenience. We moderns ask much more before we are content, than the ancients, and Edgware is designed to give us that much more. [4]

The labour-saving kitchen had been made possible through the gradual expansion of electrification. Whereas in 1910 only one in five of all homes had electricity, this proportion rose to three-quarters of all homes by 1939. Of these, 30 per cent possessed vacuum cleaners and 80 per cent electric irons. Analysis of house advertising in a 1926 newspaper reveals that the desire for a labour-saving kitchen and bathroom came very high on the list of the most frequently mentioned items, and 27 advertisements out of a total of 52 referred to houses having electric lighting. [5]

In her study of the reasons why buyers had purchased homes in 1929 and 1936, Brenda Innes was told by the original purchasers that the thing they liked best about them was the bathroom. 'But it was not only the functional aspect, even of bathrooms, that weighed in their choice.' Innes found that they had been used to adequate bathrooms in their previous homes but this time the builders 'had succeeded in appealing to something more subtle than just basic requirements'. She described the bathroom in the 1936 'Suntrap' house built by Henry Boot on the Bromley Manor Estate as a 'glamorous achievement of coloured glass panelling', possibly based on the 'Vitrolite' panelled bathroom, kitchen and laundry, featured in the 'All-Electric House' exhibited at the 1934 Ideal Home Exhibition. However, to avoid any possible embarrassment to would-be purchasers, the blatant luxury of tiles, mirrors, light fittings and chromium was passed off as being 'hygienic and easy to clean'. [6]

The aspiration for modernity reached a climax when the 'Modern Homes' columnist of the *Daily Telegraph* wrote in 1935 of the revolution in housing resulting from the invention of helicopters: 'this type of machine is capable of landing vertically upon the roof of a house. A roof hangar may, therefore, take the place of a semi-detached garage.' [7]

The balancing act performed in hanging on to the past whilst grasping for all the advantages of modern living keeps recurring within the pages of the various Ideal Home Exhibition catalogues of the time. In 1927 the Prime Minister, Stanley Baldwin, made a speech at the Society of Arts when he exhorted the builders and architects of the day to look back to English cottage architecture for inspiration. The exhibition catalogue approved of Baldwin's speech but cautioned: 'A wealth of oak beams cannot excuse an inconvenient bathroom. An imposing gable does not make up for inadequate guttering.' The catalogue declared that exhibition visitors would find 'beneath the artistry with which the lessons of this fascinating housing display are clothed [the domestic architecture of an older England], there is an abundance of new ideas.' [8]

As Paul Oliver shows in Chapter 5, the families that initially settled in the new estates were pioneers, building a new frontier. Those who had 'staked their claim in Edgware' (or wherever) had left the familiar landmarks of a Victorian terrace for an estate where everything, except the odd surviving tree, was strange and new. Therefore, they needed all the security they could obtain. This came from friends or neighbours or emerging local institutions, but stability and a sense of continuity also came from their home itself, with its 'ancient and modern' ambivalence. Gordon Allen was right when he said in 1934: 'What the

The ambiguity of the labour-saving, modern house within the shell of the fortified castle (*Daily Telegraph*, 1935)

'Bathroom with geyser and other convenient gas-heated appliances'
(from *The Complete Home Book*, 1937)

average purchaser wants as regards the elevations of his house is a question of psychology rather than art.'[9] The Tudor beams and leaded lights spoke of linkages with a distant and splendid English past, far removed from any thoughts of Europe and the Great War. Similarly, the new kitchen appliances and bathroom chrome were symbolic of a brave future, advancing away from the grime and drudgery of the kitchen and scullery in the house they had recently vacated.

In 1927 the Ideal Home Exhibition included a version of the *Sun-Trap House in the Tudor Style* which was built by the Potters Bar Estate.[10] The description is interesting since it summarises the contrast I have been describing between old and new, and it also relates to the second spirit of ambiguity.

Closed and open, winter and summer, private and public, lazy and energetic, introvert and extrovert; there is a long list of contrasting attitudes or opposing requirements which are commonplace experiences. Traditionally the contrast could be symbolised, on the one hand, as the desire to retreat into a cave and, on the other, to escape into a world of light and air. When applied to the semi-detached house these ambivalent emotions were expressed in the desire for a cosy, inward-looking home, a withdrawal from wartime memories, or the fear of future hostilities, from smoky towns, or even perhaps, the routine pressures of work. Whatever the motivations, many small builders accommodated these contrasting and often conflicting requirements with considerable ingenuity. They were in good company since some very talented architects before them – Soane, Mackintosh or Lutyens – had positively revelled in attempting to design contrasting spaces in close proximity. But once again the idea was repugnant to the Modern purists reared on the uncompromising doctrine of 'consistency' that emerged from the Bauhaus.

The ingredients that formed the images of retreat or liberation were rich and varied. To achieve the former a repertoire of Tudor beams, panelling, stained glass and brick hearths was developed, as Paul Oliver shows in Chapter 7. There could be highly explicit images of security, such as the hanging chain fences which protected the 'castle' from intruders. In contrast the house also contained images of freedom. To 'escape' into the open air, large openable windows were necessary. Dr C. W. Saleeby of the Sunlight League asserted in 1927: 'None but the Sunlight Home can be ideal'. He gave home owners specific guidance: 'Walls are deplorable necessities in such a climate as ours, for protection against wind and rain'; he nevertheless admitted they were 'Wholly desirable for privacy', but he warned 'the exclusion of light and air is disastrous', and continued enthusiastically: 'Wherever possible windows should be open. . . . All windows of apartments inhabited by children, or women, or men or cows or chimpanzees or horses or orchids, or any other valued living thing, should be glazed with the new glass – ''Vitaglass''.' This, claimed Dr Saleeby, was a miracle product that admitted 'as no ordinary glass . . . the ultra-violet rays in sunlight without which we cannot live'. [11]

In 1934 Raymond Unwin gave some guidance to the designers of suburban housing estates. He described the ambivalent requirements of the 'Winter-and-Summer house': '[the designer] feels the comfort or discomfort of the fireside round which the folk will gather in the winter, or the window to which they will all be attracted on summer evenings.' [12]

The inward-and-outward-looking house was a microcosm of the basic ambiguity of Suburbia. For the cosy inward-looking lounge, one can read the closely packed, claustrophobic inner town or city. Similarly, the occupant wanting fresh air could move beyond the open windows of his home to the wide open country beyond. The residents of the suburbs needed the security of the familiar town, whilst wanting to escape into the countryside. Many believed that in both their houses and their locations they had the very 'best of both worlds'. Costain's advertised their housing in 1936 with characteristic ambivalence: 'London's most rural estate – Perivale Wood . . . overlooking Horsenden Hills and Selbourne Bird Sanctuary . . . yet Ealing Broadway with its shops, schools and places of public entertainment is close at hand'. [13]

The third ambiguity was the need to remain an individual within a crowd: the necessity to express personal identity, yet never in such an ostentatious manner as to cause offence or isolate a family or house from the wider community or people or street. To achieve this objective two extreme positions had to be bridged. One was the strong image of the repetitive Georgian terrace expressive of community and town, a form of corporate, civic pride. However, as Ian Bentley observes in Chapter 4, it is even more likely that the suburban home was a reaction against another communal image – the council-house estate with all its associations of conformity, orderliness and anonymity. Gordon Allen wrote in 1929 of the public's hostility to 'brick boxes with slate lids', of 'houses in rows' and what he called 'that ugly high effect', which was in contrast to a 'pleasing cottage-like, low and spreading appearance'. [14] Then again in 1934 he observed the suburban dweller's reaction against the council-house style: 'It is safe to say he desires his home to look different from his neighbour's and, above all, unlike the municipal house, owing to his sense of social dignity.' [15]

The 'communal image' was in sharp contrast to the anarchy of houses (perhaps in some wealthy Victorian suburb) where every dwelling proclaimed the self-assurance and independence of its proud owner. This was achieved by various means: physical detachment from other buildings, as well as varieties of

HERE ARE TWO ROADS.
GIVEN FREE CHOICE . . . IN WHICH

WOULD YOU PREFER TO LIVE?

The Ministry of Health presented a loaded comparison between a
tree-less, rain-soaked suburban street with sewer-vent pipe (*top*) and a
sunny, green council estate (from *Houses We Live In*, 1939)

OPEN YOUR WINDOW TO THE TONIC AIR OF KENT'S HEALTHIEST ESTATES!

Illustration below shows Morrell's latest addition to their SUPERB PROGRAMME of LABOUR SAVING LUXURY HOMES.

This is the C5 DE LUXE TYPE. £780 FREEHOLD. 18/2 WEEKLY. £1 SECURES.

Accommodation includes Canopied Front Door Entrance. RECEPTION HALL with deep windows. LOUNGE with deep bay. DINING ROOM has French windows, High Pressure Boiler, etc. Super KITCHEN equipment includes quarry tile floor, automatic copper and wringer, specially designed Kitchen Cabinet, etc. Chromium Easy-Clean fittings. The THREE LARGE BEDROOMS include pear switches, built-in cupboards, etc. TILED BATHROOM has cased bath, heated towel rail, shaving cabinet, chromium mixing taps with shower, etc. Many power and gas points for convenience. Long secluded garden. Double entrance Gates and room for Garage. Unspoilt country surroundings.

Winchester Park Estate, Bromley, Kent. Served by three Railway Stations nearby at Bromley South, Bromley North and Shortlands. **Wickham Woods Estate,** together with Coneyhall Estate, has Hayes Station nearby, served by Morrell's Luxury Coach Free to Residents and Visitors. **Garden Estate, Petts Wood, Kent,** and **Chelsfield Park Estate, Chelsfield, Kent,** right alongside the Stations. **Old Mill Farm Estate, Orpington, Kent,** is served by Orpington and St. Mary Cray Station. All have fast and frequent electric trains to City and West End. Also **Dorchester Park Estate, Herne Hill, S.E.24.** Detached Residences from £2,000.

On a Morrell Estate the joy of healthy, drudge-less living can be yours for as little as 11/2 per week!

Morrell's new Wondervalue Homes De Luxe are indisputably to-day's record Value—alone made possible by Morrell's Gigantic Scale Methods, which pass the savings effected on to you. Prices range from £479 Freehold to £1,895. Repayments from 11/2 Weekly. Terms inclusive—No Extras. Houses have room for garage, and Purchasers' furniture is removed FREE within a 25-mile radius.

★ COUPON.—FOR FREE HOME GUIDE AND TRAVELLING VOUCHERS, WRITE TO:—Desk No. N1, Morrell (Builders), Ltd., Terminal House, Grosvenor Gardens, S.W.1.

Name ....

Address ....

....

MORRELL'S
Estates at BROMLEY PETTS WOOD HAYES WEST WICKHAM ORPINGTON & CHELSFIELD·KENT

Morrells appealed to the young housewife and the 'joy of health and drudgeless living' in Kent (*Daily Telegraph*, 1935)

material, size, and overall form. And if this was insufficient, large dividing walls and hedges could be inserted between houses to eliminate any doubt about who was who. Estate developers were well aware of the desire for individuality and advertisements invariably illustrated houses isolated from the inevitable neighbouring house that was doubtless lurking no less than two 'garage spaces' away. One aerial perspective in a *Daily Telegraph* advertisement of July 1935 went to the extent of only drawing one side of the semi-detached house. [16] The managing director of one of the largest building firms, John Laing, held the view that detached or semi-detached houses were infinitely superior to the terrace; in fact they replaced it. He reflected on the historical process: 'In the early nineteenth century . . . people were satisfied with the continuous terraces of houses displaying regularity in elevation and similarity in design. . . . Today, although the principles of pleasing planning underlying such are retained, uniformity is not now encouraged, most people preferring to live in a detached or semi-detached house.' [17]

The bridge between the subtlety (or boredom) of the terrace or council estate and the flamboyance of the detached villa was accomplished by an extensive range of architectural devices. The semi-detached house was obviously a primary element in balancing individual (or semi-individual) expression with that of the community or street. Another device was to modify the ridge roof with its end gables, an image that strongly reinforced the horizontal form of a street. In the suburbs this was frequently changed into a series of hipped roofs. While it succeeded in maintaining the street image (if in a diluted form), it also emphasised the individuality in a home (or pair of homes) as the roof sloped inwards from its eaves. Inevitably this subtle identification was unappreciated by architects and planners. Patrick Abercrombie (later to become the author of the Greater London Plan of 1944) believed that suburban housing site-planning, 'tends to lead to a sort of *uneasy compromise*' (my italics). 'The individual house and the long terrace give way to the semi-detached villa, perhaps the least satisfactory building unit in the world.' He provided just two reasons for such a judgment: 'the closeness of the dual units makes individualistic treatment fussy, whereas their repetition produces an inescapable monotony of mass.' [18]

At a much smaller scale the desire for self expression was fulfilled in various ways, including different colours of paintwork, in house names and in door furniture. The bronze Cornish piskie door knocker, purchased during a Tintagel honeymoon, or the sheer variety of the front gardens with never a repeat layout underlined the uniqueness or independence of the owner. But such emphasis was at a very different scale from its Victorian ancestor. In these large villas the 'independence' or 'sense of identity' was part and parcel of the architecture,

Housing in Hastings, c. 1935 – each pair of semis to a different design
(Ian Davis)

A pair of semis in Edgware with swept gables, hipped roof, corner first floor
windows, box-framed 'Tudor' detail and brick bays; 1934 (Ian Davis)

whilst in the case of the suburban home, it was largely up to the owner to create his own mark as Ian Bentley indicates in Chapter 6. This personal expression was normally discrete, controlled and respectable. In the period of Dunroamin there was none of the boldness that was to come in the 1960s when the Do-It-Yourself movement gathered steam.

Probably the most frequent attack on the suburban house is the charge of monotony. As early as 1909 C. F. G. Masterman complained of 'miles and miles of little red boxes in little silent streets in number defying imagination'. Yet within this suburban desert: 'Each boasts its pleasant drawing-room, its bow-window, its little front garden, its high sounding title — "Acacia Villa" or "Camperdown Lodge" attesting unconquering human aspiration.'[19] George Orwell shared Masterman's dislike of such repetition when he wrote in his novel *Coming Up for Air* in 1939: 'Do you know what world I live in', he asked, 'Ellesmere Road, West Bletchley? Even if you don't, you know fifty others exactly like it.' Orwell did not consider that semi-detached Dunroamin differed from council estates: 'You know how these streets fester all over the inner-outer suburbs. Always the same long, long rows of little semi-detached houses . . . as much alike as council houses and generally uglier.' In similar manner to Masterman thirty years before, he noted with irony the way such houses had been made personal:

> The stucco front, the creosoted gate, the privet hedge, the green front door. The Laurels, the Myrtles, the Hawthorn, Mon Abri, Mon Repos, Belle Vue. At perhaps one house in fifty some anti-social type who'll probably end in the workhouse has painted his front door blue instead of green.[20]

Robert Sinclair believed that a close relationship existed between a mass-produced house and a mass-produced man.

> From the moment that he enters what is called without irony a 'hall', he does almost exactly what the man in the next house is doing. There is no overt contrast with the home life of the Londoner, yet London contrives to rule him in his most intimate moments.[21]

Each of these writers was critical of the lifestyle engendered by the suburbs. They had noticed the expressions of territory or ownership and either regarded them with snobbish contempt, or at best affectionate disdain. What wasn't in doubt was their attitude to the repetitive 'monotonous, identical and ugly' form of the suburban houses. But the question remains: had they actually looked in detail at any suburban street? Some *were* monotonous, but others were varied, houses were rarely identical after just a few years of occupation, and the charge of ugliness is of course a relative term. What is apparent is that many builders were aware of the need to avoid monotony. One large builder in the London area, Harold Neal, wrote in 1934: 'In estate development our chief aim has been to avoid monotonous repetition in layout, roads and houses. To achieve this each house is designed separately and treated as an individual unit.'[22] At its best a suburban street achieved the same kind of subtle balance between unity and independence that can be seen in the High Street of an historic English town, where houses of differing periods and of diverse materials jostle together within a wide variety whilst retaining a cohesion. In addition to this architectural achievement the home provided at a social level privacy and fulfilment, giving the occupants a sense of identity without being isolated from their neighbours or the surrounding community.

Although utopian reformers always dream of a classless society where the baser human weaknesses of envy, snobbery and the aspiration for social status are neatly eradicated, the reality is of course that such emotions are alive and well and some would have us think that they particularly flourished in Dunroamin. Whether the accusation is valid that the suburban middle classes had a greater preoccupation with visible status than those living in Bond Street, or for that matter Old Kent Road, is impossible to know, given the absence of detailed contemporary writing, but there is a plentiful supply of visual clues to be gained from a stroll down any suburban avenue.

'The assumption that every Englishman was, or felt that he was a disinherited country gentleman accorded reasonably well with the image of some inter-war suburbs.' John Burnett has argued persuasively the accuracy of this opinion. An explanation of such an attitude was the very rapid growth of the professional classes from 744,000 in 1911 to 1,493,000 in 1951. The growth of non-manual occupations resulted in the middle class increasing from 20.3 per cent of the total population in 1911 to 30.4 per cent in 1951.[23] Burnett has reminded us that, 'despite these trends towards a more egalitarian society, the home continued to be, as it had in the past, the most significant mark of social differentiation and the most significant symbol of social status.'[24] The expanding middle class formed the bulk of those who purchased homes which became manifestations of their new property-owning status. Each semi-detached house was called upon to demonstrate in unmistakable terms to the other occupants (and particularly to parents and relatives) that they were now far removed from any image of the poverty in which many had grown up. In Molly Hughes' account of her family's life between the wars she recounts how 'Mrs "Semi-Detached" was thrilled at the prospect of becoming one of the superior people on the Ridge-way'. [25] And yet, despite such aspirations, these purchasers were considerably poorer than the Edwardian middle class that preceded them. The result was a further ambiguity (the fourth in the list on page 79) – an image of affluence, yet on a shoestring.

The origins of these images are difficult to define with any accuracy. For some, they no doubt amounted to a scaled-down version of a splendid upper-class country house (or at least its lodge), for others to a recollection of the style of the Victorian or Edwardian suburbs that fringed the immediate outskirts of most towns. The estate agents were sensitive to the imagery and pampered their would-be purchasers with the certain knowledge that they were both the inheritors of upper-class values, and even their estates. At the top end of the housing market the Central London Building Company urged people to move to 'London's lovelier district' in 1926. This was the parkland area of Kenwood on Hampstead Heath. Prospective purchasers were reminded of their inher-itance: 'the unspoilt loveliness of old-world gardens – as delightful now as when Baroness Burdett-Coutts was in residence'. Bromley local newspapers in 1934 contained tributes to 'public-spirited people leaving the district for Sussex, Devonshire, etc'. As they vacated their estates, tempted by lucrative prices, the developers were quick to use the ex-landowners' names in their advertising. Peter Way has commented: 'Many of these homes were built on the very land of the displaced squires, as the builders were pleased to point out. Every one of these new homes was built to satisfy the very same dream that the squire enjoyed there . . .' [26]

E. Howkins declared in the 1926 *Estates Gazette* that 'Attractive names will prove helpful in disposing of both land and houses'. The names of both streets and estates strongly emphasise the dream of *rus in urbe*. An examination of advertisements in just one 1926 newspaper indicates that out of a total of 52 estates offering houses 31 had specific names, and 16 of these ended with 'Estate' or 'Park'. Some of the estate names related to the previous landowner: 'Montague Gardens' probably to land sold by Lord Montague of Beaulieu, or the 'Chandos Estate' in Edgware, identifying links with the Earl of Chandos and his estate in Cannons Park. Many of the names have strong rural associations: 'Bramble Town Road', 'Holly Lodge Estate' and 'Barn Hill Estate'. In addition, five took their names from trees or plants and three were named after hills. In the Cannons Park Estate, built in Stanmore by Laing, streets were all named after John Laing's childhood haunts in the Lake District. Finally in the newspaper sample two of the estate names have religious or monastic connotations – 'St Stephen's Church Estate' or 'Whitefriars Estate'.

Just as the developers left their mark with the naming of estates or roads, the first occupants named their newly acquired homes. Together, this collection of names of estates, streets or homes provides a useful and probably accurate indication of the most important values of home owners. House names seem to indicate a greater preoccupation with whimsy than status-seeking, and contain a strong romantic streak; although they do encompass significant associations with 'superior people' – the concern for middle-class status. There is also the love of the outdoors, in particular rural, lakeland or sea-side locations. The longing for security is expressed in our book's title and others in similar vein such as *Bakome*. Other names, including *Bryn Newwydd*, refer obliquely to the years of early marriage and home-building. One estate in South London was called Beulah Park, derived from the Hebrew word for marriage or fulfilment, but far more common were all the names that recall honeymoon locations or twinned first names. *Ronilda* or *Gladroy* may well have made the critics despair but for a young couple in their first home they were as symbolic as the exchange of their wedding rings. At the very height of the boom in house building, in 1935, a *Daily Express* publication told its readers: 'Never before has there been such a demand for well-built, scientifically planned houses. A new consciousness of home-making has been born. Men and women are equally enthusiastic. Together they study house plans and schemes of decoration: together they devise ways and means of owning homes of their own . . . .. It gives them a sense of security and comfort and intimacy essential to real family life.'[27]

Within the home, the desire for true middle-class status was rather compromised by the impossibility of affording servants. It is doubtful if any of the early occupants of Dunroamin had ever lived in homes with maids, cooks or butlers, but their image of a middle-class home was incomplete without them. The pages of *Ideal Home* and the exhibits of the Ideal Home Exhibition portrayed the good life which was never complete without a servant problem. A special design feature of a house in the 1927 Exhibition was a soundproof service hatch between the kitchen and the dining-room which was designed to 'avoid conversations in the dining-room being overheard in the kitchen'.[28] The same Exhibition contained a novelty item which managed to combine rural connotations, definitions of territory, surrogate servants and associations with the aristocracy: 'garden boot-scrapers in the form of a pair of terrier dogs on guard'. G. Malle & Son Ltd of the Euston Road were happy to provide them to purchasers' choice in reinforced concrete or cast-iron.

The layout of the servantless house, with its kitchen next to the dining-room, enabled the housewife to cook meals without the embarrassment of being seen at work by visitors. Brenda Innes has noted that this was a vitally important social convention of the time. [29] Eventually the domestic appliances, Hoover vacuum cleaners and washing machines, would not only take the place of domestic helpers; they become obedient servants that never answered back or listened at keyholes.

A further characteristic of the search for visible status or affluence can be seen in the form and details of the house. This became a gallery of objects and ideas that were intended to further the ego of any would-be purchasers. But the meaning of such details eluded most critics. For example, an architectural correspondent of *Good Housekeeping*, G. Bryant Hobbs, wrote in 1933:

> These 'poor' houses generally stand self-revealed by their multiplicity of details – gables, bay windows, brackets, leaded lights and, in fact, all the trappings that suggest a house to a person who has never before had occasion to think in terms of architecture.

From this lofty position he then patronisingly suggested: 'This is really not strange, any more than it is for a child at its first party to be captivated by everything edible that it should not have!' [30]

However, another architect, Gordon Allen, writing in the following year, was aware that these 'trappings' had more to do with the 'image' of the house than with architectural notions. He described the process of designing a simple pair of semi-detached houses: 'The elevations have been treated in such a way as to suggest one large house, instead of two small ones.' [31] The front façade of the house was all important. Unlike Le Corbusier's Villa Savoie, designed as a Platonic volume with no distinguishing elements to identify front, rear or back, the semi-detached home maintained a clear distinction and hierarchy between front, side and rear walls. This differentiation referred to public and private areas, to visible and (almost) hidden walls, to ornate and plain surfaces and to articulated and flat planes. The subtleties in the ordering of these elements are so commonplace that their familiarity guarantees that they remain unnoticed. For example, we would not expect bay windows and gable ends on the rear wall of a house; we subconsciously know the rules of the game without being able to recite them.

As the visitor or purchaser moves closer to the semi-detached house, one image after another seems to reinforce the preoccupation with status, or 'keeping up appearances'. He is greeted by the incongruous sight of a single gate immediately next to a double gate for access to the garage. It is immediately obvious that one of these gates would easily suffice, but the conspicuous excess is a pointed reminder of the multiple entrances to Chatsworth or the Edwardian suburban semi. Beside the notice 'No Hawkers, No Circulars', there is

'Tradesmen's Entrance'. Both speak in unmistakable tones of authority and superiority. Even the curve of the concrete drive to the front door provides a distant echo (for those that are not Hawkers or Tradesmen) of the approach to a country estate. The drive ends at the porch, which may be reminiscent of a Doric portico, or a church lych gate. Once inside the front door the room names of Hall, Lounge, Dining-Room and Scullery, as well as the oak panelling on the wall or parquet flooring, are all reminders of splendid predecessors. That all of this could be achieved for £650, with a £10 deposit, was regarded with some justification as a great bargain, and it is doubtful if housing costs for the ordinary man (when seen as relative to incomes) have ever been as cheap in English history.

The epilogue to the many ambivalent qualities of the suburban house was exemplified in the 'Suntrap' house. In this fifth of the layers of ambiguity listed on page 79, once again, a subtle balance was achieved between the image of a house in the eyes of a house buyer and that of the supporters of the Modern Movement. Peter Donner wrote in 1942: 'They have accepted the Modern Movement in a *moderate form* [my italics]: horizontal windows, no mouldings, no ornament', then he adds the note of compromise 'but a door canopy and a hipped roof'. [32] The archetypal image of the Villa Savoie had been tamed and made almost palatable for English consumption. The roof solved the problem of where to put the water tank and how to cope with the English weather. But at a deeper level such houses destroy the rigidity of the cube or rectangle which remains intact when they have flat roofs.

In addition to these five ambiguous expressions found within the design of suburban houses and estates, there were also fundamental ambiguities in the way the houses were advertised to the buying public. Several of the national daily newspapers (the *Daily Telegraph* in particular) devoted regular space for home advertisements. Within the London area, one of the main ways of reaching the house-buying public was via the pages of the *Evening News'* 'Homeseekers' Guide' which included a weekly section of up to four pages of home advertisements. A comparison between the *Evening News* of 19 February 1926, after the worst of the housing shortage, [33] and the same paper a decade later, 22 February 1936, [34] reveals some significant changes that occurred during this decade.

The illustrations of the homes are particularly illuminating. In the early sample they take the uniform line-drawing format with over 30 carefully drawn perspectives (with a fair proportion in pure elevation). The overall impression was one of discrete orderliness. However, in 1936 a far bolder approach was

93

AFTERWARDS   DECREASING TO
£54   £36

Lease 99 years.
Ground Rent from £9 10s.
Few minutes Station and Shopping Centre. Tram

From a page of the 'Homeseekers' Guide'
for 19 February 1926 (*Evening News*)

THE HOMESEEKERS' GUIDE

Houses, Bungalows, Flats and Land in Town, Suburbs, Country and by the Sea

THIS week-end will see a great increase in the number of visitors to the new housing estates—all anxious to find a new home before the spring.

The great aim, in many instances, will be to get settled this side of Easter and thus celebrate the first great holiday of the year in possession of the ideal home.

At the moment the problem is where to direct the search and in this you have the invaluable assistance of the wide range of property offers on this page.

From such a varied selection it should be a simple matter to spot the home and surroundings which appeal to you most.

By following up these suggestions at the first opportunity you should be able to secure the exact size and type of home to suit your requirements at a price you are willing to pay.

Before long the spring home seeking rush will have gathered force and it will not be quite such a simple matter to solve your problems.

By making the most of this day and the opportunity presented, day and to-morrow you should be able to bring the quest very quickly to a satisfactory end.

From a page of the 'Homeseekers' Guide' of a decade later, 22 February 1936 (*Evening News*)

adopted. The precision had gone and photography was being used to accompany such brash slogans as: 'Start 1936 on the Right Lines – choose a Costain built Home on the Preston Manor Estate'. Localised competition seemed to be taking place within the North-West London Region: Taylor Woodrow claimed their estates were 'Best in the North-West', against such cries of 'See Belmont Farm First' or 'Ideal Homes in N.W. London' and 'You haven't seen the Finest Value until you've visited the Nash Estates at Rayners Lane, South Harrow and Eastcote'. Oakcraft Estates on the Kingston By-Pass ('The Pleasant Estate') advertised their houses with the less-wealthy buyer in mind: '.''Home'' and you pay weekly only 9s 9d.' These houses were offered from only £390 to £465, with a drawing of the home symbolically superimposed on a cloud with radiating sunrays, no doubt matching its front gate.

In the text of the advertising, prominence was given to such practical matters as the time it would take to get to Charing Cross, as well as precise details of room sizes. In sharp contrast, in the drawings and photographs of houses the only hint of a real-life situation came in the form of scudding clouds, sunbursts or a judiciously placed poplar, and people were noticeable absentees. The whole scene is portrayed in these pictures as a form of idyllic fairyland. Cutlers of Harrow wrote a brochure in 1930, *Ideal Homes in North Harrow*. They described the mysterious pleasures in store for: 'Pedestrians who delight in rambles, the region might be called Enchanted Land. Footpaths opening into pleasant escapes from crowded throughplaces into the solitude of nature are very numerous.' [35]

These builders were skilfully communicating two very ambivalent issues: information on costs, room sizes, etc, whilst the buyers' emotions were assailed by images of the peaceful rural life all of 59 minutes from the city smoke. Although the newly built local by-pass could be referred to in the text, neither cars nor traffic jams were drawn or mentioned. Whilst schools are indicated there is never a trace of a cycling child. When it came to the actual style of house being offered there was no deception. The precisely drawn illustrations indicate the range and style of houses on offer. The 1926 sample indicates 52 types of houses available, of which seven were detached, eight terraced, with the remaining 37 being semi-detached. In comparison 27 house types were offered in 1936, none of which was detached, one was a flat, five were bungalows and the remaining 21 were semi-detached. The vast majority of all the illustrations were of semi-detached houses in a wide range of styles. It is noticeable that the *text* of each advertisement, almost without exception, ignores the question of house style though a large proportion of the invective against these houses was on stylistic grounds, a loathing of various 'bogus styles', with particular abuse for the 'Tudorbethan style'.

An examination of all the houses illustrated in these samples from 1926 and 1936 reveals a strong preference for the hipped roof. Out of a total sample of 31 illustrations from both periods only four (in 1926) are of ridge roofs. The entry position in almost all of the houses was on the front façade to the side. In only two samples, again in 1926, this pattern was changed to doorways on either side of the party wall. But perhaps the most striking result is that out of the sample of 31 illustrations there are fourteen different styles of house. Even where the same style persists, as for example with the eight hipped-roof houses with hipped gables (in the 1926 sample), there is a wide variety of differences of detail, such as wall finishes, types of glazing, front walls, etc. This range of choice was a characteristic of both the 1926 and 1936 samples. The difference was that this diversity came in 1926 from a very large number of small firms (70 in this paper), which in 1936 had been consolidated to just 25, but the total included large contractors offering a wide repertoire of house types. Hilbery Chaplin Ltd, 'London's leading Estate Developers' of Golders Green, offered no less than 40 different types of house. But others could exceed this range, for example Morrell's ('You'll remember Chesfield as the finest estate you have ever seen') were offering 61 house types. John Laing offered 40 house types on their Edgwarebury Lane Estate in Edgware in the late Thirties. However, this was something of an exception; the average from the 1936 sample was of ten house types for each building firm.

In 1935 Wimpey's used a 'fill-out' advertisement which their 'Home Experts' would carefully consider before advising on the most suitable Wimpey estate. They include such matters as whether the prospective buyer wished to live north or south of the Thames, where he worked, did he want to live near or far out in the country. They asked questions about children needing elementary education, and whether there were any babies, 'rendering necessary a park within pram distance'. They also wanted to know of church connections ('indicate denomination'), the current expenditure of a family on rates and rent and whether the family wanted a large garden. The final question asked prospective buyers to indicate whether they worked for various bodies including the Civil Service, the Gas Light and Coke Co. Ltd, or in the teaching professions, etc. Such questions as prices and payments, services within the home or community were obviously the issues to which Wimpey's attached the most importance,[36] and these issues are underlined in the surveys of advertising.

In the 1926 sample the most important item was the cost of houses. Forty-nine out of the sample of 52 listed their prices; however over half of the sample gave greater prominence to the easy terms for paying the initial deposit. Various inducements were offered to prospective buyers, such as £5 to secure the house, with the balance of 10 per cent deposit on completion. Only one agent referred to the long-term security of the investment describing its virtues for 'thrift and provision for your future'.

After details of house prices the important information in the 1926 sample was the proximity of the nearest station. Thirty-three out of the sample of 52 referred to this with thirteen providing details of train times to various locations in central London (three even went so far as to describe the cost of a season ticket). A special point was made by five that the train service was electric. Nine referred to the local bus or tram service and its closeness to the new housing.

The next most important piece of information was that about electric lighting, with half of the sample referring to this. Twelve of the 27 also referred to gas light in addition to the electric services. Only four made reference to electric power points, and just one commented on bells. Then came fourteen advertisements referring to separate WCs, followed by fourteen houses with garage space (only three actually provided them). The first references to the quality of planning or construction are well down on the list. It is obvious that advertisers had the housewife in mind with their references to labour-saving kitchens, hot and cold water, gas stoves and tiled bathrooms and kitchens.

Turning to the 1936 sample, out of a total of 34 all included reference to house costs and financing arrangements. Ten out of the sample referred to the choice of house types (an item which did not occur in 1926). The proximity of the shops and station came next on the list, followed by details of train times to London. Next in priority there was reference to 'No legal charges', and a location in 'unspoilt country'. Finally, the only items to get five mentions out of the complete sample were the proximity of local schools and a bus service.

In 1935, at the height of the house building boom, 76,112 firms of contractors were registered in Britain. In 1930 no less than 84 per cent of all firms employed ten people or less, whilst only 1.5 per cent employed between one and five hundred men. [37] At the lower end of the scale there were many with minimal expertise. However the firms to survive into the 1930s normally had grown up out of a building craft tradition. T. F. Nash (later to become one of the larger builders in North-West London) was originally a carpenter. He set up his business in 1922 and by the outset of the war had established a flourishing firm producing 'The Finest Value in any London Suburb – Acknowledged Nash Houses'. An indication of the fusion of values between builders and their customers was the fact that Nash, as well as other builders in North-West London, for example Ben Cutler and E. W. Comben, all lived in the houses they had built. Comben & Wakeling originated in 1892 but its main growth occurred between the wars. The company operated from Wembley, using headed

The competitive nature of house-selling in the 1930s is evident from a comparison of advertisements of 1926 (*above*) and 1936 (*below*) (*Evening News*)

Advertisement for Wates, indicating their wide range of house styles in 1935 (*Daily Telegraph*)

A new development being laid out at Ruislip in the early 1930s. The Show House (*right*) has been completed prior to building, and 'Sold' notices are already stacked in readiness by the site hut (London Borough of Hillingdon)

notepaper with a gabled suburban house superimposed with the exclamation 'Awake Wembley!' By 1934 the firm was building on four estates, totalling 190 acres, in East Finchley, Hatch End and Kenton. The average annual output was 230 houses. In 1935 the firm's advertising used a Miss Helen Burke, 'Home Expert of the *Sunday Pictorial*'. She sent 'every woman a message': 'They're honest houses – well-planned, well-built – so labour-saving and so practical as to delight a housewife's heart. Outside and in they are a joy.' She proceeded to compliment Comben & Wakeling: 'The builders have remembered everything, even the laying out of the front gardens with lawns and shrubs, and rose and flowering trees.' Her testimonial ends with the exclamation: 'Here are homes – not merely houses. You have but to see them to appreciate the difference.'[38] This advertisement is an interesting reminder that builders were able to recognise by the mid 1930s that selling appeal had to be focussed on housewives.

At the other end of the scale from the vast number of small firms, a few 'giants' emerged through the housing boom of the Thirties: Costain, Wates, Taylor-Woodrow, New Ideal Homesteads and Wimpey. The approach of one major company, John Laing, to house building was comprehensive and vast in scale. In the mid 1930s they employed 800 men on their housing projects on what would now be called 'package deals'. Laing's chose and purchased the land, and in a rather perfunctory manner 'negotiated' with the relevant local authority. (A more accurate description of the process was 'informing' the council of their intentions.) They laid out the roads, in some cases naming them as well as landscaping their grass verges. Company architects (or hired private practitioners) designed the homes within a very specific framework provided by John Laing. The homes were built and each garden was provided with a fruit tree out of Laing's nurseries. The houses were then sold through the firm's own marketing organisation or via local estate agents and if purchasers needed help the firm would arrange their mortgages with a collaborating building society. In the later years of the Thirties Laing's went on to build shopping parades in all their major housing estates. The national progression did not stop there; the next step was to build industrial estates in Queensbury in North-West London and Boreham Wood in Hertfordshire. These provided local employment for the residents of the homes they had built. The factories and shops were then rented out by Laing's property company, who shrewdly remained the landlords.

John Laing's pride in his firm's house designs and estate layouts stemmed from his own deep interest (some of his colleagues called it meddling) in every detail of the design and costing of the estates. There is no doubt that his architects were given rather precise briefing as to what was required from them, and this included design decisions. Thus the completed estates were a very accurate reflection of Laing's own taste and values. These emerged from a childhood in the Lake District. His father was a hardworking, non-conformist builder and John shared his simple pleasures in an open-air life with a very strong family loyalty. These values were readily transferred to his house building, and he once reflected that this had been the 'happiest and most successful part of our business'. [39] The particular characteristics of Laing estates were variety, extensive planting and sensitive road layouts designed to preserve existing landmarks or trees. He wanted moderation, simplicity with no 'falseness', so there was a particular aversion to the use of fake half-timbering on his homes. 'We find that on the whole', he reflected, 'the public exhibit judgment and taste in that they desire simplicity of design and warmth of colour . . ., they dislike meaningless ornamentation'. [40] Such authoritative claims were altogether different from the pronouncements of the various critics, since Laing, like all successful contractors, possessed very detailed knowledge of what form of estate, or what form of house would or would not sell. The convergence of Laing's taste and that of thousands of buyers is hardly surprising since Laing (unlike planners and architects), had never been educated away from popular attitudes and values.

Whilst Laing's were offering their rather austere homes for sale, neighbouring estates were successfully marketing Tudor Estates or 'Ultra-Modern' 'Suntrap' homes. This extensive range of house types from various estates was further expanded by the range of designs offered by each builder. In part, this variety was a result of the large number of competing building firms, from the giants like Laing to the five-man concern. However big or small, each firm wanted to market a product which would be distinctive from that of a competing firm, as recognisable as the difference between an Austin or Ford car. Even today the windows of suburban estate agents offer houses with the name attached of the original builder.

Did the characteristics of suburban life, the green fields, grass verges, cheap and varied homes, 29 minutes from Charing Cross, measure up to the rich copy of the 'Homeseekers' Guide'? The answer must be positive. Over 70,000 builders, as well as legions of developers and estate agents and a not inconsiderable quantity of architects deserve belated credit for a housing revolution achieved in just two decades. Perhaps the dominant characteristic of these semi-detached houses was their ambivalence. And as we have seen there was nothing furtive about this preoccupation; the art of ambiguity that was highly developed in Dunroamin became a positive celebration, expressed in the content, form and detailing of these houses.

Housing estate in Elstree built in 1938 by John Laing, showing the
austere elevations, devoid of ornamentation (John Laing and Son Ltd)

The first 'Suntrap' housing, Rectory Gardens, Edgware by Welch,
Cachemaille-Day and Lander, 1932 (from *The Book of the Modern House*)

≥4≤

INDIVIDUALISM OR COMMUNITY?
Private Enterprise Housing and the Council Estate
Ian Bentley

DUNROAMIN and the Modern Movement mainstream express two contrasting visions of the good life: one stressing the primacy of the individual, and the other that of the egalitarian community. These visions conditioned the design of different inter-war housing layouts: the first through the medium of Dunroamin, and the second in council housing. Because each was so clearly identified with one particular set of values, a comparison between Dunroamin and the council estate exposes the suburban conflict of values in the clearest possible way.

Neither set of values, of course, was translated into architectural form entirely from scratch. As is usual with architectural innovation, the new values were expressed by emphasising certain features of contemporary architectural traditions, and by reacting against others. The significance of the new forms, therefore, can only be understood by comparing them with the traditions of their time.

Before the war, two distinct architectural traditions were associated with lower middle-class and artisan housing. First, there were speculative terraces, like those which we have seen at Oxford's Summertown. [1] Secondly, there was the Arts and Crafts tradition, pioneered by C. F. A. Voysey and M. H. Baillie Scott, which strongly influenced both the early cottage estates of the London County Council, such as Old Oak, Hammersmith (1909–14), [2] and the Garden City schemes of Barry Parker and Raymond Unwin as developed at New Earswick (from 1902), at Letchworth (from 1903) and at Hampstead Garden Suburb (from 1905). In the event, both Dunroamin and the local authority suburb drew more from the Arts and Crafts/Garden City tradition than from the pre-war speculative terrace.

Part of the reason was a concern for public health, aroused by an awareness of the disparity between the health standards of different classes which had become clear in the course of wartime recruiting experience. In terms of public health, the Garden City design tradition had obvious advantages over the pre-war speculative terraces. Its low density contrasted favourably with that of the terraced layout, as did the fact that its houses were usually designed with living-rooms opening straight into gardens. In contrast, the living-rooms of pre-war terraced houses were usually separated from the garden by a dingy backyard, fitted in alongside a back extension housing scullery, WC and coal store. At least some aspects of the Garden City tradition, therefore, appealed to both private- and public-housing developers; and this breadth of appeal was strengthened by the fact that the design principles underlying the tradition, as developed by Parker and Unwin, could be construed in two quite different ways. On the one hand, their work could be seen as highly ordered, its constituent parts fitting into a strong overall scheme. On the other hand, though, those same constituent parts were often designed to have strong identities of their own; so that it was equally possible to read the overall design as the additive result of the interactions between them.

This ambiguous relationship between the whole and the part is found, at all scales, in Parker and Unwin's pre-war designs. At the largest scale, it occurred as the tension between urban design and architecture in many of the illustrations to Unwin's *Town Planning in Practice* of 1909: for example, in the contrast between plans of an almost Classical character, and the highly picturesque images which would actually be registered by the observer. [3] A similar tension between whole and part appears in many of the partnership's hypothetical housing layouts, in which the underlying system of order rests on the repetition of free-standing houses, each expressed so clearly as a separate unit that it threatens the integrity of the overall pattern. [4] At a still smaller scale, the same ambiguous relationship between whole and part, between order and picturesque confusion, was characteristic of the design of individual houses. For example, as Dean Hawkes has pointed out, the complex, additive spatial vocabulary of bays and nooks to be found in the larger rooms of houses like 'The Cottage' – designed by Parker and Unwin at Newton, near Cambridge, just before the war – was generated from the intersections between highly ordered, modular systems of geometry. [5]

The buildings of Parker and Unwin could therefore be understood as texts which lent themselves, with equal validity, to different readings. First, they could be read with an eye to their complex additive nature, in which the individual, small-scale elements of the design had an important role to play in the overall scheme of things. Read like this, the image of such an architecture could be seen as the basis for a suitable expression of the individualism of Dunroamin. But there was the possibility of a second reading, different, though equally valid. Viewed with an eye to its firm overall order, the Parker and Unwin tradition

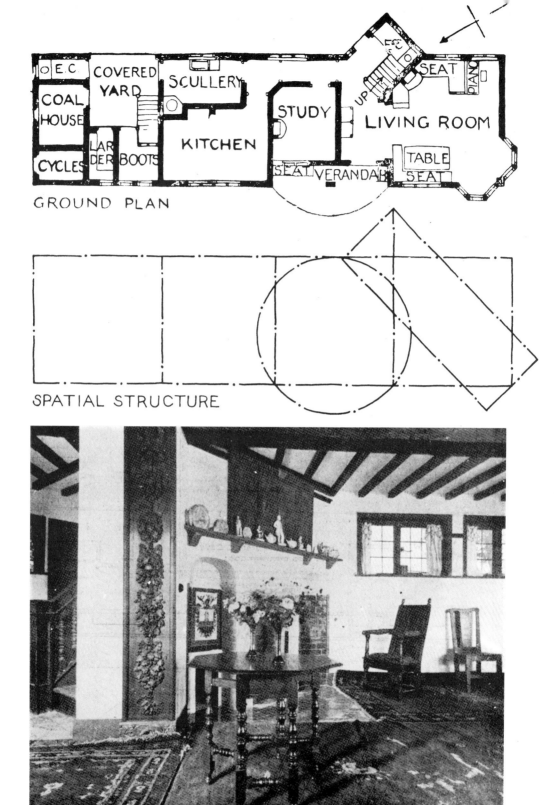

GROUND PLAN

SPATIAL STRUCTURE

Modular planning and picturesque image at the scale of the room in a
house at Newton, Cambridgeshire by Parker and Unwin, 1914 (from
Q. B. Philpott, *Modern Cottage Villas and Bungalows*, 1914)

could be seen as appropriate to that concept of the good life which held that individual behaviour should be restrained for the communal good. Architecture of this kind, therefore, was an appropriate medium through which to express the local authorities' community-orientated values.

Parker and Unwin's projects did not, of course, make up the totality of progressive housing design. That they worked within a more widespread tradition was tacitly acknowledged by Unwin himself, in 1919, when drafting the Tudor Walters Report:

> During the last 20 or 30 years . . . architects, builders and social reformers have studied the question [improvements in mass housing] and together tried numerous experiments . . . and in some districts there may now be found small suburbs, villages and estates consisting of such houses, or at least scattered examples sufficient to show the general tendency which has developed as the outcome of these efforts . . .'[6]

The Tudor Walters Report organised these ideas into a coherent body of housing practice, accessible to all kinds of housing developers. Highly influential amongst local-authority housing designers, because of its status as the official design manual, the report was also intended to influence speculative developers. As its introduction pointed out, 'It is certain that . . . a very large proportion of working-class housing will still depend upon private enterprise of one kind or another'.[7]

In practice, the report succeeded in influencing speculative development – though not in the precise direction which its authors intended – for two main reasons. First, its principles were to guide development control under the various town-planning measures of the inter-war period. Secondly, and more directly, the report's information was of great practical use to the speculative developer. Pointing out the 'absence of traditional skill and guidance, which rapidly changing conditions have largely destroyed',[8] which meant that 'unfortunately, though very naturally [contractors] . . . have largely accepted the type [of housing] which had grown up in the period of neglect'[9] before the war, the report proceeded to fill the gap in expertise with an intensely practical body of advice, based on a hard-nosed attitude to development economics guaranteed to appeal to the speculative builder. The fact that the report's terms of reference were concerned with *working*-class housing[10] did little to diminish its usefulness to the speculative developer, despite the fact that he was catering primarily for a *middle*-class market. The report's information on low-density site development was at least equally relevant to the demands of the *middle*-class house-buyer.

Both the local authority and the speculative builder were therefore influenced by Tudor Walters, but they were influenced in significantly different ways. Drafted by Unwin, much of the report reflected the tension between expressions of individual and community values which has been so typical of his pre-war work with Barry Parker. Different types of developers could make their own different readings of many sections of the report, and could draw selectively from them to meet their own needs. Where it dealt with site layout principles, however, the report's advice was not open to different interpretations. Buttressing its arguments with down-to-earth economic calculations, Tudor Walters was unambiguously in favour of low-density developments, with some twelve houses to the acre in suburban locations, and with road costs reduced by the use of such devices as culs-de-sac. Similar advice, with particular emphasis on the increased costs of roads and services which resulted from higher densities, continued to be given by progressive housing designers like Barry Parker throughout the inter-war period. In 1937, for example, Parker wrote an article reviewing his own work at New Earswick, in which he came to the conclusion that:

> On every hand instances are to be found which . . . reveal in a startling way that the costs of roads provided with a view to increasing the number of houses to the acre has far outweighed any saving which has resulted from obtaining greater density, and thereby less cost of land per house. [11]

The design implications of this argument were graphically summarised in a series of plans, showing alternative layout possibilities for an area of New Earswick, which accompanied the article. [12]

Advocated by Tudor Walters in 1919, and continually supported between the wars by influential designers like Parker, this kind of low-density layout, depending on culs-de-sac for full site development, became the norm for speculative builders and local authorities alike. But this general concept was itself open to different interpretations; according to the values of different designers, it could be used as the structuring principle for places of markedly different image. And in its advice as to the desirable *image* of housing areas, Tudor Walters was ambiguous enough to encourage such different interpretations to occur. On the one hand, the report suggested the possible advantages of 'the standardisation of the elevation, if definitely used as a unit in the composition of designs for groups of cottages or street façades' [13] so as to create an overall sense of order in the development as a whole. On the other hand, it was against the 'depressing effect of monotonous unbroken rows' [14] which such standardisation could all too easily produce. But the crucial decisions as to the *balance* which should be struck, between the potentially contradictory values of standardisation and variety, was left to the reader. Through this process of selection and adaptation, Dunroamin and the local authority estate gradually developed as two quite different – and ultimately antagonistic – streams of design.

The promoters and designers of council estates, for example, placed a high value on the concepts of community and equality, to be achieved through the medium of public ownership. In effect, sweeping changes in working-class housing were proposed, with the intention of supporting the sense of community which had supposedly been lost during a century or more of exposure to the industrial town. But it was proposed to initiate the necessary reforms in housing quality within the framework of assumptions, ideas and institutions which made up the post-war *status quo*. Council housing therefore suffered from the dilemma inherent in all reformist undertakings: its attempts to promote community values were frustrated by the need for estates to be developed within the same economic framework which had, itself, done so much to destroy those values in the first place.

For example, the concept of the estate as community motivated attempts to bring together families of different sizes, and people of different age groups, within it: 'It is generally agreed that to cover large areas with houses, all of one size, and likely to be occupied by one class of tenant . . . is most undesirable' [15] said Tudor Walters. In practice, however, the local authority had to minimise the financial risks of its housing investment. It was therefore under pressure to aim at the middle of the potential housing market, rather than building for minority groups; [16] though there was usually some variation of house size on most council estates, there was almost never a variety of provision such as would have reflected the true complexity of housing demand.

The idea of the estate as community also led to a concern with the provision of social facilities: 'suitable sites should . . . be reserved for larger houses, shops and business premises, schools, places of worship, clubs, institutions, and for open spaces, playgrounds etc.' [17] But the report's reformist stance made it necessary to justify such provision in market terms:

> If suitable sites were selected, the letting or selling of some of such sites might be made to contribute to the economic results of the scheme. For example, the large number of houses must create a demand for shops and confer a special value on sites suitable for such a purpose. [18]

In practice, with a 'market' approach such as this, only minimal social facilities could be provided, except on those rare estates – such as Manchester's Wythenshawe – which housed enough people to support them through the market. Far more often, the communal provisions could consist of no more than a recreation ground and a few shops. Attempts to develop community values through the design of estates with mixed communities and an abundance of shared social facilities were doomed to failure. At the most fundamental level, the efforts made to promote community values were negated by the economic framework within which estate development had to operate.

At a more detailed level, less likely to have important economic implications, the desire to express the idea of community conditioned many aspects of the form of the council suburb. The public spaces of the estate were conceived as positive elements in their own right, rather than as mere left-over spaces between the buildings. This had several implications. First, it encouraged the use of a variety of spatial forms – the cul-de-sac, the close, the visually enclosed curved street and the parkway – in addition to the straight streets typical of the pre-war terraced suburbs. Secondly, it led designers to emphasise the *junctions* between public spaces as places in their own right, thus strengthening the unity of the public realm of the estate as a whole.

The importance given to public spaces also meant that more money and design effort were allocated to them. Often they were landscaped, and were far larger than was strictly necessary for circulation; whilst the desire to make them places to *be in* rather than merely spaces for *passing through*, encouraged designers to give them a closed quality. This reinforced the economic arguments for the cul-de-sac; which also had possibilities for social engineering of a kind which had been implicit in the philanthropic housing tradition since Victorian times. The cul-de-sac's enclave quality enabled residents to exercise surveillance over the activities taking place there; and this encouraged the more respectable tenants to control undesirable activities, much as the sharing of sanitary facilities in the Peabody blocks had done half a century before.[19]

At a smaller scale, the search for expressions of community led council-house designers to favour terraced layouts. This preference did not arise from reasons for economy; the need to take archways through terraced blocks to provide access from the front road to the back gardens – the arrangement advised by Tudor Walters – made the terraced layout more expensive than the semi-detached alternative would have been, as the report itself admitted.[20] Despite this economic disadvantage, terraced layouts were very effective for expressing the idea of community, because of their potential for creating strongly enclosed public space and for linking individual dwellings into unified compositions.

The further linking of terraced groups, to promote a sense of unity at a still larger scale, was specifically advised by Tudor Walters; the report included

The use of the cul-de-sac to form enclosed public spaces at Oxford City Council's
Marston Road Estate, Oxford, 1935 (Graham Paul Smith)

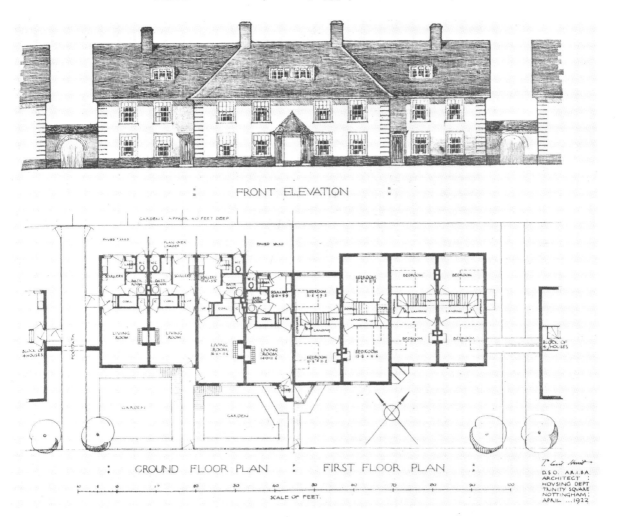

FRONT ELEVATION

GROUND FLOOR PLAN : FIRST FLOOR PLAN

SCALE OF FEET.

Unification of several council houses in one composition, for small sites in Nottingham.
Low-cost standard type proposed by T. Cecil Howitt, 1922. Several houses have their
sole living rooms used as circulation space (*The Builder*)

diagrams showing walls and outbuildings used as links which 'tend to remove the objectionable appearance of the repeated gaps' between the ends of the terraces.[21] However, such attempts to link houses into appropriate express- ions of community ran counter to the individuality of separate front gardens. Appropriately, therefore, Tudor Walters showed interest in the American system of communal landscaping to the fronts of houses, which eliminated private gardens altogether; but – somewhat regretfully, one feels – the report concluded that: 'In this country . . . there appears to exist a general desire for some enclosure'.[22] The necessary private enclosure could itself be used as a unifying element: 'If suitable types of hedge are planted, they will very soon grow so as to afford an effective screen.'[23] Following this lead, the unifying potential of the neatly trimmed privet hedge, publicly maintained to a uniform height, was exploited on many a council estate.

Much design effort was also devoted to making strong visual links between the individual houses *within* the terraces, so that their individual expression was lost in that of the block as a whole. Horizontal links across the frontages of the houses, binding the whole together, were strongly emphasised. Window heads and sills were often lined up, whilst the linking potential of long uninterrupted ridges, eaves and gutters was reinforced by economic arguments put forward by Tudor Walters: 'Generally, it is better to run the eaves in an unbroken line immediately above the first-floor window heads and avoid the numerous expenses entailed . . . when the roof is broken by domers and flats.'[24] Applied elements, such as bands of render, brick plinths and string courses, completed the repertoire of linking techniques. In contrast, vertical elements – which would have tended to emphasise the *individuality* of the separate houses – were rare. Even where bay windows were used – as, for example, in some of Tudor Walters' house plans – they were invariably one storey high, and were therefore horizontal rather than vertical in emphasis.

The same desire to avoid vertical elements had a strong influence on the way in which terraces were related to sloping sites. The vertical implications of stepped roof lines were usually avoided, and much design ingenuity went into accommodating level changes within the houses, either by using plinths of varying heights, with steps up to the front doors of the downhill houses, or by taking the ceilings of the uphill houses into the pitch of the roof. On extreme slopes,

> where there is much fall in the length of a group of houses, expensive and ugly steps in the roof may be avoided by using a type of low house at the high end of the groups and at the low end adopting another exceptional type of design having extra bedrooms on the second floor partly in the roof.[25]

The drawing which Tudor Walters used, to illustrate this treatment of steeply sloping sites, [26] shares with all the report's elevations a loosely Neo-Georgian style, like that which Unwin had used in the design of his wartime housing scheme at Gretna. Because of its wide repertoire of linking elements, such as long horizontal roof lines, string courses and plinths, the Neo-Georgian style had great potential for joining terraces of houses into a single unified composition, appropriate as an expression of the idea of community, whilst its simple regular forms – suggesting economy, rationality and order – were highly appropriate to the needs of the local authority in its rôle as corporate architectural patron. Its ability to express both community and rationality ensured that Neo-Georgian replaced the earlier Arts and Crafts tradition, as *the* public-housing style during the inter-war period.

In addition to this stylistic standardisation, the planning of the house types on each estate was usually standardised, for management reasons, to a small range. Since all the houses on the estate could hardly be designed to cater for families of the same size, there was bound to be a certain minimum variety of house design, echoing the range of different family sizes. If attempts had been made to introduce a *greater* variety of house types – for example by providing dwellings with different plans for families of the same size – then people eligible to live in a house of the particular size concerned would have been likely to have preferred some of the options available, and disliked others. To make sure that the council was seen to treat tenants impartially, therefore, the typical council estate used a minimum range of standardised house plans. All the houses on the council estate, therefore, were similar to each other when first built; and the mechanics of public ownership ensured that they would *remain* similar even with the passage of time. If tenants wished to make alterations to suit their own idiosyncratic requirements they needed the permission of the council, as landlord. And the council, needing to ensure the continuing market appeal of the dwellings, was usually unwilling to allow any but the most minor alterations to be made. In any case, there was no mechanism for compensating the tenant, when he vacated the dwelling, for any increase in value brought about by the alterations which he might have made. There was, therefore, a positive financial incentive for tenants to leave their houses alone.

Even the process of maintenance did little to break down the original similarities between dwellings. For example, it was simpler for the council to arrange for all houses to be repainted at the same time, and in the same colour. In any case, the fact that council houses were viewed as long-term investments and were therefore usually designed with a view to low maintenance, meant that even the most individualistic of painting programmes would have had relatively little effect.

At all scales therefore—from the layout of the estate, through the form of its public spaces, to the design of the housing itself—the council estate spoke the language of community. Even *inside* the houses, one main living-room often served as a through-route to other rooms: unable to be closed off for completely private use, it emphasised the high value which designers placed on reinforcing a sense of community even within the family group.

In contrast Dunroamin, underpinned as it was by an individualistic philosophy, placed a high value on private ownership, and on social mobility as the key to individual development. Each of these key concepts—individualism, private ownership and social mobility—was reflected and reinforced, in specifically architectural terms, by a design tradition which differed in every detail from that of the council estate.

The demand for expressions of individualism led to an emphasis on the one-family house as the basic unit of design. From such houses the whole estate was built up in an additive way, with little attempt at producing any *overall* sense of order. Appropriately enough, in view of the fact that public things were thought of as less important than those which concerned the individual, the public spaces of the Dunroamin estate were rarely designed positively, as significant places in their own right; indeed, the public realm usually consisted only of a road system. Designed for maximum economy, this served merely to connect one house to another, and to join all of them to the surrounding world. Unlike its local-authority counterpart, it was designed for passing through, rather than for being in; its blankness focussing attention on the *private* gardens which fronted on to it.

This negative character of its public realm, perfectly consistent with Dunroamin's individualist philosophy, was emphasised by the fact that few speculative estates were built with either community facilities—except those, such as cinemas and shops, which had commercial viability—or with any significant landscaping of the public space. The rare exceptions are almost always from the later 1930s, by which time the effects of the Depression and of competition amongst speculative builders as market saturation approached, had killed off many smaller developers. Writing in 1936, John Laing spelled out the requirements for success in the speculative housing field:

> Any person coming into the business now, and desiring success, must be prepared to invest large sums of money in land, bought in bulk, and in materials, purchased in the most favourable markets. Then . . . he must be satisfied with a small percentage of profit, and trust to a large turnover to make the business successful. [27]

A firm of the size of John Laing and Son, used to manipulating demand through intensive advertising, felt that it could *influence* events rather than merely react to them. With an interest in the maintenance of social stability as great as that of any local authority, firms like Laing's reacted to the 1930s social troubles by themselves taking a paternalistic approach to housing, attempting to express and reinforce the concept of community through the design of their estates. Experienced in the building of council housing, it is not surprising that Laing's themselves adopted various characteristics of the local-authority estate, such as positively designed, landscaped public spaces, in their own developments. John Laing even went so far as to approve of Georgian design when he spoke of the 'principle of pleasing planning' underlying London's early 'continuous terraces of houses displaying regularity in elevation and similarity in design.' [28] Yet Laing was under no illusion about what his customers wanted: 'uniformity is not now encouraged, most people preferring to live in a detached or semi-detached house'. [29]

Carried to its logical conclusion, the Dunroaminer's search for individual expression would have pointed towards the detached dwelling but, in the face of cost constraints, the semi-detached became Dunroamin's norm. In choosing this format, in preference to the terraced layout which had been normal in the pre-war speculative suburbs, the builders of Dunroamin were to some extent following the lead of Tudor Walters. Semi-detached layouts were used to illustrate several of the points made in the report, which also stressed the fact that, 'Generally speaking, it will be found less expensive and more convenient to provide access to the back garden of each house from the one front road by means of a side path', [30] rather than from a separate rear service access. Though the report went on to show that terraces could use this side-path arrangement, by making archways through the terraced block, it admitted that this would add to costs. [31] Economic logic therefore reinforced the purchaser's desire for a clear expression of the individual home, both factors supporting the semi-detached format: the little evidence we have suggests that the two factors were probably about equal in importance. [32]

The adoption of the semi-detached format interacted with several other factors to generate the design of the typical Dunroamin two-storey house. There was an overwhelming preference, on the part of purchasers, for houses to have two living-rooms in addition to the kitchen. [33] Potentially, this conflicted with a second prime design consideration: the importance of the back garden as a safe place for children to play in under observation from the house, [34] which ruled out the traditional pre-war speculative plan, in which a rear extension allowed the house to have a depth of three rooms from front to back on one side, but cut off the garden from the most intensively used of the living-rooms by a passage-like backyard.

Since rear extensions were to be avoided, the front-to-back dimension of the house was fixed at a depth of two rooms. Given this fixed plan depth, the need for a narrow frontage to reduce road costs led inexorably to the adoption of a two-storey house type – referred to by the influential architect and housing writer Gordon Allen, in 1936, as 'the universal plan for housing containing three bedrooms' [35] – in which the ground and first floors were of equal area. A three-storey design would not have further reduced the frontage, would have been both difficult to plan, and uneconomic because of the larger area of internal circulation space required. For a given plan area, the alternatives of a 'chalet' or bungalow would have needed still wider frontages.

With the two-storey semi established as the norm, much of Dunroamin's architectural interest centres on the ways in which different builders expressed the individuality of each home. In one sense, paradoxically, the potential of the semi was greater in this regard than that of the fully detached house: the expression of individuality implied the expression of individual *importance*; and the pair of semis, with its greater mass, lent itself more easily to expressions of importance than did the smaller bulk of the detached house. Perhaps for this reason, the symmetry of the pair of semis, carrying with it further implications of importance, was firmly maintained: rarely, if ever, were the two halves of the pair given different architectural treatments, except in terms of minor details such as stained-glass panels.

In addition, this use of symmetry lent a closed, complete quality to the pair of semis, effectively marking it off from its neighbours on either side. Emphasis on the pair as a *separate* unit was reinforced by other design characteristics: first, by the frequent use of the hipped roof – reiterating the closed, finite quality of the pair – and, secondly, by qualitative differences in the treatments of the front, back and side walls of the house. The fronts and backs, orientated towards the Dunroaminer's private domain, were treated as positive architectural elements. Here were used the house's highest-status external materials; and here too was lavished the greatest amount of design consideration, with care taken over matters like the relationships between solids and voids. The sides, however – fronting onto the neighbouring houses, across the 'five- or six-foot gap' of the architectural critics' suburban horror stories – were treated very differently. Usually lower status materials were used; and the placing of doors, windows and drainage pipes had a careless quality. Enclosed by walls of this negative character, used as a low-status tradesmen's entrance, and possessed of an adverse micro-climate, [36] the space between the semis resisted any tendency for the observer to conceptualise architectural links across it between neighbouring houses.

The above-discussed design characteristics emphasised the separateness of the *pair* of semis, as the largest – and therefore potentially most prestigious – block with respect to which the *individual* dwelling could symbolically hold its own without being overwhelmed; but other design features developed to display the importance of the individual house *within* the pair. To emphasise the separateness of the two halves of the basic symmetrical block, two rules – one negative, and one positive – were usually obeyed by Dunroamin's designers. The negative rule prohibited any emphasis on the *centre* of the pair; to avoid underlining the integrity of the block as a whole. Front doors were usually placed as far apart as possible, at the *edge* of the block. The alternative arrangement, with entrances paired in the centre, is less often found, though it has advantages in terms of acoustic privacy and of the grouping of bathroom plumbing. The need to avoid emphasising the centre of the symmetrical block gave another reason for rejecting the Neo-Georgian style. Nothing could have been less appropriate for Dunroamin than Raymond Unwin's 1936 recommendation to speculative house designers to 'mark the centre with a point of emphasis, an extra storey, pediment or what not.' [37]

The second, more positive method of expressing individual dwellings was to provide each with its own strongly articulated focal element, usually a two-storey bay, large enough to draw attention away from the unifying symmetrical outline of the pair as a whole, particularly in sharp perspective, as seen by people walking or driving down the roads of the estate. The frequent use of variations in the form of bays – and other elements such as porches and oriels – expressed as strongly as possible the individuality of houses otherwise identical in design. In this respect Dunroamin went far beyond the limits suggested by Tudor Walters, totally ignoring the report's stern admonition to remember that: 'The proper corrective of monotony does not consist in an endless variety of different and unrelated parts or designs.' [38]

The use of the two-storey bay to differentiate individual houses was one of Dunroamin's most pervasive characteristics: 'The bay window must be accepted as a *sine qua non*', said the architect and writer Alwyn Lloyd, in a 1936 article advising architects on effective methods of co-operation with speculative builders. [39] To some extent, though, the effectiveness of the bay began to break down under the economic pressures of the late Thirties. Experiments with the simple and potentially cheap forms of Modernism sometimes led to the linking of the two separate bays into a single element which, because it was central to the *pair* of houses, thereby lost its differentiating function. Where

The visual importance of small design variations to emphasise the individuality of each pair of semis. These 1930s houses ignore the style of the adjacent Hoover Factory on the Western Avenue (Graham Paul Smith)

The notorious Cutteslowe Wall, Summertown, 1938 (*Oxford Mail and Times*)

possible, site topography was turned to advantage in differentiating the two halves of the semi-detached pair. When sited alongside a sloping road, for example, the pair was sometimes split on its centre, so that the two houses were at different levels. Examples of this kind have long been used, by architectural critics, to demonstrate Dunroamin as the absolute nadir in terms of design; but from the point of view of Dunroamin's *own* values, this splitting of the semi-detached block – whether consciously sought-after or arrived at on purely pragmatic grounds – constituted an intelligent use of the site to maximise the individual expression of the two houses in the pair.

So far, the design characteristics which I have discussed have been direct reflections and reinforcements of Dunroamin's individualist values. Many arch-itectural consequences also followed from the Dunroaminer's urge towards house-ownership: the speculative approach to building houses for sale, which made home-ownership a widespread possibility, had a dynamic of its own, which placed constraints on the types of houses which were built. Aiming at the centre of the potential house-buying market, so as to reduce the risks inherent in catering for any more specialised body of purchasers, the speculative builder concentrated heavily – at least until the later Thirties – on the three-bedroomed house. As a general rule, therefore, most Dunroamin estates as built showed little variation in terms either of age-group, income level or dwelling size, a major departure, as we have seen, from the advice of Tudor Walters.

This tendency towards standardised house types and family characteristics was due not only to the needs of the speculative developer, but also to those of the Dunroaminer himself. The value which he placed on self-improvement had obvious implications in terms of upwards social mobility; and his house was the most obvious medium through which the Dunroaminer could express his current social status. If his standing improved, he could move to a new home, appropriate to his changed circumstances. Consequently, he had to look upon his house as a commodity, which he might need to sell on the open market in order to move to a more desirable location. As well as being concerned with his house's *use* value – its value as a pleasant and convenient home from his own point of view – he had to be concerned with its *exchange* value. This emphasis led the Dunroaminer, like the speculative builder – and like the building society, whose *only* interest was in exchange value – to want his house to be attractive in as wide a market as possible, even if, perhaps, it did not suit his personal taste as closely as it might have done. The economic implications of individualism therefore led, somewhat paradoxically, to a certain conservatism in house design. The resolution of the underlying conflict between this conservatism and the contrary urge to-wards individual expression gave Dunroamin much of its architectural interest.

For whilst the basic layout of the speculative semi was remarkably conservative, the precise interpretation of that layout, through the detailed forms of roofs, bays and porches, was extremely varied. Indeed, it was precisely the basic *conservatism* which brought the detailed expressions of *individuality* into focus.

His concentration on exchange values also meant that the Dunroaminer had to ensure that his house would *maintain* its value, partly a function of the characteristics of the house itself, and partly to do with the quality of the environment in which it was situated. The Dunroaminer was therefore moved to maintain his house, and its gardens, to a high standard, in the process adding much individual expression to the basic Dunroamin format. He also placed a high value on the selectness of his environment, which had two main implications: one for house design, and one for estate layout. For example, the relatively low status accorded to the council tenant — by the council tenant himself as well as by the owner-occupier [40] — turned the Dunroaminer strongly against any suspicion of council-house styling in his own home. Bewailing this fact, the planning barrister, Sir Leslie Scott KC, referred in 1936 to the 'demand for the kind of house . . . which is bought just because its exterior is so different from the decent exterior of the council house that the casual observer must see at a glance that its owner is *not* living in a council house.' [41] Most local authority estates were designed in a rather stripped-down version of Neo-Georgian; so Neo-Georgian was perhaps the *least* frequent stylistic influence in the Dunroamin estate. [42]

The Dunroaminer's economic need to protect his environment's social status implied a requirement for the estate layout to discourage activities with lower-class connotations, such as children playing in the street, or even the presence of working-class people, except in a service capacity. This further boosted the popularity of the cul-de-sac layout, for two reasons: since the cul-de-sac led nowhere, the only people to be found in it were the residents themselves, and those with business there; whilst its enclave character made for easy surveillance of street activities.

The Dunroaminer's desire to segregate his environment from areas of council housing was vividly illustrated, in 1934, by events in the North Oxford suburb of Cutteslowe. An area of private housing, called the Urban Housing Estate, was built on land purchased from the city council who themselves developed a council estate on adjoining land. Originally, the two estates were linked by a pair of roads, but soon disputes arose. A resident on the private estate complained of chalk graffiti and 'children and dogs everywhere' in the council estate. [43] Claiming that links with·the council housing lowered the value of their own development, the builders of the Urban Housing Estate constructed walls, seven feet high with iron spikes, across the roads at the estate boundary. Passions ran high; one city councillor, taking the part of the council tenants inconvenienced by the walls, said that on visiting the site he had seen 'this high wall with barbed-wire entanglements and behind it, cut off like wild animals or savage creatures, there was a collection of citizens. . ... The people are herded behind walls and barbed wire like Germans in a concentration camp.'[44] Though the council tried hard to get the walls removed, the Dunroaminers of the Urban Housing Estate were equally determined to see them stay. It was not until 1959 that they were finally demolished.

The Cutteslowe walls made it clear that by 1934 Dunroamin and the council estate had become very different environments, each, at least potentially, hostile to the value implications of the other. This fact was made all the more striking by two fundamental *similarities* between them. First, they both grew from the housing experiments of the Garden City movement, as summarised in the Tudor Walters Report. Secondly, they housed residents who, in objective terms, were often more similar than their marked differences of self-image would have allowed them to believe; even the people who lived on opposite sides of the Cutteslowe walls were not dramatically different, when measured against the Registrar General's 'objective' categories of social class. Well over a third of the private residents of the Urban Housing Estate fell into the same 'skilled occupation' category which encompassed the majority of Cutteslowe's council tenants.[45]

Since they grew from the same design tradition, and since they housed populations not dramatically dissimilar in objective terms, the strong and consistent differences between Dunroamin and the council estate can only plausibly be explained in terms of the different values which inspired them: the vision of the free individual as against that of the egalitarian community.

⇒5⇐

GREAT EXPECTATIONS

Suburban Values and the Rôle of the Media

Paul Oliver

To consider fully how the values of Dunroamin were recognised and portrayed during our period is virtually impossible; too much is irreclaimable. At best one can but sketch some of the attitude-forming and reflecting elements in the media of the time, and in particular, their bearing on the physical environment and contemporary perceptions of it. Any such discussion can reasonably start with the services that made the effectiveness of the suburban expansion possible.

Suburbs in the Thirties relied on regular transport, and the confidence that the trains would run on time was one of the bases of suburban life. The sound of the seven-o'clock, or eight-o'clock 'hooter' – the factory siren which, at a firm like Kodak, indicated that the workers should be at the gates – reminded Dunroamin's commuters that the day had started. They went on the 8.05 or the 8.14 or other trains which ran with clockwork precision, and 'travelled up' with friends, with whom the sharing of the *Daily Express* or the *News Chronicle* provided a framework for discussion.

This railway-dominated culture both emphasised, and reinforced the importance of the commuter network. To many travellers going to 'business' or 'the office', the companionship of the railway train 'compartment' was that of 'the club'. Different textiles on the upholstery, sepia photographs of Striding Edge or Tintern Abbey and even the name plates on the engines of the LNER or LMS emphasised individuality, encouraging allegiances. Nevertheless, cross-country rail (or, to a lesser extent, bus) travel was inconvenient. The pattern of transport was essentially from the suburb to the inner city.

Though such identification was less apparent in the omnibus system, even here the 'General', later, the 'London Transport' buses, with their bright red cellulose and gold lettering, established regular routes, to which many suburbs served by them became linked. The bus conductor, with his clip of coloured tickets and ticket punch or waist-held clipping machine, was a sufficient symbol of authority, stability and punctuality for 'bus conductor sets' or 'outfits' to be sold as children's play uniforms. Regularity and punctuality within the transport system reinforced expectations as to dependability and security within the suburbs.

By 1930 the number of horse-drawn vehicles had been reduced to a quarter the total of a decade earlier, but there were still over fifty thousand on the road. Throughout the period, United Dairies and other large milk concerns, and many small and local ones, delivered the daily milk round from horse-drawn floats; horses drew mobile grocer's carts, stacked with soaps and cereals, and with buckets dangling at the tailboard where paraffin for oil heaters was dispensed. 'Totters' – known in the suburbs as 'rag-and-bone men' – cried their incomprehensible calls on the still suburban air, leading their plodding horses and sometimes ringing a bell, which clamorously challenged the strident tinkle of the Walls Ice Cream 'Stop-Me-and-Buy-One' vendor with his tricycle refrigerator. Like the brewers, even builders' merchants used horse-drawn carts to bring their materials to the sites where the new rows of semis were rising above foundation level. Old, lumbering steam vehicles were also in evidence: immense traction engines and steam-powered road locomotives noisily puffed their way through suburban arteries. Private motoring still had the elements of adventure, in spite of the growth in popularity of the motor car. In 1938, a Ford Popular could be purchased for under a hundred pounds, and the garage became a required adjunct to most new homes. The car was not used for going to work; it was principally a leisure vehicle, for picnic trips into the Surrey Hills or to a beauty spot like Burnham Beeches. It provided freedom, mobility, but its purpose was to bring the family back to the home as much as to escape from it.

The suburban environment of the inter-war years was one of considerable overlap in technologies and patterns of living, made more evident by the conjunction of urban and rural ways of life on its outer fringes. So, in quiet suburban roads, craftsmen set up their pitches on the pavements. The rush-and-cane seats of broken chairs were swiftly repaired or remade by street-corner caneworkers sitting on hessian sacks; knife and scissors grinders with wooden carts in tow, used their cycle power to sharpen blades. Here on the new streets the lighting was frequently electric, switched on at dusk in a sudden blink of illumination that reflected off the autumnal mist. But in the suburbs built in the Twenties gas street lighting was common; the short lamp standards with their inclined prisms of glass topped by metal ventilator finials, stood with one arm outstretched to receive the ladder of the lamp-lighter. (In 1960 the writer's own suburban street in Harrow was still visited twice daily by the lamp-lighter.)

Beyond Dunroamin the social inequalities of the time impinged lightly on the

Rayners Lane, Pinner before development in the early 1930s (from
Dennis F. Edwards, *Metro Memories*)

Haymaking in the fields backing on to Rayners Lane and Marsh Road,
Pinner, late 1930s – the small boy with a loaded pitchfork is Paul
Oliver (*left*), and the same location in the 1940s when garden trees and
bushes had matured and the fields had been made into a park (*right*)
(W. N. Oliver)

suburbs, which were inhabited largely by people who had struggled and saved to escape the stresses of central urban living. But in the suburbs nearer to the rural regions, the rural poor were still in evidence. Gypsies brought black-eyed children to the doors to sell clothes-pegs from large baskets or to pin 'lucky heather' to a reluctant lapel. They were still dressed in long, flowered dresses and peasant scarves. Tramps were less romantic. There were many, sleeping rough under the hedgerows or in improvised shelters. The 'tramp's hut' was a familiar part of the rural scene on the suburban edge. Many did casual work or begged. They were sometimes suspected of stealing, but though there were thefts in Suburbia, the scale was small and the stealing petty. It was some indication of the security that Dunroamin's 'defensible spaces' of closes, crescents and 'drives' afforded, that the depredations of the legendary 'Flannelfoot' were the more serious crimes that were of general report.

Dunroamin was secure because of the strong social bonds that were established between the generations of suburban settlers. They were not lonely people in a lonely crowd; anomie was not the characteristic mental state of the new migrant to the suburb. Excitement, exhilaration, pride in laying down a deposit that would lead to home ownership – these were among the dominant emotions. For most new arrivals what they had now was infinitely better than what they had left. On a newly established suburban estate it was especially important that relationships with other new residents were made. The sense of participation in a new venture encouraged visiting – and the scrutiny of each new property that was being occupied. With no established structure for social intercourse, new ones were devised. Especially important was 'the Club': frequently, social life was focussed on the tennis club, with dances and other fund-raising activities, cementing relationships as well as financially supporting the unit. Cricket clubs, with fixtures arranged with other suburbs, were as popular. Golf or bowls had their adherents, partly identifying age as well as wealth. In Rayners Lane, the Rayners Lane Cricket Club was second to the Rayners Lane Camera Club, whose premises in the cellar of a new shopping parade were given a modern treatment by a local architect, who designed the projection room and screen, installed incidental lighting and obtained second-hand tip-up seats from Gaumont-British. [1] A doctor was the first president; his wife, like other wives, acted as an usherette in beach pyjamas. Members' films – black and white on 9.5 mm – were shown, together with rented films like *White Hell of Pitz Palu*.

In many suburbs amateur dramatics provided an important focus for social life, often as an extension of church or school activities, but also as independent organisations such as Pinner's popular, and typically named, 'Vagabonds'. Gilbert and Sullivan companies were also to be found in many suburbs, putting on their productions in school halls or even on the stages of the larger cinemas. Though the appeal of the church was already diminishing, many churches still had substantial congregations. New Methodist and Baptist churches were built in simple brick structures in the suburbs, and here and there Christian Science Reading Rooms appeared. All these provided the means for new arrivals in the suburbs to meet socially, but for the middle-aged, the single or the elderly taking the dog for a walk was as effective a means as any of making the casual contacts that could lead to stronger social ties. The comparatively neutral but apparently inexhaustible themes of animal welfare, feeding and training provided the necessary conversational basis for initial overtures.

Other important social links were welded through meetings with neighbours and conversations over garden fences and hedges. But in the early phase of a suburb it was the children who provided the flux. Common interests in the education of their children brought young couples together to discuss the merits of schools in the neighbourhood. Bonds were formed among children playing in the parks, climbing trees or scrambling over the foundations of new developments and housing sites. Their parents were soon drawn into the new relationships, and were willing participants in the establishment of neighbourhood identity through the network of friendships formed.

Male and female rôles were clearly defined: the man was the breadwinner, his wife the home-maker. His responsibility was to bring the income that would support wife and family, and in Dunroamin there was discomfort if 'his wife worked'. Exceptions were principally professional: women doctors were gaining some ground, women teachers were accepted. But the responsibility to the growing family was paramount, and any woman who had a job was likely to be regarded in some degree as neglecting her home; [2] certainly the sight of children waiting on the doorstep for parents to return invited censure by giving such children 'tea'.

At the weekends it was assumed that the husband might work in the garden or do home improvement jobs around the house. He had the popular periodicals like *Practical Motorist* or *The Woodworker* to help him, while the sewing and knitting which was part of every woman's domestic evening occupation was given guidance in *My Weekly, Woman's Own*, or among the somewhat more expensive periodicals like *Good Housekeeping*.* Dunroamin was seldom directly depicted in women's magazines, although the scenes of domesticity could be interpreted in suburban terms, like the settings against which models posed which were

---

* It must be remembered, however, that magazine circulation in the Twenties and Thirties was comparatively small; mass readership was a Fifties phenomenon. *Woman*, for example, had a readership of 75,000 in 1938; in 1952 this figure had grown to $2\frac{1}{4}$ million weekly, and $3\frac{1}{2}$ million seven years later. [3]

transposable to the suburb. Room interiors showed standard lamps, deep easy chairs, pouffes, fireside rugs, occasional tables and recess bookcases of similar character in numerous publications like *The Home of Today*. [4] When families were incorporated in the drawings and photographs the wife was usually seen doing the housework in an overall, making pastry in the kitchen in a pinafore and sitting in sensible clothes by the fireside, her pipe-smoking husband opposite her and her children, with the family cat, at their feet.

Generally the children were shown playing: the boy with his Meccano set or Hobbies outfit, the girl with doll's house and dolls. Through such imagery the persistence of the rôles and the focus of domestic life around the symbolic hearth, was continually underscored. At a more subliminal level, the children's values and their reflection on their future rôles were reinforced in their reading matter, whether it was in the conventional, grammar-school seriousness of *The Children's Newspaper*, the *Boys Own Paper* and the *Girls Own Paper*, or in the 'twopenny bloods' of the *Hotspur*, the *Wizard* or *The Rover*, and their counterparts in *Girl's Crystal*. Too much has been written of the Frank Richards booklets, the *Gem* and the *Magnet*, the Biggles stories and the Angela Brazil girls' books to justify further discussion here: the fact that such publications were so widely read in Dunroamin serves to emphasise the family-centred society, and the clear distinctions between male and female responsibilities which were established at an early age. Adventure there was, and fantasy too, acted out through the Wolf Cubs, the Boy Scouts, the Brownies and the Girl Guides, in troops and companies which were rapidly established in the suburban areas. Their publications, their respect for authority, flag and Empire, their simplistic but earnest emphasis on activity, health, self-reliance, hierarchy and obedience, combined to reinforce the conservative values of the suburb as they assimilated them from their parents.

The regularity of the trains which was often as important to the school-children as it was to their fathers, stimulated a fascination for locomotives with which boys wholly identified. To the familiar question: 'What will you be when you grow up?' the stock reply was 'An engine driver'. It was of little account that few boys did become engine drivers; what was important was that, at a formative stage in their lives, they expressed a desire to participate in a rôle that was at once romantic, regulated, and of public service. Many found such an expression of their values in the jobs they finally took.

For girls it was different. Though employment as a secretary was acceptable for a young woman and, with some reservations, even as an assistant in a shop or retail establishment, girls were still not encouraged to seek careers that would take them away from home, or to share in the increasing mobility that was available to young men. Some exceptions existed, notably in the field of nursing; a young woman wishing to leave home could find some support for making a socially useful career in a hospital. The rôles available were reflected in the toy sets for girls; the bus conductor's counterpart was the 'Young Nurse' outfit with bandages, cap and pinafore, Red Cross prominently displayed. Far outweighing them numerically were the cookery sets, the embroidery sets and the collections of miniature house-ware, not excluding brooms and Ewbank, which helped to fix the rôle of home-maker and mother that was the principal expectation of a girl for her future. The designs that were represented were modelled on the current patterns, fixing their imagery and creating expectations of a home moulded closely on the familiar domestic environment.

Children grew up of course, but not as quickly as their own children decades later. They were well into their teens before puberty and adolescence, and pre-marital sexual encounters often did not advance beyond innocent 'petting'. If the debutantes on whom the gossip columns reported each season were expected to 'come out' at eighteen, in the suburbs a large proportion of young men, and most young women, who did not go to university celebrated their 'twenty-first' at a function organised, at the local Conservative Hall or similar venue, by their parents. The years of family unity were therefore long, even though the number of children in the average family had been lowered. This meant that the annual cycle of the years could be followed to a routine punctuated by short holidays and celebrations: St George's Day, Whitsun, Empire Day, August Bank Holiday, Guy Fawkes' Day, Remembrance Day and Christmas. Every year the family went for a two-week holiday, often to the same place – Bognor, Bournemouth, Shanklin, Little Holland, Scarborough or other middle-class resorts – to stay at a boarding-house which was acclaimed as 'home from home'.

And when they returned it was with protestations that 'there's nothing quite like your own home'. For if social relationships had been established with neighbours and new-found friends, it was nevertheless a home-centred society which Dunroamin fostered. Though the regular summer holiday, the Christmas festivities and the long vacations of the school-children somewhat changed the regular pattern of the week, for most of the year the weekly rituals were carefully observed. Monday was washday, Tuesday was for ironing. Depending on which was 'half-closing day', Wednesday or Thursday meant shopping. Cleaning, vacuuming, dusting came on Thursday and Friday – upstairs one day, downstairs the next. Fish on Friday, a roast for Sunday lunch – the regularity of the weekly cycle was observed by the shop-keepers, exploited by advertisers: 'Friday night is Amami night' was a shampoo firm's slogan which became a catch-phrase of the period. For husbands working in London the early departure for 'the office' in the mornings and the late commuter train at the end of the day, meant a limited time only with the younger children. Weekends were precious, even though Saturday morning working was still expected from civil servants and by many commercial offices. Playing with the children, cutting and rolling the lawn, going for a hike or for a spin in the family Morris Eight were valued weekend pursuits.

As for the year and the week, so for the day: its pattern of kettles of shaving water, hurried departures for train or bus, taking the children to, and meeting them from, the school (on foot – few women were car drivers), tea and home-work and an evening by the fire listening to the wireless, accented by a multitude of small and individual gestures of family ritual special to every home, was no less than what most families wanted or expected. In this the wireless played an important part for, though the morning and the evening papers were bought by the commuting husband, the radio provided a vehicle for mass entertainment and information that all the family could share. Empathising with Larry the Lamb in *Toytown* on *Children's Hour*, or joining in with *We are the Ovaltinies* from Radio Luxembourg, was part of the experience of being a child in the Thirties. Older children listened with their parents to *In Town Tonight* or *Monday Night at Seven*, or laughed at *Band Wagon* which, in spite of its name, gained much of its humour and its appeal from the near-suburban flat which Arthur Askey and Dickie Murdoch purported to keep on the roof of Broadcasting House.

The question arises as to the extent to which Dunroamin's values were shaped by, or reflected in, the new mass media of the time, which grew in parallel with the growth of Dunroamin. Radio had developed rapidly from the cat's whisker days of 2LO and the formative period of the BBC. With Lord Reith establishing a stratification in the corporation that was not far removed from the social strata of society at large, the upper echelons of the hierarchy determined the content of radio productions, talks, discussions and entertainment. The result was an almost total disregard of the suburban way of life in any way which revealed an understanding of, or a sympathy for, its values. When, and this was rare, the suburbs were mentioned at all, it was in terms of disparagement, as Ian Davis has shown in Chapter 1. There was no competition,[5] and the effect of market forces did not apply. Under the firm control of its Director General, the BBC obeyed the mandate of its charter: 'To educate, inform and entertain'. A cartoon in the *Melody Maker* showed Auntie BBC spanking a child representing 'the Listening Public' and saying 'There brat! Whether you like it or not your mind's got to be elevated!'[6] But with no 'Letters' programmes, no phone-ins, Dunroaminers had little capacity to make their values or their wishes known; instead, they marvelled at the wonder of the wireless and were entertained by Lew Stone or Henry Hall, informed by Stephen King-Hall, and educated whenever it was possible. If there was any real recognition of life in the new suburbs expressed in the plays, talks and features broadcast by the BBC in the inter-war years it is now virtually beyond recall.

Throughout the Dunroamin years the cinema was without exception the principal vehicle of commercially provided leisure. Before the Depression in 1926 there were some three thousand cinemas open in Great Britain. With the worst of the Depression over, the entertainment industry expanded its cinema building programme and by 1934 there were 4,305 cinemas open, with a total seating capacity of some 3.8 millions. [7] Within the next five years a new cinema was being opened, on average, every three to four days with the large chains, including ABC, Odeon and Gaumont-British, opening High Street cinemas of ever-increasing luxury. Grandly named the Regal or the Royal, the Palace or the Plaza, The Ritz, Dominion, Embassy or Roxy, they proclaimed their assumed status as palaces for the people. [8] The cinema interior was a sham and it was recognised as such; textured and sprayed in gold and green or blush, the plaster interiors were modelled and sculptured in exotic forms.

As early as 1934 the annual admission to British cinemas had topped 900 million, with gross takings of nearly £40,000,000. By 1942 admissions had reached $1\frac{1}{2}$ *billion* and they continued to climb (it was not until 1957 that admissions dropped to the 1938 figure of a thousand million). [9] Within the middle and working classes of Britain the cinema was the mass popular entertainment; there is no means of ascertaining the precise figures of suburban cinema attendance, but there seems no reason to doubt that it was less here than elsewhere.

Averaging more than five hundred productions a year, Hollywood's studios were supplying Britain with 80 per cent of the films shown in its cinemas, the proportion even rising during the Second World War. [10] The standbys of the High Street Odeon and Gaumont were comedies, glamorous musicals, western and gangster films and historical dramas. American films could not be expected to reflect the mores of English suburban life, but the British product, though largely confined to making B features, could reasonably have shown something of Dunroamin's life and people, who supported the film industry by paying for a substantial proportion of the thirty million seats every week. Instead, there is scarcely a glimpse of suburban life in the output of the times; working-class city suburbs and the inner-city slums of the poor had a greater chance of being shown. The country houses of the wealthy, the streets of Belgravia were contrasted with the narrow alleys of the industrial Midlands. Every upper-class hero had his comic cockney counterpart, but Dunroamin's middle-class England was virtually absent from the screen, and was to remain so even during the war years of realist and propaganda films made by the Crown Film Unit.

There had been documentaries in the Thirties but few, if any, even hinted at the suburbs. They concentrated, importantly enough, on contemporary issues in films like *Housing Problems, Workers and Jobs* or *The Smoke Menace*. [11] Undoubtedly the newsreels, projecting a succession of uncontroversial and chauvinistic images of the contemporary world, accompanied by a self-satisfied commentary which took an amused, superior view of other races, reinforced the conservative values of Dunroamin. But curiously, the suburbs were rarely represented even on the newsreels; news happened elsewhere, and unless there was an unusual crime of passion there, which was rare, Dunroamin was unlikely to be featured. In this the newsreels reflected the attitudes of the commercial film makers.

Research in the influence of films on the audiences of the Thirties was rare. With the help of *Picturegoer*, J. P. Mayer conducted one survey in 1945. Of 67 detailed replies to the question: 'Have films ever influenced you in regard to personal decisions and behaviour?' only one, by a nineteen-year-old girl who had seen 1,350 films, even speculated on the possibility of the cinema having any influence on house design and internal planning: 'Of course the kitchen mostly appeals to me, being a woman, but I daresay it will appeal to some men too in the way of comfortable rooms, better lighting system, and where there is no help needed for such a house, such as helping wife or mother to wash up, or carry coals as she is tired of doing it herself. Also it must be pleasing for a husband to come home from work, to a neat and pretty wife, owing to many labour-saving devices, than to a wife who is tired and looks it too.' [12] Influences on fashion, make-up, manners and social behaviour were acknowledged by most of the 19 men and 49 women who responded with letters. Fashion, by definition, is ephemeral, and Dunroamin's occupants were very willing to accept new styles, new language, new clothes, provided they made little impact on the permanent elements in living. These were represented by the house, the garden and the furniture, and in these areas fashion, while not entirely without impact, moved far more slowly. Though the suburbs illustrated in Hollywood films were glamorous and spacious, glimpses of the more affluent corners of middle-town America, or of Californian sun-drenched housing, made little impact on Britain's suburbs. The gardens that were hedged with privet and low walls were not altered to accord with the picture presented in the Andy Hardy situation comedies of grassy slopes, uninterrupted by boundaries of any kind, which linked one New England styled house with another on either side. The American

Cleaning the family Morris Eight. The plot width allows for both garage gates and separate garden gate (BBC Hulton Picture Library)

Hollywood influence in fashion and hair styles did not extend to breakfast china or the decoration on the lampshade, c. 1940 (BBC Hulton Picture Library)

house with its porches, verandahs, rocking chairs, door screens, played no part in shaping the houses of Dunroamin in the 1930s.

Inside, where the elements could be changed more rapidly, there could have been visible more influences of Hollywood. Success in the sale of cocktail cabinets was probably directly attributable to American inspiration, as were mirrored niches and recesses with flower arrangements before them and the glamorising of the bedroom dressing-table and wardrobe. American bathrooms and kitchens with labour-saving equipment, too, seemed glamorous, even if their scale on film hardly reflected the dimensions of a suburban bathroom in outer London. But the characteristic studio re-creation of the American suburban interior, which often doubled the domestic volume familiar in the average American middle-class home, created spaces that had no points of comparison with Dunroamin's twelve and fourteen-foot living-rooms.

Hollywood was fascinated by Britain and its version of the British, the interest fuelled by a sharp awareness of the financial rewards of keeping alive British enthusiasms for film. But in spite of this, not even the war-time *Mrs Miniver*, which purported to depict British middle-class life and was intended to repair some of the damage done by the class stereotypes, made any acknowledgement of the millions living in the streets and houses of Dunroamin.

For the inhabitant of Dunroamin there was little in the world depicted on the screen in either the Hollywood or the British product to remind him of home. The cinema, therefore, can be seen as having performed its customarily identified rôle as providing escapist entertainment which accorded with the atmosphere created by the cinema interiors. What was the effect of this on values in Dunroamin? It would have not been surprising if the suburbs had sired a generation of neurotics, of paranoid inhabitants who would have had good reason for believing that the world had totally ignored their existence. Instead, Dunroamin was remarkably consistent throughout the Thirties and Forties, having less than its proportional share of social problems, and a low incidence of murders and suicides. [13] Dunroamin was, like all of Britain, class-conscious to the extent that the suburb was predominately middle middle-class and preferred it that way. It was jingoistic, staunchly British, committed to 'decent' values that centred on the home. In the films Dunroamin found reinforcement for its world-view—not as portrayed on the screen, but rather as it could conclude from the evidence presented to it. The westerns depicting migrants, settlers, newly established townships, heroes that arrived with no details of their past, all together forming a community, bonded by the railroad or linked by the express stages, reflected, if only dimly, suburban audiences' own situation. All around Dunroamin was being erected. The wooden scaffold poles provided the skeletal frameworks within which the new housing estates were growing within walking distance. The fact that bad men, rustlers and sheriffs shot out their disputes did not detract from the parallel. Instead it served to fortify the sense of the honest, rapidly established community while vicariously providing the excitement that the law-abiding reality did not.

Fortunately for Dunroamin's inhabitants the British film industry was small and cliché-ridden, pre-occupied with the romantic past or the contemporary upper class; fortunately too, the documentary film makers were committed to their demands for social reform and improved housing for the poor and the lower economic levels of the working class. And fortunately likewise, Hollywood had no knowledge of the British suburbs and could not act out its fantasies and its dramas in that context. So Dunroamin was spared, in the greatest and most immediate visual mass medium of the time, the falsifications that would have come with the cinema's depiction of its way of life. Instead it could take strength from its position, witnessing the upper-class and lower-class stereotypes enacted above and below its own, centrally placed, position. With the emphasis on worlds, periods and classes that were not its own, Dunroamin was securely located. Far from being unnerved by neglect, it was fortified, reassured as to the fundamental rightness of its values and the unassailability of its endeavour to found a new kind of community.

One is left with an impression of stability, conservatism, resistance to change. But this, in an important sense, was not wholly the case. Dunroamin required the dependability of established value systems because the adventure of home-making in its atmosphere of expansion, growth, construction and consolidation was itself so unsettling. Trees were being felled, materials transported and unloaded, timber-pole scaffolding erected and brick walls raised all round. Speculative builders, often small concerns employing only a few 'brickies', 'chippies' or 'sparks', laid out the foundations of new groups of houses. Their dimensions seemed impossibly small when the trenches were first dug; the clay piled high on the patch that would one day be a garden was mixed with rubble, broken bricks, sawn-off lengths of joists, floorboards and eventually, picture rails and banisters. Warm-hued Doulton-ware jointed pipes plotted the lines of drains and soil disposal; curb-stones standing on plinths of concrete indicated where the footpaths would be. The landscape one month was very different six months later. New schools, new shopping parades, new libraries, even new churches altered the suburbanscape at an unprecedented rate. In such a world of upheaval and physical transformation Dunroamin needed the assurance of constancy of values.

The dynamic, unfolding, changing environment of the suburbs spread out from the city centres, expanded into the country and consumed the farm-lands: confidence in the dependability of suburban values was all-important. Dunroamin's occupants wanted a stable milieu for their family-focussed culture, and it was fortunate for its growth and survival that there was neither within it, nor in its exposure to mass media, any serious threat to its security. Threats to the security of the suburb were more serious at the national, or rather international level. The 'September Crisis' over Czechoslovakia in 1938 brought Britain to the very edge of war, and trenches were dug in the grounds of schools throughout the country. As Britain lumbered inexorably towards the conflagration, it was apparent that Dunroaminers would be called upon to defend the world they had shaped, and the values that they cherished.

=6=

THE OWNER MAKES HIS MARK

Choice and Adaptation

Ian Bentley

PREVIOUS chapters have shown the intimate connections between the forms of Dunroamin and the philosophy of individualism. These connections give a special value to the study of Dunroamin at present, for there is widespread concern—both lay and professional—about Modern Architecture's apparent *lack* of interest in the individual. The growth of corporate patronage and the division of labour in architects' offices together ensure that most buildings are designed with no contact between architect and user. This situation is reflected and reinforced in architectural education: students are trained to design for imaginary users who can make no active design contribution. Through their experiences of both education and practice, therefore, architects are used to thinking of lay people as passive consumers of the built environment.

Though deeply entrenched, this attitude is now beginning to be seriously questioned; groups outside the profession combine with rebel elements within to argue that people should be treated as active participants in the built settings of their lives.[1] The adoption of this active view of man implies changes in architectural values; the extent to which a building can support its users in the pursuit of their own objectives—what, in this chapter, is called its *responsive-ness*—becomes a touchstone of architectural quality. Founded on a vision of the free individual, with strong implications of responsiveness, Dunroamin is an interesting environment to explore in search of ways in which the concept of responsiveness might condition physical design.

Responsiveness is an attribute of the relationship between the user and his environment. The level of responsiveness of any particular user-environment relationship therefore depends upon the characteristics of the *user*, of his *environment*, and of the mechanisms by which power is channelled between them. Of these three areas of concern *power* is at once the most fundamental in terms of importance, and the simplest to understand: all things being equal, the greater the power the user can bring to bear on his environment, the greater will be his ability to use that environment to support his own ends. Power, of course, may be channelled through many media: particularly important, so far as the built world is concerned, are the channels of economics, of legal tenure and of technology.

In economic terms, the Dunroaminer was usually better off than his local-authority counterpart, which meant that he could more easily mould his environment – house and garden – to suit his own requirements. His economic power was also given greater *leverage* through the mechanics of legal tenure. Because he owned the freehold of his home, the Dunroaminer could alter it as he wished, unconstrained by tenancy agreements.

So far as technology was concerned, no startling new developments were made available to the Dunroaminer. Power tools were not yet available to the home handyman, and most hand tools and materials were still produced with the expectation that their users would be skilled tradesmen. The traditional brick-and-timber fabric of Dunroamin was, however, extremely well-matched to the more easily-used tools available to the Dunroaminer. Only simple carpentry skills, with occasional bricklaying, were needed for the minor adaptations likely to be made when the house was new.

Reinforcing this good match between building technology and available skills, the Dunroaminer *himself* was changing; he was beginning to use more effectively the power available to him. The extent to which he could exercise power largely depended on factors such as class, wealth and intelligence, over which the Dunroaminer himself had no immediate control. To some extent, however, it depended on his *understanding* of the power available to him, and of how it could most effectively be deployed. This understanding was fostered through the growing numbers of books and magazines on carpentry, furniture-making and gardening produced for the home handyman,[2] many with sections on 'buying your home', advising on the complexities of solicitors, building societies, and surveyors. The more practical skills taught in such books were consolidated as part of schoolboy lore; the large range of fretwork and carpentry sets, produced by Messrs Hobbies Ltd, became highly popular as Christmas and birthday presents.

Of the three issues which determine the responsiveness of the man-environment relationship – the user's knowledge, the power which he commands and the physical design of the environment itself – the last is the most complex. The extent of an environment's responsiveness depends on the degree – possibly negligible – to which it helps or hinders its users in achieving their own objectives. Potentially, at least, this helping or hindering process operates at any or all of the levels at which users and their environments interact. As perception psychologists point out, it is useful to distinguish three such levels: those of physical form, use and meaning. [3]

The distinctions between these levels become clear when they are related to Dunroamin. At the level of *physical form*, the house and its garden might be perceived as an *object*, or commodity, by an estate agent trying to sell it. Its only *use*, to a property developer trying to buy it, is as a potential building site; but it is still a home to the people who live in it. To the president of the local residents' association its *meaning* might be 'individual values'; whilst it means 'bad taste' to an architect living in a gentrified Edwardian terrace nearby.

Each of these levels of interaction between the user and his environment corresponds to a level of responsiveness. At the *form* level – the level of the physical fabric – an environment's responsiveness depends on the extent to which its user can create, adapt or modify it in a physical sense. A high degree of responsiveness in *use* implies an environment which can be used in different ways according to different users' aspirations.

Responsiveness at both these levels represents the environment's *potential* for supporting users' wishes in terms of forming and using it. The practical realisation of this potential is conditioned by what the environment means to its users, for meaning mediates between the physical forms of buildings and the ways in which they are used, modified and understood by those who dwell in them. The environment's meaning can therefore support or inhibit responsiveness at all three levels.

So far, for the purposes of clarity, each level of responsiveness has been discussed separately. In practice, however, it is artificial to consider one level in isolation from the others. Increasing responsiveness at one level may, in practice, imply reducing it at another, as later examples will show.

Examples of responsiveness at all levels are to be found in the speculative suburb. For example, Dunroamin offered its users the potential to alter their physical environments if and as they wished. One way in which the user could initiate such changes, in addition to the obvious course of making physical alterations to his house, was by merely moving to different surroundings. *His* environment was then physically different, even though *the* environment, viewed as an artefact, was unchanged.

Dunroamin offered more choice of this sort than did the council estate which was its only significant rival in the field of new housing. In nearly every locality during the period between the wars there was just *more* of Dunroamin than of its local-authority counterpart. [4] Furthermore, in the earlier post-war years, speculative developers had not yet coalesced into big firms capable of developing large schemes; often, therefore, Dunroamin estates were smaller than local

The Dunroamin House: Planes of Choice

PLANE OF CHOICE	EXAMPLES	CHARACTER-ISTICS	RANGE OF CHOICE	PRICE 1920s & 30s	FREEDOM OF CHOICE
First the house as habitable shell	3-bedroom semi. 4-bedroom semi. Also bungalow; chalet in some districts	Permanent, structural. Privately owned or sometimes rented	Variations of plan; with/ without garage outbuilding. Plot sizes	From £450–£900 normal. Higher in 'select' areas	Limited by district and numbers of builders
Second repertoire of alternative major features	Windows, bays, gables, porches	Semi-permanent, distinctive, large-scale. Seldom changed	As offered by builder. Often 5–10 types	As offered by builder; might add £100–£150 to price of house	Restricted to variants offered by builder
Third repertoire of alternative details and fixtures	Stained-glass windows, tiled fireplaces, bath-room suite	Distinctive, non-structural. Changed very rarely	10–50 variants of each might have been offered by builder	£1 (stained-glass)–£20 (fireplace)	Controlled by availability from builders' merchant
Fourth items of primary function	Cooker, carpets, bedroom suite, dining-room suite	Large, heavy. Could have been moved. Occasionally might be replaced	5–20 variants obtainable in large stores	£20 or above, according to quality and style of materials	Considerable, conditioned by store stock and transport
Fifth articles of secondary function	Radiogram, toaster, standard lamp, electric fire	Practical, portable. Might have been changed, parts might have been replaced	10 (radios) to 50 (light fittings) available in local shops	£2–£5	Extensive, local shops and stores. Delivered or carried
Sixth accessories of symbolic function	Ornaments, pictures, bird table, garden figurines	Portable, decorative. Often not durable. Frequently supplemented	100s available in shops or as souvenirs	2s.–£2 or above	Unrestricted choice. Travel (e.g. holidays) might have extended it

authority ones, and were consequently scattered on a variety of different sites within each locality. This gave the Dunroaminer a locational choice whose importance was implied by contemporary advertising; particularly in London, whose great size gave a maximum of locational choice, advertising stressed the competing amenities of each site, emphasising considerations such as nearness to transport, leisure facilities, or healthy rural air.

Dunroamin also offered its dwellers a variety of possibilities for direct physical intervention in the forming of their environment. Indeed, a large part of the Dunroamin milieu consisted of gardens, towards which the dwellers usually *had* to adopt an active rôle: each had both to design and to construct his own, and strong social pressures made it likely that he would constantly maintain and update his plot. A contemporary Do-It-Yourself book was almost certainly correct in summarising most people's attitudes as follows:

> Countless thousands of Englishmen endure, cheerfully, aching backs and weary limbs, that their tiny gardens may be gay in spring and summer with bright flowers and shrubs. They could get exactly the same effect by paying a gardener a few shillings – but would it mean the same? Assuredly not. [5]

The layout of the Dunroamin estate maximised the contribution of these individual design efforts to the image of the place as a whole. The low density of about twelve houses to the acre ensured an openness of layout, so gardens made up a large part of what was seen from the public road. Their impact on the Dunroamin image was increased by the spatial relationship between the street, the gardens, and the houses. A large part of the garden space was screened from the public realm, behind the house itself, to provide space for private family activities: the front garden, therefore, was used primarily for display.

Though some Dunroamin front gardens were relatively large, because of fortuitous differences in site depth, their owners did not arrange them as their counterparts in Victorian or Edwardian suburbs would have done. The earlier determination to create privacy, with massive planting and high railings, gave way to the use of the front garden *purely* as a symbolic zone. With elements such as rockeries and flower beds, the layout of the front garden rendered it unuseable except for symbolic purposes; whilst the street boundary was defined by low walls or fences, unable to create privacy, and treated as sculptural display elements in their own right. Even the least inspired display was evidence of the support which Dunroamin's layout, in association with the cheap, malleable technology of the rockery and the flower bed, gave to the self-expression of the people who lived there.

The back garden was also an arena for the exercise of creativity; but it was

Front gardens were usually designed so that they were useless for anything but symbolic purposes. Gnomes sit beside a rockery 'pond', near the Western Avenue, London (Graham Paul Smith)

The potential of the back garden as an area where the Dunroaminer could make his mark was emphasised in many 1930s contemporary books of household information (from Sid G. Hedges, *Universal Book of Hobbies and Handicrafts*)

directed towards different aims. If the front garden was where the Dunroaminer confirmed and expressed his self-image for all to see, the back garden was where he made a private world, designed for the requirements of family life. Since these needed privacy, high lap-boarded fences were usual. Closer to the house, the fence was often raised above its customary five feet, to afford greater privacy for the concrete terrace which invariably projected some six feet from the french windows at the back of the house. Sometimes these fences were provided by the builder, but often his efforts were regarded as inadequate: 'The erections of the builder are often of the flimsiest nature – anything that will pass muster for a fence is put up to sell the house', said a contemporary handicrafts manual. [6] In such cases, fences were further raised by the householder himself, with an open-work trellis, rising to a height of eight feet or so, over which roses would be trained. Ostensibly this was the purpose of the trellis when it was discussed with the neighbours, though its first function was probably to afford greater seclusion.

The garden itself was usually divided into two zones, distinctly different in character. One zone, near the house, was designed for sitting out in good weather, and for looking at from the house most of the time: it was laid out to provide a variety of sensory experiences, through the sight and smell of plants and flowers. The other part of the garden, further from the house, was informal and utilitarian, often devoted to vegetables and to the compost heap. It was screened from the house by a trellis or pergola, usually made by the householder himself. As an act of personalisation providing an important part of the view from the house, it also amplified the effects of other, less obviously significant acts of choice, enabling the roses and clematis which were trained over it to take on an architectural scale and importance. Both parts of the garden often contained shelters, in the form of summer houses or more utilitarian sheds, either built by the householder from drawings available in the considerable number of books of the period which gave household hints and tips, or else chosen from the extensive ranges marketed by firms such as Boulton and Paul.

The house itself offered other planes of choice – summarised in the chart on page 139 – each of which increased responsiveness at the level of the physical fabric. Sometimes, though by no means always, the purchaser could choose between houses of slightly different plan arrangement – different *habitable shells* – within the boundaries of one estate. Choice at this plane was somewhat limited in the true Dunroamin estate; but the same could not be said of the roof forms, bays, oriels, porches and the like – a *repertoire of alternative major features* – which formed a second plane of choice, and which could be added to transform it from a shell into a home. Paradoxically, indeed, the very *consistency* of the basic shell ensured that any major features which *did* differ from house to house would show up all the more clearly, in terms of distinguishing each from its neighbours, so as to provide a variety of perceptibly different houses from which the purchaser could choose. The degree of variety thus provided, by means of the repertoire of alternative major features, was often very great, as Ian Davis shows in Chapter 3. Such features were not normally incorporated into the house at the purchaser's special request: for reasons of construction management, they were decided upon by the builder.

At a smaller physical scale, however, Dunroamin incorporated a third plane of choice—a *repertoire of alternative details*—which could be added to suit the individual purchaser. Internally, choice at this plane covered such items as fireplaces and kitchen and bathroom fittings, all of which could be ordered from catalogues or seen at the builders' merchants. Externally, the repertoire covered elements like colour schemes, together with the detailed forms—though rarely the positions—of doors and windows. Paradoxically, the choice of doors and windows was increased by the developing rationalisation of the building industry. The easy availability of a wide range of industrialised components, including elements such as leaded lights and stained-glass panels, made it easy for the builder to offer this repertoire of alternative details to an extent which would have caused impossible management difficulties if every component had been individually designed and made.

Despite the wide availability of industrialised building components the possibilities for alternative details were, in absolute terms, fairly restricted; but the usual elements of choice were carefully positioned so as to maximise their impact, both for the family and for visitors. Coloured-glass panels, for example, provide frequent cases in point. These were too costly for use in every room; so they were placed in the most public positions in the house, such as in the front room bay, and in the front door. Another adroitly chosen location was the staircase window, positioned in the circulation space linking together all the rooms in the house to ensure the maximum impact; particularly during the important ritual by which lady visitors went upstairs to leave their coats on the bed.

Personal choice at a fourth plane was introduced by furnishing with *items of primary function*: large, expensive elements such as cookers and bedroom suites. The selection here was broad and was limited only by the stocks of the furniture stores and suppliers of domestic equipment. Because of the relatively high cost of furniture, it was seen as a long-term investment; which meant that choices were conditioned by considerations of serviceability and durability. The upholstery of the settee, the resilience of the interior-sprung mattress, the dimensions of the wardrobe or the capacity of the kitchen copper boiler were functional constraints on choice which were offset by their imagery in fabrics, wood veneers, enamel or chrome finishes.

Rugs and smaller items of furniture, from nests of occasional tables to the radio, gramophone, standard lamp, coal bin, book-case, bathroom scales and hall umbrella stand, were all encompassed within a fifth plane of choice. *Articles of secondary function*, they were less necessary to the efficient running of the home, but were substantial and desirable items which raised the comfort level attainable. They were consumer commodities, in that they could be replaced within the bounds of reasonable expense.

A sixth plane of choice was afforded by *accessories of symbolic function*. Offering the greatest freedom of choice, these were impermanent objects, such as light fittings, shelf ornaments and flower vases; pictures, prints and souvenirs of holidays and novelty shops, purchased with little regard for utility. Ephemeral and decorative, their relative portability meant that they could be obtained from sources at a considerable distance; and they could be moved about the house, stored, or simply removed with a freedom that was scarcely possible with the more expensive furniture or the semi-permanent aspects of house decoration.

The ability to make a personal impact on the home environment through the purchase of small items was certainly not unique to Dunroamin, nor to the inter-war years. There were, however, significant developments in the design and production of furniture which effectively *amplified* the impact which could be made with them. As Paul Oliver shows in Chapter 7, the marketing of the three-piece suite, for example, and the production of many ranges of objects, of different function and scale, but incorporating the same stylistic motifs, were typical of the period.

Sets of matching items of this kind formed the basis for acts of personalisation of a sufficiently large scale to take on significance in relation to the scale of an entire room. Superficially, the Dunroaminer's attachment to matching sets of furniture and other items might appear unremarkable; the Georgians, after all, had designed their interiors to produce an effect of stylistic unity. But the Georgians were interested in stylistic unity for *its own sake*; and in order to achieve it they were prepared to accept — indeed, they eagerly embraced — the idea of subordinating each element in the design to the overall theme of the room. The Dunroaminer, on the other hand, happily mixed his three-piece suite and his matching sets of decorative items with all sorts of *other* elements, which were often very different in stylistic terms. His intention was not to achieve stylistic unity, but rather to make correspondences between relatively small items in such a way as to increase their impact in *whatever style he wanted*. Certainly most three-piece suites were not, in any meaningful sense, stylistically similar to the flat plastered, anonymous box which was the usual Dunroamin room of the 1930s, depending for much of its effect on the wallpaper or paint chosen by the householder himself. Indeed, it was the very simplicity of the box, lacking in intrinsic formal interest, which ensured the maximum impact for the householder's own scheme of decoration.

So far as the main living-room was concerned, the basic box shape was usually articulated by a picture rail, a bay window and a fireplace, each of which had its rôle to play in terms of increasing the responsiveness of the room at the level of physical form. The picture rail, for example, made it easy for the householder to hang such items as prints, family photographs, or mirrors; or home-embroidered panels which could be made up with the minimum of special skill, using the range of pre-marked patterns widely available. Gradually, however, the picture rail began to seem less desirable. It suffered heavily in the fierce campaign against 'dust traps' which was waged in the taste-forming popular magazines and home-decoration books, which also promoted a wider knowledge of the simpler handyman techniques such as plugging and fixing to walls. Taking advantage of these more widespread abilities, manufacturers began to develop new types of wall-hung objects, such as flower vases and flights of plaster mallards, which could not easily be hung from the picture rail, but needed more solid fixings direct to the wall. Gradually, these convergent influences reduced the popularity of the picture rail during the later part of the inter-war period.

The bay window and the fireplace, unlike the picture rail, were retained as important elements in main living-rooms throughout the Dunroamin period, though their forms changed in detail under the simplifying influence of the campaign for the labour-saving, dust-free home. Bay and fireplace – both large and obviously permanent architectural elements with connotations of importance – were used to enhance the significance of the personalising impact made by the cheap, small, ephemeral items in whose selection the Dunroaminer had the greatest freedom of choice. The bay window in the front room, for example, amplified the *public* impact of such items. Thrust out towards the public realm, often with a tiled sill convenient for plant pots as well as for the display of ornamental objects, the design of its every detail evolved to maximise the bay's potential for display.

For example, detailed examination of a typical Dunroamin bay shows that there is a continuous gradation of scale between the largest perceived element – the overall form of the bay itself – through an intermediate scale represented by its roof, main structural mullions, and tiled or rendered skirt, to the glazing bars which define smaller openings; and finally to the patterns of the net curtaining material – whose intricate systems of folds constituted a popular art during the inter-war period – at the smallest scale of all. Having this gradation, in which each element is related to the next above and below it in the hierarchy without large differences of scale, the bay differs radically from the typical picture window of later suburbs – large, without glazing bars, and set straight into the plane of the wall. The relevance of this distinction becomes clear if we compare the settings which both the Dunroamin bay and the picture window provide for the objects on public display within them.

Apart from curtains, most items readily available for public display needed, for practical reasons, to be small and portable: vases, brass donkeys, potted plants and the like. The Dunroamin bay, built up from architectural elements at a variety of scales, is capable of providing an *appropriately* scaled architectural frame for the display of both large and small objects. Large objects – the curtains – relate automatically to the scale of the entire bay; whilst the smaller decorative items are appropriately framed in the smaller scale of the glazing bars. Because each of the variously scaled objects on display is provided with architectural settings of appropriate scale, they all appear to be *part of* the perceptual structure of the bay itself; they are, so to speak, *incorporated into* the architecture, rather than appearing merely as superficially applied ancillaries to it. The effect of the later picture window is very different. Exposed in the naked space of such a window, small displays are dwarfed. Overwhelmed by the scale of their architectural setting, they dwindle into insignificance.

There are two important differences, in terms of their contributions to responsiveness, between the bay window and the fireplace. First, the fireplace enhanced the significance of small personalising objects in the *private* realm, within the house itself. Also – unlike the bay, whose design was chosen by the builder – the fireplace was itself an element in the *repertoire of alternative details* which contributed to the third plane of choice. Given the hearth's significance as a prime symbol of home, its choice was itself an extremely important act of personalisation. Despite these differences, however, the fireplace was conceptually similar to the bay, if only because it increased responsiveness through the manipulation of architectural scale. Some Dunroamin fireplaces were complex pieces of design when viewed in this light. Some of the products of the popular Claygate range, for example, incorporated numbers of differently scaled brick shelves and niches, capable of providing appropriately scaled settings for the display of objects of various sizes. Even the simplest form of tiled fireplace, from the 1930s, projected sufficiently from the wall to be used in this way, whilst the commonest form of simple tiled design – the Art Deco influenced ziggurat – had small niches formed by the recessing of its top corners. The whole fireplace thus became a display unit, which enhanced the importance of the displayed objects

Mantelpiece, picture rail and plate shelf maximise the impact of small objects in this 1920s interior. By the 1930s extra shelves and recesses enabled such objects to be incorporated within the symbolically important family hearth (see lower illustration opposite page 176) (from W. Frost, *The Modern Bricklayer*)

The standard Dunroamin plan, with all rooms kept free from circulation routes (from *House Building 1934–36*)

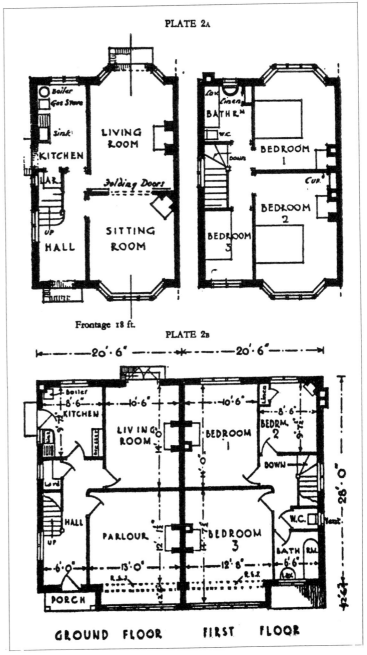

in two ways. First, since it was an element at a scale midway between that of the room itself and that of the kinds of objects likely to be displayed, it set up a scale continuum which enabled the small objects to be perceived as *part of* the architecture of the room itself, rather than being merely superficial additions to it. Secondly, the small personalising objects placed on it gained significance by association with the importance of the hearth as prime symbol of home.

The examples of the bay and the fireplace clearly show responsiveness at the level of form; the objects on display made physical alterations to the fabric of the house, both internally and externally. But in both examples, the levels of form begin to interact with that of meaning: it was the symbolic importance of bay and fireplace which increased the *impact* made by these small and ephemeral physical alterations.

Similar interactions between different levels of responsiveness – this time between the levels of form and use – show up in the arrangements which were sometimes made for combining together the Dunroaminer's two main living spaces. Some developers took over the Edwardian practice of providing folding screens between the main rooms of large houses in order to produce a more malleable layout, able to be adapted by each household to suit its own lifestyle. This was clearly a device for increasing responsiveness at the level of form, because of the ease with which the householder could change the physical form of the house. But, because the changes made were easily and quickly *reversible*, the range of different activities which the space could accommodate – and hence its responsiveness at the level of *use* – was also increased.

Advanced versions of this idea were to be found in some Dunroamin estates, for example in houses developed by Bysouth Ltd at Enfield during the 1930s. In their type 'A' house the two main ground-floor rooms were separated from each other, and from an intermediate zone of space, by folding doors, an arrangement which allows four different combinations of space to be used. Even without such devices, the planning of the speculative semi provided for a high level of responsiveness in use. In terms of the size and arrangement of its rooms there was considerable scope for accommodating a variety of uses – even non-residential uses – without the need for any but the most minor of physical alterations: as a doctor's surgery, shop, or nursery school, for music teaching, or a play group, for a chiropodist, or a dentist, and even as a funeral parlour.

This degree of flexibility in use was made possible by the fact that Dunroamin's main rooms were usually about twelve feet square, more or less; and were thus examples of those average-sized rooms which, according to recent research, can accommodate some 80 per cent of common human activities.[7]

Flexibility in use was also enhanced because circulation within the house was arranged so that access between rooms, and to common services, did not disturb the privacy of any individual room.

Sometimes, this circulation system also gave direct access to a side-located garage; to produce the most flexible of all versions of the speculative semi. The garage – usually measuring some nine feet by sixteen – was itself an average-sized room if a little on the narrow side. It could, of course, be used for car storage; but if, like many Dunroaminers in the 1930s, the householder had no car – or if, even as a car owner, he had a better use for the space – then the garage could house many other activities. It could be used for a wide variety of hobbies or games, or become a workshop, or – with the large garage doors removed and the opening filled with a more domestic arrangement of window and wall – it could form an extra sitting-room or bedroom.

Even without a garage, the 'average-sized-room' layout of the standard speculative semi also made possible a variety of patterns of use at ground-floor level. The traditionally-minded could keep to the pattern of parlour (for special occasions) and living-room (for general family use); whilst participants in the general inter-war move towards informality of lifestyle could dispense with the parlour, using the two rooms as 'lounge' and dining-room. The other rooms in the house – particularly those upstairs – were relatively less flexible in use, for cost constraints ensured that all of them – except perhaps for the principal bedroom – were significantly smaller than the optimally flexible average size. There was therefore insufficient space for any activities other than sleeping or studying: since upstairs rooms were in any case culturally constrained to night-time use, this reduction in flexibility was less important than it would otherwise have been.

The Dunroamin layout also promoted responsiveness in use through the closeness of its links between house and garden. These links enabled the garden to be used as an extension of the living space of the house, in a way which had been impossible with the pre-war speculative house, because of the obstruction caused by its long rear extension. A terrace outside the back living-room, to which it was linked by glazed french doors, now encouraged the use of the garden for sitting out in fine weather; and the fact that the kitchen windows now overlooked the garden made it possible (to reiterate an important point made in Chapter 4) for the housewife to supervise the play of young children. For the first time, they were able to indulge in really *messy* activities within their home territory.

Except for the considerable advantages of easier access to the rear by means of its side approach, and better links between house and garden, the spatial layout of

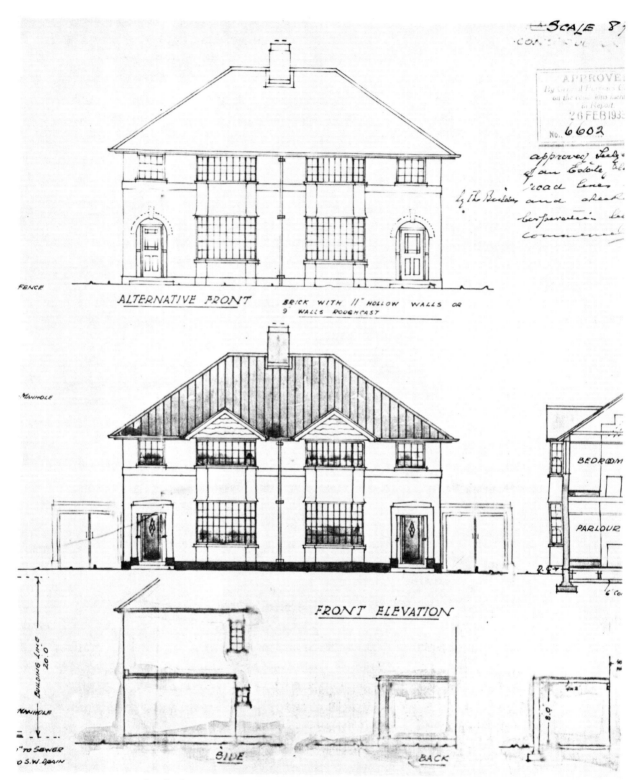

ALTERNATIVE FRONT

BRICK WITH 11" HOLLOW WALLS OR
9 WALLS ROUGHCAST

FENCE

SCALE 8

APPROVED
26 FEB 193
No. 6602

FRONT ELEVATION

SIDE

BACK

BEDROOM

PARLOUR

MANHOLE

BUILDING LINE
20.0

MANHOLE

1" TO SEWER
O S.W. DRAIN

Standard Dunroamin plans with differently designed bays, roofs and
porches, and with garages as optional extras, Cowley Road, Oxford;
by Ephraim Organ and Sons, 1932 (Oxford City Library)

the Dunroamin semi – except in its more expensive, garaged version – probably represented little advance, in terms of flexibility of use, over the speculative, middle-class house of Victorian and Edwardian times. Nonetheless, it was certainly better in this regard than many of its council-estate counterparts, which frequently sacrificed the privacy of the main living-room by using it as a circulation route to other parts of the house. Its advantage over many of the smaller Modern Movement houses, which carried this council house arrangement a long step further with their radically open-planned living spaces, are obvious.

In terms of meaning, too, Dunroamin promoted a greater degree of responsiveness than its local-authority or Modern Movement counterparts. Because meaning mediates between physical forms and the ways in which they are modified, used and understood by those who dwell in them, the meanings of the environment can support or inhibit responsiveness at the levels of the physical fabric and of use, in addition to determining responsiveness at the level of meaning itself. So far as the physical fabric is concerned, connotations of *permanence* and *completeness* in buildings tend to inhibit the making of alterations to them, whilst connotations of *impermanence* and *incompleteness* have the opposite tendency. At this level, therefore, meanings which support responsiveness are subversive in relation to many 'high-architecture' traditions: they are – at least potentially – in conflict with the classic notion of architectural quality as typified by buildings 'to which nothing can be added, and from which nothing can be taken away'.

Dunroamin's connotations vary considerably as between the front and the back of the house. At the front, there are many implications of both completeness and permanence. For example, the overall mass of the pair of semis, as seen from the street, is strongly symmetrical; in plan, the semi-circular bays seem finite and closed in form; and the front usually has materials of high status, put together with obvious care for long-life. These connotations of completeness and permanence inhibited the making of major alterations. This was appropriate, given the public nature of the front façade as the primary definition of the public realm. It was also appropriate to the Dunroaminer's need to conserve the image of his environment in order to maintain the value of his property.

Even at the front, though, individual creativity was merely kept within strong constraints, rather than being completely denied by the connotations of the form. The front of the house contained some *impermanent* materials, such as paint, which *had* to be regularly renewed; so far as these elements were concerned, Dunroamin's complex form increased the choices with which the householder was presented during the process of routine maintenance. First of all, Dunroamin often required more maintenance than its rival the council house, which was designed as a long-term, local-authority investment with the need for low maintenance regarded as an important design determinant. In addition, Dunroamin's complex form ensured that maintenance had to be applied to a relatively large number of perceptibly different elements of the building: porches, bays, gables, applied half-timbering and so forth. Each time the need for maintenance arose, the householder was faced with a decision: should the half-timbering on the gable be painted out, or should it be painted up to emphasise it? Should the front door be painted all one colour, or should its panels and mouldings be picked out separately?

At the front of Dunroamin, then, the connotations of the form were such as to contain individual creativity within appropriately narrow limits. At the rear, however, the situation was different; here, the householder could be as idiosyncratic as he liked, within wide limits, without affecting the value of his neighbours' property. At the back, therefore, the connotations both of completeness and of permanence were far weaker. The fenestration had less obviously formal intentions, for the window sizes and positions were determined largely by the need to achieve a convenient interior. If there were variations in terms of the status implications of the materials used, then it was at the back that the inferior ones were to be found. If the front was in brick, or rendered with the occasional facing brick peeping through to suggest quality in the hidden parts, then the back might be in plain roughcast with its implications of relative cheapness and impermanence. There was no need to provide the *disciplined* outlet for creativity which was afforded at the front by the complex pattern of parts requiring regular maintenance. Appropriately enough, they were largely absent.

Dunroamin's connotations also supported responsiveness at the level of meaning by expanding the *range* of meanings which the house could have for its users. As Ian Davis has discussed in Chapter 3, the builders of Dunroamin used ambiguity to enable the speculative house to carry a range of different connotations, from which the Dunroaminer could draw support for his individual system of values. For the speculative builder this was a valuable concept: this kind of ambiguity, or *multivalence*, was likely to make his buildings seem appropriate to the slightly differing values of a wide range of people. The use of multivalent forms therefore broadened the house's market appeal. The point here is not that the speculative builder consciously designed multivalent houses; rather, it was a developing tradition of such buildings which survived best when subjected to the discipline of the highly competitive speculative housing market. As might be expected, therefore, Dunroamin evolved from relatively unambiguous beginnings in the years after the First World War, towards ever greater multivalence during the later 1930s. The earlier post-war semis still sufficiently resembled the pre-war speculative 'Queen Anne' to evoke the multiple response of Moyr Smith's 'pure English, pure Flemish, pure Italian'; whilst they also reflected the high value placed on individualism and – with simple Neo-Georgian as the council housing style – Dunroamin's complexities came to stand for private enterprise too.

The earlier versions of Dunroamin, with pitched roofs, bays and evocations of half-timbering, also had strong connotations of tradition; but from the mid 1930s designers drew on the International Style vocabulary to produce a further level of multivalence. The new combination of pitched roofs, bays, but clean white walls and streamform corner windows still alluded strongly to its more traditional forebears, continuing its traditionalist, individualist, private enterprise messages. But now it carried other messages too. It had connotations of modernity *and* traditionalism, cosiness *and* the bracing values of the open air, as well as hinting at the Riviera holidays which its owner would one day like to take.

Dunroamin's ambiguous connotations have always offended most architectural critics. Since the First World War, architects – whether classicist or modernist in persuasion – have valued purity and consistency of form, using the word 'ambiguous' as a term of abuse. Other levels of responsiveness have also flouted architects' values. Flexibility in use, for example, is diametrically opposed to the functionalist's aim of tailoring forms closely to particular activities; whilst the idea of encouraging (or even allowing) the user to modify his home attacks the Bauhaus notion of 'total design' which is buried so deep in the foundations of the Modern Movement. The speculative builder's success in achieving some measure of responsiveness, at all these levels, may be one more reason why the architect – perhaps irritated by the nagging of a faintly troubled conscience – has hated Dunroamin so much.

The tourist promenade deck of the *Orion*, 1935. Its functionalism
appealed to Modern Movement architects (Peninsular and Oriental
Steam Navigation Company)

By the late 1930s the ambiguous image of Dunroamin had often
become both traditional *and* modern, as in this 1934 Costain estate at
Selsdon, Surrey (Graham Paul Smith)

$$\Rightarrow 7 \Leftarrow$$

THE GALLEON ON THE FRONT DOOR

Imagery of the House and Garden

Paul Oliver

IF there were many planes by which the house-owner in the suburbs could exercise choice, and make his mark upon the environment, two questions arise on the significance of the specific elements he could choose or employ and on their meaning. How were the values of Dunroamin expressed throughout the house, and how did they meet their occupiers' deep psychological needs, in comparison with the values embodied in the houses of the Modern Movement?

Paradoxically, both Dunroaminers and the architects of the Modern Movement were obsessed with the benefits of the open air. It was the exodus from the cities rather than the growth of the population which promoted the expansion of Dunroamin. The cities were dirty, the slums iniquitous, the Victorian terraces cramped and ill-lit. Tens of thousands of tons of refuse were dumped daily in the adjacent wastelands, the rivers were open sewers, the city air was polluted with sulphur. Solid impurities in the air above central London in the mid Thirties fell at the rate of 475 tons per square mile per annum; heavy smoke haze covered Westminster for a third of the year.[1] Suburban living offered space, low densities, gardens and access to the countryside. The emigrant from the city could rejoice in raising his family in clean and humane surroundings.

With the new awareness of the benefits of sunshine, fresh air and exercise, the architecture of the advocates of Modernism might have seemed to be the ultimate aspiration of the middle class. Clean lines, bright interiors were among the virtues of the new architecture. 'When Webb designed Red House for Morris, they did not worry much about the sun; today we all crave for the sun, light and air', wrote Marjorie and C. B. J. Quennell. They illustrated Wells Coates and Pleydell-Bouverie's 'Sunspan' house built at the Ideal Home Exhibition at Olympia in 1934 and showed how a 'revolution' had taken place outside and in. 'The Victorian sitting room was rather like a junk shop with innumerable objects which had to be dusted day after day. "Away with them",

155

say the young designers, ''we will have everything glittering and clean''. So they are experimenting with chromium steel, glass and cellulose paint, and their furniture is fitted in as part of the fabric.'[2] But the 'Sunspan' house was not a success with Dunroaminers any more than were the houses by Skinner and Tecton and other exhibitors at the Modern Homes Exhibition at Gidea Park that year.

Flat roofs, curved glass in the fenestration, chromium steel and 'everything glittering' with white metal and cellulose paint, were not what the suburbs wanted. The Quennells unintentionally indicated the reason in *The Good New Days* (1935), showing the deck of the Orient liner *Orion* with its davits, air-ventilation tubes and deck machinery above the caption: *Cleanliness and Space*. There were family likenesses in the Peckham Health Centre interior and the boiler house at Battersea Super-Power Station.[3] Propagandists for the Modern Movement invariably made the same correlations between functionalism, industrial equipment, glass and chrome, sunlight and air.

Through the Twenties and Thirties the factories were developing at a pace only paralleled by the growth of the suburbs themselves. Between 1925 and 1932 nearly eight hundred factories opened or extended in Greater London. S. Vere Pearson recorded in 1938:

> The facilities for up-to-date factory buildings, with ample floor space on one level (preferably the ground level only), suitable for modern methods of mass production, have often, no doubt, been the chief attraction of the outer suburbs. Most of the factories are producing goods for retail consumption, such as clothing, furniture and electrical apparatus. . . After the War, but mainly since 1925, development received a new impetus extending to certain areas such as Slough, Greenford and Park Royal, mostly in the trades relatively thriving throughout the post-war period.[4]

In these new factories 129,610 persons found employment. Some 551 new factories opened in England in 1936 alone, and of these two-fifths were in Greater London and a fifth in the North-West of England. The *Economist*, which published a supplement on London in 1937, noted: 'The Development of the new factories has followed a clearly marked radial plan along the main arteries of transport. It is transport which has made West Middlesex the favoured area for industrial development,'[5] the largest developments being 'in the triangle enclosed between lines drawn from London to Watford on the north-west and Slough on the west. The advantages of this area can be seen at its new industrial centre, Park Royal,' with its LMS and GWR railways, 'two ''Tube'' railways to bring its labour, and a brand new arterial road. The arterial road is perhaps the greatest attraction, to judge by the factories that line the Great West Road, the Edgware Road and the North Circular Road.'[6]

To walk around these roads today is to see very clearly demonstrated why Dunroamin did not take to the 'Sunspan' house or other 'modern' estates. They were built with an imagery close to that of the factories where many of Dunroamin's population in the lower economic group worked, or with which the more affluent suburbs no longer wished to be associated. The large windows with horizontal glazing bars, the flat roofs, the white walls and hard, spartan exteriors and functional interiors were unwelcome in the home; the images that the suburbs required for the domestic environment were not those of the factory, however much 'cleanliness, sun and air' might be coupled with it.

The suburban semi was a complex reaction against a number of other house forms: it was opposed to the image of the Victorian terrace, with its 'collective' associations beneath a single roof, and from which many of the lower and middle class had come; it was contrary to the style of the factories with their heartless, anonymous, technical efficiency; it was against the style of the Continental Modern Movement, whose 'machine-for-living-in' aesthetic was inimical to the picture of domesticity; and it challenged the style of the municipal housing estate, whose upper middle-class champions, in a not untypical rôle-reversal, had spent their childhood in individualised housing and who now aspired, for the masses if not for themselves, towards a collective image.

Imagery was at the heart of the matter: what the advocates of the Modern Movement required was an architecture whose imagery spoke of the new era, of functional, rational, practical living in a machine age, coupled with an ideological commitment which sought equality, communality of spirit and the repression of individualism. What the new Dunroaminer sought was an imagery that spoke of home, of family, of stability and of individualism. Modernists were prepared to clad their brickwork in render that appeared to be concrete for the sake of the image the new architecture projected; the Dunroaminer saw no incongruity in having his home clad in the symbols of domesticity. The two positions were opposite sides of the same coin, but could never share the same face. The printing presses were on the side of the Modernists, when the invective was let loose, but the symbols through which Dunroamin could communicate its values were expressed in the building itself.

As members of a community the suburban household had an effect on the image of the suburb in which they lived. That identity was achieved through the totality of hundreds of individualised environments; there were many constraints which exercised a measure of control on the family idiom while contributing to the unity of the suburb. Some of these were legislative: building lines, width of paths and roads, depths of gardens and standardisation of front-ages. The administrative confusion in which many of the suburbs developed might have left loopholes for individual enterprise but the complex of authorities made it difficult for the householder to know the restrictions under which he was living. As the North Harrow Ratepayers Association complained in 1932, its members lived under a parish council in Pinner, a rural council based at Harrow Weald and a county council at Westminster. Their gas supply came from South-West London, their electricity from North London, the Colne Valley Water Company supply came from Bushey in Hertfordshire. The head post office was at Harrow, the police court was at Wealdstone, the county court at Watford, the bankruptcy court at St Albans and the workhouse was at Edgware.[7] With a bishop at Willesden and the parish church at Pinner even the spiritual welfare of North Harrow was dispersed; a few years later some of the municipal incongruities were straightened out and the modern church of St Alban was built. 'One of the best of its style in England', wrote Nikolaus Pevsner.[8] 'It looks like a factory,' the local residents still say.

In spite of, even because of, this confusion in official identity, many suburban communities cared for their crescents, drives and avenues. The better laid-out ones had young ornamental trees and grass verges between the footpath and the road; some had beds of shrubs in addition. At its Pinner end, Rayners Lane, for example, had a grass verge edging the road, then a strip of beds set with berberus and flowering shrubs where stood, until recently, the elm trees that marked the old field line. The pavement, of pinkish-hued slabs, was edged with macadam and a storm-water channel set by the low walls and chain posts of the front gardens. Admittedly this was a well-favoured road, but many suburbs had streets with boundaries of some variety, lined with cherry or other trees and grass verges, which softened the transition from public domain to personal one.

Prospective house-buyers wished to be part of a community in which their own dwelling did not set them apart or alienate them from their neighbours and eventual friends; they wanted to choose houses that were, within their means and the choice available, identifiably their own homes. Solutions to this double and somewhat contradictory demand contributed both to the 'same-ness', the 'monotony' of which some commentators complained, and to the 'individuality gone mad' which others condemned.

Though the repeated criticism of Dunroamin is that it is dreary and monot-onous this is justified only by those that see monotony in the fact that all the houses in a road, or a group of roads, may be in semi-detached pairs. Far from being faceless this repetitiveness of the semi-detached house is like the repetitive characteristic of faces in a crowd. Human faces have a morphological similarity in the disposition of features, dimensions of ears and nose, eyes or mouths that makes even a centimetre of variation seem, on occasion, to be grotesque. As the human features gain their individuality by being complex aggregations of a multitude of minor, even virtually indistinguishable variants from an unspecific norm, so the semi-detached house gains its individuality from a multitude of small personalisations of paintwork, curtains, treatments of brickwork or doorways. Family likenesses may be recognised in groups of dwellings erected by one builder; or they may even be found unexpectedly in nearby suburban streets, giving a dimly felt sense of common ancestry. Identification by reading the subtle signs that distinguish one pair of homes from another is analogous to the spotting of the faces of relatives and friends in a school photograph: the clues are recognised at a subliminal level. They read as individuals to a member of the class; to others they may remain indistinct and unidentifiable. It is at this subliminal level too, that the identity of each house within the symmetry of the semi-detached pair is communicated. To the owner, as to his neighbours, the small details of house and garden are all-important. In architectural terms, as perceived by the designer, they may be insignificant but to the occupant they have a very different meaning: they express the values important to him.

Limited though the potential for expression was in the basic house as shell, the form of the roof, its texture and colour, conveyed associations of significance. The physiological parallels with the human head made the hipped roof more rounded and complete than the simple pitched form. Compared with this the flat roof appeared brow-less, missing the cranial balance that the additional height supplied. It was bald and exposed, devoid of the protection of a pitched roof.

For these reasons the semi was favoured with extended gables from both the hipped and the pitched roof. As the span of the pitched roof extended over the semi-detached pair the single gable emphasised the individuality of the single dwelling. In some instances the gable would be 'bonneted' (a term which acknowledges the anthropomorphic physiognomy of the house), the pitch of the roof being echoed in the slope of the gable, which was generally fully tiled. Another popular form linked both gables and swept them down with long, extended eaves to the front porches and doors of each house, containing them within a protective embrace and conveying a sternly affectionate image, with a certain rectitude in the timber slats that were usually affixed at regular verticals on the façade.

Gables were commonly placed over bays which pushed out the space of the front living-rooms. Though in practical terms the bays admitted more light into the rooms and afforded greater opportunities for occupants to watch the passing show in the suburb's quiet streets, they performed another rôle. Just as the body

Anthropomorphic imagery of the house; Hendon, c. 1934 (Ian Davis)

Carefully detailed semis at Hale, Cheshire, 1922. Quoins and
architraves are defined in brick against pebble-dash (BBC Hulton
Picture Library)

can be a symbol for the head, so the physiognomy of the suburban house could also project a body-image. The swelling bosom of the bay windows combined to communicate maternal warmth. Such curves dominated the necessarily recti-linear elements in the façade so that the swelling breasts of the bays eclipsed the masculine associations of a rigid formalism. There were, of course, alternative details in the second plane of choice which conveyed a more male image, but the feminine forms dominated. When square, rather than round bays were employed it was often in association with arches over the recessed porches. The body orifice of the front door was frequently curved, sometimes with the arch continuing to form a large segment of a circle and often with an aureole of brickwork to emphasise the opening. The feminine forms of typical semis, before which the front garden was spread like a trim apron, had connotations of the mother as home-maker so important in the period. The woman's place was not only in the home; the home was a woman.

Many suburban houses were assertive statements of these symbolic forms, emphasised by the use of tile-hung bodices or economically bejewelled with a cluster of tiles applied to the wall surface. But others were embellished beyond such economical treatment of their masses with additional layers of associ-ational imagery which brought further dimensions of reference and meaning. Occasionally this decoration would be through the use of glazed tiles with Oriental or Spanish connotations. Such overt details irritated the critics of Dunroamin.

Among the many potential targets of all aspects of the imagery of the suburban house, it was the allegedly 'Mock Tudor' or 'Tudorbethan' detailing which appears to have upset designers and 'men of taste' the most. John Gloag asked in 1934:

> Why are you, or perhaps your neighbours, living in an imitation Tudor house with stained wooden slats shoved on to the front of it to make it look like what is called a half-timbered house? Those slats have nothing to do with the construction of the house. They are just applied as ornaments. The house does not look like a real half-timbered house and it never can. It has been built in quite a different way from a real Tudor house. Why do we live in this sort of half-baked pageant, always hiding our ideas in the clothes of another age?[9]

Later, in 1938, Anthony Bertram attempted to answer his question, or rather, had it answered for him.

> Probably the popular love for the Tudor, whether genuine or bogus, is based on fear and a wish to escape. When I was broadcasting I had many letters that said quite frankly, 'The suggestion of those quiet old days gives us the restful atmosphere we seek in our homes.' This is self-deception, because of course the old days were far from quiet, but it is

not surprising. These are insecure and frightening times and I believe that economic depression and the fear of war are the chief promoters of the Tudoresque. [10]

George Devey, Ernest Newton, and C. F. A. Voysey were among those distinguished nineteenth-century architects who used timber framing in Tudor-inspired houses, [11] but it was Baillie Scott who won favour from Raymond Unwin with a Neo-Tudor development at Hampstead Garden Suburb that would please 'lovers of oak and honest English timber'. Unwin believed that 'to people who like houses of the suburban villa type these will not appeal.' [12] But in the suburbs that were to develop some fifteen years later, the Neo-Tudor, on the contrary, appealed greatly. Structural timber framing as such was neither necessary nor was it encouraged; there were bye-law restrictions to prevent it. But the artificial timbering on porch or gable, which commenced at sill height or the first floor, related the suburban semi to the well-publicised Garden Suburb developments. In fact the extent of the use of Tudor detailing was related to the amount of money that could be spent on it within the total budget for the house. Hence it was the more expensive houses, detached and standing in larger plots of ground in Sutton or Hove, Epping or Epsom, which had extensive use of simulated timber framing. Some examples had extended storeys at first floor level with jettied construction.

For the Dunroaminer the essential importance of the applied timbering was to make the house familiar and symbolically 'right'. A gable without timber radiating from the centre in simulation of a king post and braces, or without vertical planks pinned to imitate regular studding, often seemed naked and incomplete to the owner. The application of a little unnecessary detailing was in itself evidence of a kind of richness, an assurance that the materials had not been pared to the minimum.

It was this disregard for veracity, this unashamed sham which so incensed the critics. But frequently they were more irritated by the symbol of Tudor associations than by anything excessive in the treatment of the building. Often the Tudor references were so minimal and oblique as scarcely to be identifiable; they did not need to be more. For the curious fact was that while the artificial framing on the expensive houses was imitative, being denotative of specifically identifiable Tudor details, the planks that were nailed to the exterior of Dunroamin's houses were hints only, connotative of uncertain echoes of the Tudor style rather than direct imitations. Thus they were symbolic at more than one level: symbolic, not descriptive, of the Tudor tradition; and symbolic of what appeared to the middle class, three centuries later, as Britain's greatest period in history.

162

Houses with jettied first storey, Eastcote Park Estate, Middlesex,
c. 1934. A new development is being built at the left (London Borough
of Hillingdon)

Lower-priced housing, North London. Individual identity is established
by bays, gables, porches and varied texture (Ian Davis)

Poised between a recent history, which for many was best forgotten, and an uncertain future; anxious only to secure a worthy home in a good, clean environment for a growing family, the occupant of Dunroamin's semi-detached was happy with the echoes of Britain's Tudor past and largely oblivious of the ironic observations made as to his taste. Blurred, inaccurate, romantic, patriotic, the 'Tudorbethan' timbers, leaded lights to casement windows, chevron and herringbone pattern brickwork on the more expensive detached houses were all triggers to the responses which the mythological Elizabethan age evoked.

On the ordinary suburban semi such details as herringbone brickwork were less likely to occur. Panels between the strips of applied timber were more frequently treated with a rendering of roughcast cement or pebble-dash. As a surfacing material pebble-dash was extensively used in suburban housing, even when houses were being built for the upper end of the market. From the builder's point of view it had other advantages: cheap bricks could be used in the external walls, without the necessity of more expensive facing bricks, and could be covered by a treatment which could be laid on by unskilled labour. For the house owner the surface was permanent and could not be scrawled upon with chalks or crayons. It was therefore very acceptable functionally, but at a more subliminal level it appealed because it was indeed, stone: the shingle of the pebble-dash had a material kinship, and tactile and visual qualities which were reminiscent of castle walls rather than of fine ashlar. Distant echoes of the beach also lingered – as children playing on building sites with the piles of stone before they were used, soon discovered. Pebble-dash wall treatment had been used for a few decades before the height of Dunroamin's building period. In particular, it had been employed extensively by C. F. A. Voysey, who designed houses from the mid Eighties with white-painted pebble-dash or roughcast walls for some of his large country properties. The additional cost of maintenance made this a less appropriate treatment in Dunroamin, even though many suburban houses were 'Snowcemed'. It must be admitted though, that the indiscriminate and pervasive use of unrelieved pebble-dash in many suburbs created the least attractive of Dunroamin's environments.

Though the prospective purchaser had limited opportunities to influence the basic form or major surface treatment of his home, the third plane of choice* came with the elements that could be exchanged for others of identical size. Of these, stained-glass windows were significant, for not only were they illuminated from within, they communicated imagery to the outside world. Stained glass was

*See the table on page 139 in connection with this and the next chapter.

widely employed in Dunroamin, but its motifs were selectively derived from those favoured by the Arts and Crafts designers, and from the workshops that translated their designs or had developed their own. Many of the firms who had been influential at the turn of the century made brasses, mosaics and repoussé work as well. But their mediaevalism was too specific, locked in a past with which it could not identify itself, representative of upper-class values, and too detached symbolically from the world they were creating to suit the taste of suburban settlers. 'To my mind', wrote the stained-glass designer Oscar Paterson, 'the emotion of taste is inseparably associated with the perception of *utility* and *beauty of association*'. [13]

Oscar Paterson established his stained-glass works in Glasgow as early as 1886, and his work was a major influence on the popularisation of the medium. His designs of 1900 included cottages in the hills illumined by the rising sun, and ships on high seas. The sailing vessel or galley was also a popular Arts and Crafts motif in hammered iron and bronze. [14] Usually the galley was shown with rows of oars dipping into curling waves, passing the viewer, but the implications of slave galleys or the associations of Viking raids dimly retained in the folk subconscious made this less than popular with Dunroamin. A sailing ship with a massive sail and one or two masts was customary, the galley oars omitted. But whereas a great man-o'-war with a high stern, sailing away from the spectator, would be designed by an Arts and Crafts workshop, the symbolism that satisfied Dunroamin required that the ship was sailing towards the viewer, full canvas spread. Whether the boat was embarking on a new venture, or sailing into port was not clear; the owner could project himself into either interpretation of the scene. Essentially the ship carried himself and his family and for this reason it was important that he should not feel it was sailing away from him. With one or two sails billowing in full, pregnant shapes, the 'galleon', as it was usually termed, rode high on a tumbling sea.

Unlike the nineteenth-century stained-glass windows, few of Dunroamin's halls and staircases featured figures. Alone among the humans depicted were Dutch children or baggy-trousered Dutchmen and wide-capped, full-figured wives in pastoral settings which generally included a windmill. Undoubtedly they were easier to shape in the small pieces that the suburban window required than more slender figures. It seems likely that the timelessness of the costume commended itself, being less specifically rooted to a period, while the small children in bonnets and sabots spoke of simple domesticity. The windmill was a reminder of a period of rural industries of great antiquity, then fast disappearing. Redolent of the open air, of the cycle of the seasons, of the 'wheel ever turning', the sails of the mill were the source of the power that turned the

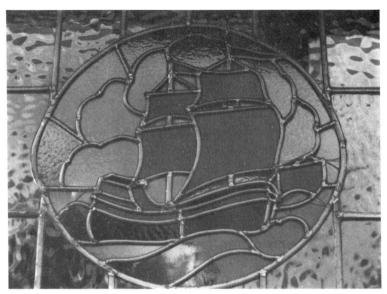

The galleon on the front door (Graham Paul Smith)

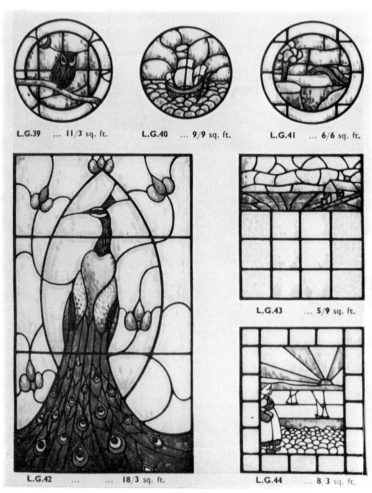

L.G.39 ... 11/3 sq. ft.   L.G.40 ... 9/9 sq. ft.   L.G.41 ... 6/6 sq. ft.

L.G.43 ... 5/9 sq. ft.

L.G.42 ... ... 18/3 sq. ft.   L.G.44 ... 8/3 sq. ft.

Catalogue illustrations from a range of leaded glazing
(UBM MAC Ltd)

mill-stones and ground the corn. The transformation to the staple of life made it a powerful symbol of fertility.

Among the most popular themes was still the peacock, the motif that had been inspired by James McNeill Whistler's Peacock Room of 1876. It became a cliché of Art Nouveau design but, though its use in Dunroamin was derivative, its symbolic value was subtly different. To order one was not unduly expensive: a peacock window three foot by five in leaded glazing and with two horizontal reinforcing bars cost around £13. Such a peacock was not depicted with tail fully spread, but as seen from the back, with its head turned to one side so that it could be seen in profile, and the tail feathers laid out in the foreground with the eyes prominently in evidence. It was not so much a symbol of display, or of achievement, as one with a fully spread tail would have been: it was more a symbol of promise – of a peacock that would one day display its whole glory. The symbolic implications were those of richness only partly revealed; of a splendour which was to come, when hard work at the office, a well-appointed home and a family had eventually been achieved. It isn't surprising that the peacock is seen against a glowing vaginal shape. Genital, budding, rising shapes surround it, flicking their semen-like tails of leaded line, all elements combining to create a potent symbol.

Offered by the trade for installation in front doors and porch windows, above casements, and most prominently and popularly, on staircase landing windows, pictorial themes were common in suburban houses. But the most frequent motifs were of conventionalised flowers, which also had their design origin in Arts and Crafts clichés. Generally they were non-specific, although lilies and tulips could be identified in the single-bloomed, tall-stemmed flowers among the designs available. Swelling on the stems, breaking out in tumescent designs at the flowerhead, or thrust centrally into spreading curves, they were symbols of sexual union and of new life. The degree to which the range of motifs was restricted by the manufacturers for the building trades must remain to some extent conjectural but, with manufacturers offering many designs from which to choose, the public helped define the range. A trade publication explained: 'Only intended to be representative of what we can supply, and special designs will be prepared at any time upon receipt of particulars of requirements.'[15]

Large coloured-glass pictorial landing windows offered some privacy from the next door neighbour's overlooking window. Smaller panes at fanlight level might carry heraldic devices: shields with diagonal bands and simple shapes, unspecific to any genealogy, implying a lineage of distinction without precise identification, in keeping with the unknown backgrounds of Dunroamin's inhabitants but with their desire for established roots. Beside the front door, vertical stained-glass windows flanked a central, often oval, motif. The builders recognised the importance of the doorway and the porch as symbols of the threshold.

But the approach to the threshold was often the owner's design decision. Around the house and its gardens the boundaries were carefully marked out and arranged with semi-permanent fixtures at the fourth plane of choice. To the front of the plot this would be most frequently indicated by a low brick wall, broken at intervals by vertical wooden posts with rounded tops. Between the posts iron chains were frequently slung from staples. Though their function as barriers was purely notional, the chains carried associations of drawbridges and symbolically helped to define the right to control the passage of the visitor to the house. The garden gate, flanked by two such posts, reinforced this function, which remained even when the privet hedge had eventually grown to the height of the chains. Access to the garage was gained by a 'drive', which was usually a concrete approach, or two strips of concrete which would take the wheels of the car. That the garage gates could serve to admit visitors did not eliminate the necessity for a garden gate, even if this was immediately adjacent to it: the coach, for which the car was the modern substitute (even its metal body was termed 'coachwork', and the 'sedan' was a popular type), required an access that was separate from the entrance for the owner.

Walking up the garden path from the front gate one had time to admire the narrow flower beds that edged it with sprays of London Pride and neat clumps of primula. Often the path would be laid by the house-owner with crazy paving, but many paths were of laid concrete symbolically scratched with a trowel to create the crazed effect. Crazy paving took its pattern from the cottage garden, but it also symbolized the creation of order out of chaos; the puzzle of fitting the pieces of random shape to a trim edge was one which pleased the suburban gardener, and once done was continuing testimony to his industry, patience and capacity to control the elements in his environment.

Little beyond the overall plot size and shape of the garden was provided by the builder, so it could also function at the fifth and sixth planes of choice. In the Thirties most front gardens consisted of an area of grass or 'lawn', and a number of flower beds. These most frequently fringed the grassed area edging the fencing, providing a dark-toned, sometimes brightly coloured frame for the canvas of the trim lawn itself.

The character of the front garden as an important element in the presentation of the Self was often emphasised at the sixth plane of choice with accessories of symbolic significance but no practical function. So the gateposts might be guarded by a pair of seated lions, whose design was already seventy years old when Dunroamin adopted them. It was based on the pair of *lions sejant* designed by the Victorian sculptor Alfred Stevens for the forecourt posts to Sydney Smirke's British Museum. His problem – how to design a lion that could sit on a space whose width was only a third the height of the animal – was solved by modelling the body from a domestic cat. This he endowed with the head, mane and paws of a lion; the resultant hybrid, which he commenced in 1858, still guards the Wellington Memorial in St Paul's Cathedral. [16] Dunroamin intuitively recognised the domestic feline within the patriotic associations of the guardian lion and bought its scaled-down replica in thousands; it does so yet.

Other garden ornaments were chosen from a catalogue offered by garden suppliers. Most of these are still manufactured from a basically limited range which has sold in millions to their innocent purchasers over half a century. Among these is the pair of storks, one erect in masculine pose, the other bent in female submissive posture, the pair symbolic of fecundity and faithfulness. Most popular of all such ornaments are the dwarfs that have been placed in gardens in Dunroamin since the 1920s. They have been the subject of irony and contempt, as symbolic of the poor taste and kitsch values of the suburb, so much so that their popularity has somewhat diminished. That they continue to be purchased in such quantities as they are is evidence enough of the potency of their symbolisms and their importance to the countless couples and families that have carefully placed them in their gardens.

Descendants of the ancient folk-lore of Scandinavian, Celtic and Germanic tradition, and peopling their mythology, they establish links with an inheritance older than Christianity. As such, their significance, if unknown to those who use their replicas as garden ornaments, belongs to the collective unconscious. But their presence in Dunroamin's gardens, while reflecting their timeless symbolic meaning, was by no means an archaism; they performed a function that was more than whimsical though their owners were unlikely to be aware of it.

Apparently popularised in Britain after the First World War, they owed their origins to the gnome gardens of the Black Forest and South-West Germany. Still imported as Heissner's Coloured Garden Figures in the late Thirties, they comprised a range of bearded little men in green jackets and pointed red hats. Some just held their stomachs or thrust their hands into their pockets; others were fishing, smoking, holding axes, pushing wheelbarrows and carrying baskets. Many were connotative of creative activity – gardening, farming, painting; others were reaping a harvest, fishermen or woodsmen. Those who reclined smoked a pipe. Most were engaged in occupations that symbolically had sexual associations. The garden was a kingdom peopled with dwarfs; the garden kingdom was the parallel of the national kingdom within the limits of the garden owner's own domain. Their form and, in their pointed caps, their colour, was phallic; the postures of the standing figures priapic. There need be no surprise at the popularity of Walt Disney's *Snow White and the Seven Dwarfs*[17] among Dunroamin's film-going public in 1938, nor even at the popularity of a recent international success, the book *Gnomes* by Huygen and Poortvliet. [18]

Garden gnomes were, and are, phallic symbols, counterparts of Tom Thumb and Rumpelstiltskin. There are no female garden gnomes; a manufacturer who produced a large number of dwarf women is said to have been left with hundreds unsold. The small pool around which the gnomes sit or recline, and in which they fish in so many gnome gardens, is a vaginal symbol. Together they express territoriality, the determination to settle and to populate the earth within the domain of Dunroamin. Though their laughing, jovial expressions may seem to invite the visitor, they inhabit the garden in a manner that inhibits any invasion. They face the road as a miniature uniformed army, at ease but watchful; laughter can be an aggressive act.

There are many other garden ornaments that summarise the values important to Dunroamin. A single garden may contain a whole vocabulary of them – such as that illustrated opposite, approached by a 'Lych gate', connotative of traditional church-going, defended by patriotic Stevens lions. In a vaguely Elizabethan costume with spreading, capacious skirt and well-rounded bosom, a matriarchal figure stands behind a yellow-hatted gnome who creates concertina music on a rock. At a totally different scale a squirrel, sitting on a trim plinth, eats nuts – connotative of thrift, industry, foresight. Before it is a brightly cockscombed cockerel, a sexually assertive 'cock o' the walk'; nearby a man in working clothes relaxes on a miniature concrete bench, representing deserved rest after the day's labours. Before him, at a naturalistic scale is a hound, alert, head raised, the counterpart of man the hunter; beside it lies a second dog, a spaniel with spread ears and large eyes, faithful, submissive, friendly, the domestic equivalent to 'woman as homemaker'. Though only a small percentage of gardens may display such ornaments and figures they are eloquent, if overtly stated, symbols of Dunroamin's values. For many, the rows of plants neatly planted at regular intervals along a path; the carefully tended and trained standard roses; or the painstakingly nurtured chrysanthemums and carnations, peonies and pansies together represent those values in more abstract terms. Diagonal paths and symmetrical flower beds, staked plants and pruned stems may represent skill, industry, nurture, care, attention and unremitting devotion, as effectively.

Wild nature was tamed in the garden, its beauty appreciated, but its excesses –

Heissner's Coloured Garden Figures (Foreign.)
Artistically Designed. Hand Painted. Weather Proof.

No. 228.

Miniature Gnomes. Set of six, 8 in. high, **2/6** each, **15/-** set

No. 630. 13½ in.
20/- each

No. 206/7. 6 in.
8/- each

Fishermen.
No. 749. 11 in.   No. 748. 15 in.
11/- each   24/- each
No. 246. 6 in.   No. 754. 10 in.
3/- each   8/- each

No. 905a. 10 in.
8/- each

No. 743. 16 in.
24/- each

Heissner's Coloured Garden Figures populated countless suburban front
gardens in the Thirties (UBM MAC Ltd)

A squirrel, a cockerel, hunting dog, spaniel and concertina-playing
gnome are among the garden ornaments that proclaim the values of a
family (Ian Davis)

such as weeds, or a tendency to produce suckers and unshapely shoots—were carefully brought under control. This was only one message to the visitor as he opened the gate and walked up the garden path. As he did so he passed from the public zone through one that was recognised as transitional but whose private character was strong enough to make a small boy retrieving a stray ball feel guilty, and wandering dogs to be admonished by their owners from the public realm of the street. Through this intermediary zone one reached the front porch, and the door that it protected.

The porch was a sign of distinction; houses without porches or with a mere flat porch roof suspended by two iron brackets, seemed somehow impoverished. A good porch might have a horseshoe arch, layered tiled shelves on either side and layered tiles forming sills below the entrance windows. It owed its origin to the porches of Cumberland and Devon farm-houses where workers could rest after honest labours and muddied boots were stored. So it also symbolised the suburban equivalent. The slightly recessed area now offered cover for wet umbrellas, and wide-necked, cardboard topped milk-bottles left by the milkman.

Typically, the front door was a sturdy affair, with three or four stiles and deep mouldings. Above the chrome letter-box an oval window would be enriched with stained glass, and more coloured glass mellowed the light of the side windows. Over the porch was an iron-framed porch light or lantern. Coach-lamps weren't to become popular until after the war, but electric door chimes were just coming on to the market. If there was an electric bell it might have a light, but those houses with oak front doors and iron hinges were more likely to have an iron ring knocker.

A rap on the knocker, a touch of the electric bell and the private silence within was broken. It was considered discourteous, peremptory, both to knock and to ring, or to knock too loudly. Then the sound of footsteps in the hall, a shadow against the galleon and the opening of the door. One knew from the conversation carried on at the step, or the invitation to cross the threshold and to come into the hall, how one related to the occupants in the privacy of their own home.

=8=

A LIGHTHOUSE ON THE MANTELPIECE

Symbolism in the Home

Paul Oliver

WHEN the front door was opened the body image of the house assumed particular importance to the occupier, who regarded an invitation to come in across the fibre mat marked *Welcome* as a special mark of favour. An uninvited step, across the sill into the hall, or the door salesman's extended foot, was an intrusion that was resented much more for its symbolic gesture of violation than for the innocuous fact of the step itself. Even when invited in, the caller had invisible layers of privacy to negotiate: the entrance 'hall'; the hall corridor, the front room.

Invitations into the kitchen, or upstairs (except to 'spend a penny' or for women guests to deposit outdoor clothes and powder their noses before a party), would be rare. The hall, the last vestige of the medieval principal chamber, was furnished to emphasise arrival and departure. It was not that, for example, the aneroid barometer, with its long pendant shape suggesting that a column of mercury was inset behind, was necessary; the office commuter would wear his bowler and carry his tightly rolled umbrella whatever the barometer indicated. But it symbolised contact with nature; a sailor's or farmer's concern with the vagaries of the weather.

Like all the woodwork in the house, the hall doors and staircase were likely to be stained, 'brush-grained' (or 'combed' as a speedier alternative), to enable the Norwegian deal to assume the quality of fine English oak. The walls would be clad with a textured vellum-coloured paper as if sheet parchment had been used to cover it. Beneath the level of the picture rail a frieze would be pasted, depicting repeat patterns of flowers and fruit or autumn leaves. They could be used to frame the entire wall panel, and corner details of sprays of leaves, vines and grapes, or squirrels, symbols of thrift, could be added. In the hall and up the

173

The front door as orifice: the body image expressed as the symbol of
penetration, Birmingham (Graham Paul Smith)

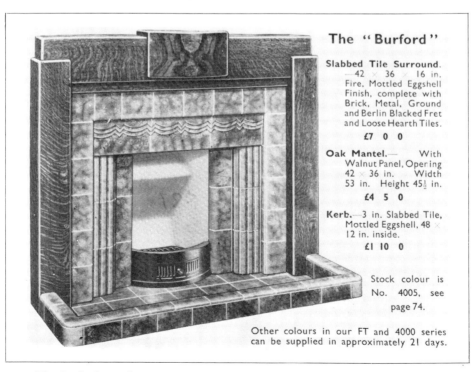

The "Burford"

Slabbed Tile Surround.
—42 × 36 × 16 in.
Fire, Mottled Eggshell
Finish, complete with
Brick, Metal, Ground
and Berlin Blacked Fret
and Loose Hearth Tiles.

£7 0 0

Oak Mantel.— With
Walnut Panel, Opering
42 × 36 in.   Width
53 in. Height 45½ in.

£4 5 0

Kerb.—3 in. Slabbed Tile,
Mottled Eggshell, 48 ×
12 in. inside.

£1 10 0

Stock colour is
No. 4005, see
page 74.

Other colours in our FT and 4000 series
can be supplied in approximately 21 days.

The Burford Fireplace Suite, 1937. Its parted curtains and ruched pelmet in
tiles provided a cinema setting for 'pictures in the fire' (UBM MAC Ltd)

staircase a darker 'Lyncrusta' relief paper, thickly embossed and suitable for sponging, would be pasted below hand-rail level. The design was frequently a scaled-down version of strapwork or wooden panelling. As an intermediate zone the hall was unfurnished for casual sitting or for anything that might encourage long discussions at the front door. But a token chair, surplus to the needs of the dining-room suite, might stand against the wall and help screen the uncomfortable, but sometimes inevitable, presence of perambulator and bicycle. Not that these failed to be a source of pride when wheeled outdoors; it was merely that their presence in the hall suggested a lack of space to accommodate them elsewhere.

It was in the sitting-room (living-room, or often, lounge) that the family could entertain friends. Whatever term was used, the sitting-room was always designed to focus on the fireplace and the hearth. The open fire, fed with shiny knobs of coal from a helmet-shaped coal scuttle, was enjoyed for its friendly glow, its warmth, and for the 'pictures in the fire' which the caves and crevasses in the embers stimulated. A 'fireside companion', crested by a galleon or Dutch children in cast brass, held the poker, brush, shovel and tongs, tools for the rituals of fire-making and tending. In front of the fire the nightly customs were enacted, the children drinking their Ovaltine by fire-loving cats – as advertisers for fuels like 'Coalite' were quick to exploit.

As both heart and hearth, the fireplace was symbolically important, and builders offered a remarkable range of alternatives at the third plane of choice. As many as sixty designs from a single supplier were available; these might include fireplace surrounds in mottled eggshell tiles, mantels in oak and mahogany and a considerable variety of colours to match – and determine – colour schemes. Typical fireplaces were spanned with arches far larger than the required openings to awaken impressions of Devon fires or inglenooks. Keystones were signified in a darker tone of tile; cornerstones and quoins were similarly indicated. Some fireplaces emphasised their ritualistic associations with shapes that recalled Aztec altars or Chaldean ziggurats, while hints of the motifs from the tomb of Tutankhamen were picked out in coloured faience. That the origins of theatre may also lie in ritual was acknowledged in fireplace designs where the tile surround was in the form of parted curtains; in some the dream-world pictures of the cinema and the pictures in the fire seemed to meet.

In front of the fireplace was the three-piece suite. Books on home upkeep would emphasise that 'we no longer need a suite of furniture', but a suite was what Dunroamin wanted: a settee and two fireside chairs, deep and comfortable. In the Twenties the suite was usually outlined with curved backs, the deep armchairs shaped in a single arc, or the drop-end Chesterfield settee with one or two. The three pieces would be covered in a durable material, but in the more expensive suites with a 'French' tapestry of rococo design, probably derived from France after the First World War. A simpler taste was expressed in calf hide, pinned to the volutes of the arms with upholstery nails; Rexine leather-cloth made a cheaper substitute on which brown velvet cushions, fringed at the edges, were placed to reduce the coldness of the surface. When a suite was too expensive, or had worn too far for home repair, loose covers sporting generous cabbage roses were in turn protected by covers for the arms and over the back.

The suite was an obsession in Dunroamin's homes; the dining-room suite had Jacobean turned legs, balled feet and Jacobean 'twist' trimmings, egg-and-dart, machine-cut or stamped mouldings and oval mirrors on the sideboard. A solid table, often with heavily turned legs, cross-braced, had leaves that could be folded down or which could be raised in the centre to enlarge the area. Dark brown and highly polished, it would have a table runner placed diagonally for artistic effect, on which would be placed a shallow bowl of hyacinths. The chairs were likely to be upright, with cabriole front legs and with seats covered with leather fixed with copper upholstery nails. Upstairs the bedroom suite was also likely to be in 'Jacobean style', a tradition of dubious lineage which further exploited the mouldings, the balled feet and dangling pendants for drawer handles which the taste required.

As with other elements in the imagery of Dunroamin, the genealogy of the Jacobean style in dining-room and bedroom suites can be traced. But its historical background, whether in terms of the authentic Jacobean details, or in their revival and popularisation, is of secondary importance here, and was of no importance at all to Dunroamin's inhabitants. From the manufacturer's point of view the Jacobean style, lighter and simpler than the Tudor but maintaining many of its details, was ideal for the scale of the smaller house. If few in the semis identified Jacobean with James I, they appreciated the symmetry of the furniture derived from the period, and were not concerned with veracity of detail; they were drawn to the *symbols* of history, not the *facts* of history. The suite had to be consistent in its own terms, demonstrably a *suite*, or group of related elements, for reasons that were more to do with the family than with authenticity.

Suites were symbols of unity and of a fully-furnished environment. To own a suite, rather than a mixture of individual and unrelated chairs or items of bedroom furniture, was to stress one's taste for order and totality; fragmented furniture of miscellaneous pieces was seen as temporary, incomplete, awaiting replacement by a full suite when it could be afforded. The suite was thus a symbol of the capacity of the breadwinner to provide for his family; it was a

Dining room and living room furniture by mail order
from Drages of High Holborn (Drages Limited)

Jacobean dining suite on 'Jacobean twist legs', 1926: 'after the style of
the 17th century . . . drop-in seats upholstered in various shades of
Rexine' (Wolfe & Hollander)

Mantelpiece ornaments, Swiss village scene, picture lamp shade,
fireside companion, home-made stool – and 'modern' mirror, in a
typical 1930s suburban living room (BBC Hulton Picture Library)

symbol too, of the completeness of the family and the hierarchy of its members. Father sat on one side of the fire in 'Father's chair'; his wife sat on the other, or embraced her children on the settee. The suite was a step towards the symbolism of the 'symmetrical family', in Willmott and Young's phrase, [1] which was already taking shape in the Thirties.

Somewhat more ambiguous was the standard lamp, whose place in the sitting-room was a combination of modern electric technology and traditional function. The stems of the standards were usually turned; extended table legs that could be made to fit the Jacobean image. That it was not a candelabra could be neatly overcome by placing over the whole standard a large, umbrella-like shade. Shades were domed or made in the form of truncated cones. Sometimes they were faceted with petal shapes, or cusped in section to provide a variety of surfaces to take silk covering or imitation vellum. Vellum panels would be stencilled with symbols of Thirties domesticity and optimism: galleons, crinoline ladies, bunches of flowers. Occasionally the latter were on translucent surfaces so that they made an illuminated picture when the lamp was switched on.

Though there was a central light with a large opaque glass bowl, on the walls in the recesses beside the chimney-breast and symmetrically placed might be light brackets, proudly displayed pieces of home craftsmanship, with the edges notched and shaved to give the impression of age; half-shades of parchment would be designed to match the other shades. On another wall would be hung triple wall-vases in green or cream ceramic, though they were used more as ornament than as practical containers for flowers.

Here in the sitting-room and dining-room the modern equipment was generally modified and decorated or embellished to suit the imagery of cottage domesticity. But different associations were required of the fixtures, equipment and articles of secondary function in the kitchen, the bathroom and the 'smallest room' (the euphemism 'loo' had yet to gain popularity). The kitchen was the housewife's domain, and was proudly considered as such. It was the first room to be inspected in the showhouses by the wife; it was the room in which she demonstrated her skills, her competence in providing nourishment for the family. The bathroom was just as clean; the airing cupboard, stacked with neatly pressed and folded linen, was kept with the door fractionally open, to 'let the warm air circulate', but also, subliminally, to express the wife's efficiency, cleanliness and rôle in the family.

The symbolism of the kitchen was strongly representative of the new concerns with health. The advocacy of certain ideas by Mrs Bagot Stack, through the success of her Women's League of Health and Beauty, and her book *Building the Body Beautiful* for all the amusement that the satin blouses and black knickers provoked, undoubtedly contributed much to the nation's health. Hiking was a widespread pastime, indulged in most by those from Dunroamin who had relatively easy access to the countryside, but were not country people. Cyclists toured the Thames Valley and their peregrinations were matched by millions throughout the country who joined in the national craze for health and fresh air.

Books of advice on home-making in the Thirties laid considerable emphasis on health, diet, keep-fit exercises, and technical aids in the home. The latter—modern gas and electric cookers, or wash boilers for instance—were closely related to the ideas of health and efficiency in the home, and were the women's prerogative. The kitchen, therefore, had to convey both rural simplicity and the practical modernity of the efficient housewife in a servantless house. The kitchen tables and chairs were simple and unfussy, the table covered with washable American cloth, the chairs a derivative of the Thonet bentwood with a shell pattern stamped on the plywood seat. Or they might be sturdy, with upturned legs and rexine-covered seats. Near them was the built-in dresser, with a glass-paned china cupboard above a chest of drawers. Derived from Arts and Crafts versions of cottage furniture, the dresser was scaled down for the suburban semi, but became an indispensable item in its equipment. Dresser and larder doors were generally painted a spring green, or with a brush-grained wood stain, both with connotations of rusticity.

Within such a kitchen the freckled grey-and-white enamel of the Ideal boiler or the GEC cooker might seem anomalous, but Dunroamin saw no incongruity in the juxtaposition of rural images and modern equipment—any more than do the suppliers of kitchen fitments fifty years later. Though a kitchen in a semi between the wars had no dish-washer, mixing machine, blender, waste-disposal unit, or any of numerous other utilitarian appliances which became comm-onplace in the Sixties, some of its equipment, such as the relatively rare refrigerator, but much more common meat safe, were articles of secondary function at the fifth plane of choice. Dishracks, bread bin, carpet sweeper, hand-operated creamer, were among them, but most of the kitchen and bathroom equipment was made up of fixtures. Certain items expressed their functional rôle though they were in use outside these functional rooms; most significant was the vacuum cleaner. Subject of the early application of the hard sell, the vacuum cleaner became one of Dunroamin's first status symbols and its salesman one of the most popular of joke characters. Like the television set of the post-war world, it communicated by signs other than its physical presence; the equivalent of the rooftop aerial was the whine of the Hoover in use. Not only was the vacuum cleaner a possession which demonstrated that a substitute for the maid or servant had been obtained; it also proclaimed that ownership of it made the hiring of

NEW GRAMOPHONE AND LOUD-SPEAKER FRETS

We have a range of 36 frets suitable for wireless and gramophone work. They are of the latest patterns, and are beautifully cut in selected plywood. The sizes are specially chosen to be suitable for the popular forms of cabinets. For the full, illustrated list see Handicrafts 1931 Annual.

No. T.378. 24ins. square, Opening 21 ins. square, ⅜ in. oak veneered ply. 5/6, post. and packing 1/3.

No. T.376. 24 ins. by 18 ins. opening 21 ins. by 15 ins. ⅜ in. oak veneered ply. 4/- post. and packing 1/-. No. T.401. Mahogany veneered ply. 4/-., post. and packing 1/-.

No. T.377. 24 ins. square. Opening 21 ins. square, ⅜ in. mahogany veneered ply. 5/6. post. and packing 1/3.

Handicrafts Ltd., Weedington Road, Kentish Town, London, N.W.5.

Taming the radio – examples from a range of loudspeaker frets (*Handicrafts*, September 1930)

Captain Dismore of Imperial Airways with his daughter in the modernised interior of their Thornton Heath home, 1938 (BBC Hulton Picture Library)

domestic help unnecessary. But though the sound of the vacuum cleaner could be heard in the street, emphasising that the house was clean and kept in good order, the housewife preferred not to be seen actually engaged in the process; while she was unseen there was still the possibility that someone else was employed to do the housework in *her* well-run home. So the cleaner, used in all parts of the house, was stowed in the cupboard beneath the stairs, a complex symbol of the transitional position of the middle class.

The wireless set presented a particular problem in the domestic ensemble, for it was the most significant twentieth-century addition to the suburban home – more so in its capacity to bring the breadth of the world to the living-room than was the vacuum cleaner as surrogate servant. But whereas the vacuum cleaner was brought out on occasion when its function was explicit, and hidden before the visitors arrived, the radio was always on display. The electric or gas home could be proudly proclaimed in the domestic centre of the kitchen where functional equipment, refrigerator, boiler or cooker were in themselves symbols of modernity and liberation; the radio on the other hand, was most likely to be in the dining-room or living-room, or, with an extension speaker, in both. In these spaces, with their Jacobean or cottage imagery, the radio was an alien element. One solution was simply to disguise it, as a drinks cabinet, or in a chest whose doors could be opened to adjust the turning knobs. But the radio was also a point of pride of ownership; its modern austerity had to be tamed to suit the home, with Jacobean mouldings around the edges of its cabinet, or most frequently, a fretwork design over the fabric of the loudspeaker. This solution coincided with the popularity of fretwork as a hobby in the Twenties and Thirties. A range of motifs was available – *Handicrafts* magazine had over thirty designs for the home craftsman to cut out of three-ply with the thin saw-blade. [2] They ranged from a lyre, signifying culture, to Peter Pan, signifying eternal youth and supported by rabbits (fecundity), to cottages or a village church and trees. But quite the most popular motif (and perhaps easiest to make) was the sunrise.

In every home there were many articles, some of them special to the suburban environment, that were to be found at the fifth plane of choice, among the non-utilitarian ornaments and objects of minor function selected for their significance to the owner. Their importance was often purely personal, reflecting an impulse, a day of contentment with the family in the country; their appeal was conditioned by the values of the group and, by their purchase and inclusion on the mantelpiece, they reinforced these values.

On the walls were to be found a few pictures, seldom to be examined in detail but contributing to the total imagery of the room. They might include popular favourites like *The Hay Wain* by John Constable, or Turner's *The Fighting Temeraire*. The appealing features of Vermeer's *Young Girl With a Turban* and the knobbly delineation of Dürer's *Praying Hands* might be seen in the company of a wind-braced *Diana of the Uplands*, the crouching faun-like figures of a Maxfield Parrish, or a Spanish gypsy fiction suavely brushed by Russell Flint. There were brass plates, relief-stamped with scenes from Shakespeare, figures before a country inn, plaster plaques of country cottages with thatched roofs and herbaceous borders in bloom; sometimes a flight of mallard ducks in shiny ceramic colours winged across the wall. Coloured photographs, in the main, came later, but an exception was the Swiss mountain view, with a log house, woodstore, flowers on the slopes and white, snowcapped mountains soaring into a deep blue sky above.

What did these pictures and their equivalents signify? Were the sailing ships, the mallard ducks, the Swiss scenes symbolic of escape and, if they were, escape from what? From the city, or from the suburbs, as some would like to think? The paintings, reproductions, and other wall decorations were symbolic of the values of the suburban community as it had established itself and was growing. The Dutch interiors, reproduced from originals by Pieter de Hooch or a modern copyist, were reflections of a stolid middle class of moderate but not ostentatious affluence; the satisfaction of the *Laughing Cavalier* by Franz Hals, the cherry-lips of Murillo's *The Boy With Cherries*, the cultivator of his garden beside a straight and steady road in *The Avenue, Middelharnis* [3] by Hobemma, the simple relaxations of the inn, all were assertions of a steady, agreeable, reliable life within the community. If the clipper ships by Somerscales were a slight up-dating of the galleons they also meant salt-spray and effort, commerce and efficiency, human endeavour with grace; the Swiss houses in the mountains were signifiers of health and fresh air; the ducks were in flight and might soon settle.

It is evident that some objects and images had filtered down from upper-class values, yet the persistence of many symbols in Dunroamin was special to middle-class Britain, and multi-layered in their implications. Though many might be dismissed as kitsch or at best, in poor taste, they were important to their owners for the values they implied. Symbols are not subject to canons of good taste and carefully nurtured concepts of quality. Symbols have meaning; sometimes they have aesthetic merit. Dunroamin was not without aesthetic criteria, though its measures of quality were often different from those of other sectors of society. Rooms were valued like gardens, if they were 'pretty'; but they were valued too, if they were 'nice'. Nice was not the same as pretty, for the pretty was full of charm, sentiment and sweetness, while nice was orderly, controlled: nice and clean, nice and neat, nice and tidy, nice and smart, nice and bright.

To 'take a fancy to' something in Dunroamin was to express one's taste.

182

Objects and curiosities might 'tickle your fancy', stimulating desire. Often the object was more than usually elaborate, a little more reckless or detailed, or charming in design, and the word 'fancy', which derived from 'fantasy', connoted both the fantasising about the object and the fantastic qualities within it. Meaning light, whimsical and moveable, applied or decorated, 'fancy' described the surface rather than the substance. It was a means by which Dunroamin implanted its own values in ornament on the sterile and the mass-produced. 'Dainty' indicated refinement; the fastidious and the selective was dainty, whether it was displayed by the cat walking carefully through the objects on the window-ledge, or the lace-work on the cushion covers or the antimacassars. The old French term *dainté*, with its associations of worthiness, had not been unduly distorted. The fancy and the dainty were more appropriate for certain times and certain places: the bedroom could be dainty, in pink, offset with white lace, the bathroom a little less so, the dining-room not at all.

Outside, the garden was nicely kept. It could be pretty rather than dainty, but sometimes it could be the subject of fancy: flower-beds arranged in fancy, that is 'fanciful' shapes; fancy borders and edging might be introduced; but as exceptions rather than as the norm. In the gardens, front and back, the symbolic possibilities of shaping the environment were greatest. Here rituals of the family outdoors could be enacted, from the cutting of the grass on Saturday evenings with the Ransomes hand-pushed mower, to the hanging out of clothes on wash-day Monday. The rear garden was a realm in which children could play, the wife could sunbathe, a husband could practise his tennis strokes or the family play clock golf and French cricket. In the back, appearances were often less important; worn patches might occur where children regularly played, but even here a display of flowers, both annuals and perennials, was still a source of pride. A rockery of rather regularly placed pieces of stone or broken concrete was often to be found in flower beds on a slope. A rockery had its own aesthetic, not attempting to appear as if an outcrop of rock had broken through the earth level unexpectedly in this suburban environment. Symbolically signifying the wilder parts of Dartmoor or the Lakes, it was scaled down to miniscule size and kept under modest control, a setting for ice plants, aubretia and a miniature mountain tarn.

The garden was seldom complete without its furniture and ornaments, though here the Englishman's cottage could be realised with wooden seats, and rustic tables. Garden fixtures at the fifth plane of choice, affirmed the permanence of settlement and values through the passage of the years. Bird-baths, sundials and bird-tables came in a wide variety of forms, made in genuine or reconstructed stone, or in the case of bird-tables carved in wood, with thatched roofs. The sundial, marking the slow progression of the day, soundlessly, dependably, eternally, conveyed a sense of peace and constancy in a far from changeless world. Designs for pergolas and arbours revealed the eclecticism that was characteristic of Dunroamin; trellises that bounded sections of the garden or opened up small vistas were often in the ever-familiar sunray pattern.

Without doubt the sunray device was the most ubiquitous of Dunroamin's symbols. It appeared in scores of contexts. Frequently it was to be found on garden gates, as a disc in one corner with rays expressed as flat planes extending across the gate. Sometimes the same motif on the gate would be made in thin lengths of strip iron, or even in tubular metal. It was frequently to be found in the front door, as panels or sometimes as an iron frame set against the main structure. Stained-glass sunrises in door windows were a commonplace. The traditional transom of Georgian design had used radiant lines which required little to transform them into the sun, and doubtless this played its part in the popularisation of the sun motif. Balustrades, garden fences, door panels, even brickwork employed the same device with astonishing frequency. Within the house it was likely to be found in the glass of the kitchen dresser and worked in appliqué on the teacosy. Lampshades almost inevitably encouraged sun devices, with the light shining through obscured glass in the hallway or outside the front door. Radiant designs appeared on thick hessian doormats, and glowed cheerfully on fireside rugs.

But it was the fireplace within the house, not surprisingly, which most frequently bore the sun symbol. So close was the association of the sun with the flame and heat of the hearth that it was possible for fireplace designers to use triangular- or diamond-shaped suns, which considerably economised on cutting and shaping tiles, and still evoke the symbol. Often the radiant lines that pointed to the outer extremities of the fireplace required only a hint, a mere cluster of three wedge-shaped 'rays' to convey the theme.

Perhaps the oldest symbol employed by mankind, it struck deep notes of meaning in the folk memory, but its persistence in the Twenties and Thirties was especially related to the new craze for sun-bathing.[4] The fascination for sunshine was related to the contemporary concerns for a healthy environment which had encouraged hundreds of thousands to move from the cities to the suburbs. Though sun symbolism had an ancient history, its popularity in the taste of the day gained a considerable boost with the opening of the tomb of Tutankhamen in 1922. Interest in its treasures and in Egyptian art generally provided new decorative elements in the design of jewellery and luxury enamelled-metal goods. But the symbols of Re and the depictions of the Aten were always of the sun at its zenith, with the sun god extending from its rays blessing hands with the life-symbol of the ankh at the fingertips.[5] This was not the symbol as Dunroamin

Curved windows, Art Deco chevrons and white render of a late
Thirties 'Suntrap' house. The garden wall retains ziggurat motifs and
the gate displays sunray symbolism (BBC Hulton Picture Library)

employed it. There were no blessing hands, no use of the ankh. The sun of the suburbs was essentially a *rising* one, signifying a sunny future, the dawn of a new day.

Both high-style architecture and Dunroamin expressed, through symbols, the obsession for sun and fresh air of the times. But the former used the metal railings, white paint, flat or platonically curved surfaces and porthole windows of the cruise ship, referents that had little meaning in the suburbs. Yachting and cruising were the pursuits of the wealthy and if Dunroamin joined in the current fad for sailor songs it was less ready to accept the abstract cues of nautical details in its houses. The sun was not hinted at: it was clearly stated in line, colour and shape.

In Dunroamin the adventure had been undertaken and the sun was rising to bless it. A setting sun was not unknown, but it was rarer; the implications of the end of life, of the oncoming night were too melancholy. The prevailing spirit was captured by the popular songs of the day, in many of which the sun, if not rising, was at least appearing from behind the clouds. The Depression years were not easy ones for new families but optimism was reflected in the songs that were broadcast on the BBC or sung in the Hollywood musicals, *Happy Days Are Here Again* 'the skies above are clear again . . .' composed by Yellen and Agar for the film *Chasin' Rainbows. Gold Diggers of Broadway* in 1929 produced *Painting the Clouds With Sunshine* and the air was soon filled with *The Sun Has Got His Hat On*, 'sing Hip Hip Hip Hooray, the sun has got his hat on and he's coming out today' and invitations to 'come over *On The Sunny Side of The Street*'. From the Diet and Shwartz song *New Sun In The Sky* in *Band Wagon* of 1931, to the *Sunshine Serenade* by Jack Lawrence of 1939, there was a succession of clouds, blue skies and sunshine songs to match the popular imagery of Dunroamin's coloured glass and garden gates.[6]

Such a motif was common at all levels of society in the period of Art Deco design, but, as in the case of the Deco 'fountain', not all the familiar devices of high-style decoration were to be found in Dunroamin. Similarly, the symbols popular in Dunroamin were not necessarily those of the design profession working for its élite clientèle. In Dunroamin certain motifs appeared in a variety of settings, both outdoors and in. The lighthouse, for instance, might be fashioned in concrete to stand on a prominence in the rockery, turned and polished in Purbeck marble to function as a doorstop, glow from a cliff in a stained-glass picture window, or stand as a phial of coloured sands on the mantelpiece. Its symbolic significance was often far greater than its recognisable character as sign. The stoppered, sand-filled lighthouse became a favoured object on the shelf, a memento of a family holiday, a testimony to the industry and artistry that went into making its strata of coloured sands. As a lighthouse it was a symbol of the home as defence against the elements, of enlightenment and influence; while its phallic form at a subliminal level was symbolic of fertility. Within the simple object, a Dunroamin family could find comfort in its confirmation of the values of family, industry and domesticity.

The concept of home was reinforced in innumerable ways in Dunroamin. Cottages, which the tile-hung, small-gabled, Tudor-detailed, red-brick, leaded-light fitted, bottle-glass doored, herbaceous-bordered Dunroamin houses echoed, figured prominently in ornaments and ephemera. Teacosies were made in the form of cottages; calendars, biscuit tins, chocolate boxes, plaster wall plaques all depicted cottages. Boxes for letters and shoe brushes might be designed in cottage form, teapots and marmalade jars were formed as china cottages or bore pictures of them. Cottages and cottage gardens, descendants of the writings of Gertrude Jekyll, indigo-drawn for transfer to linen, were embroidered on tray cloths or pieced together on jig-saw puzzles. Images of the home and the values that were associated with it abounded: the Englishman's home was his cottage, not his castle.

Such examples can be grouped in sets, and in many cases may belong to that set only: the bird-table could be a thatched house but never a sail-boat. Others could only be acceptable in one context: fishing and smoking gnomes are to be found in the garden, but never in the house. Even the galleons that sail the stained-glass windows do not venture on the garden pond. It is obvious that some symbolic elements such as the garden gnomes readily make a set, a set which is extendable, but not indefinitely; there may be car-driving gnomes in children's books, but not among the garden figurines. What they say in the language of gnome postures and activities is expressed in perhaps two dozen characters. The set is virtually finite. Other garden ornaments—storks, squirrels, sundials, bird-baths—may be grouped in two or three symbol systems. But the imagery, though greater, is not infinitely extendable either. Some may be added by Dunroamin's own home craftsmen who may make waist-high, wind-turned smock mills, or may couple a set of small blades above a weather-vane to drive a frantically sawing manikin by a small crank. It is a range that is encompassable and which excludes a multitude of alternative possibilities that might have reflected the characters in popular films or other media.

It might be revealing to list the constituents of the language which embrace not only the garden ornaments but the shelf ornaments as well; which include the motifs on the radio and the fireplace, and encompass the tapestry on the living-room suite and the embroidery on the table runner. But though Dunroamin liked its sets, and sought to obtain its suites, it was not averse to

The interior of the 'Suntrap' house illustrated on page 185, with flowered antimacassars on the modern suite and imitation coal on the electric fire in front of the fireplace. The radiogram stands in the window bay (BBC Hulton Picture Library)

Confusion of the codes: Jacobean-style writing desk, Corinthian (Nelson's?) column lampstand with 'Oriental' shade, painted kingfisher and smiling fretwork cat, c. 1930 (BBC Hulton Picture Library)

mixing codes. If a sunrise rug were spread before a ziggurat fireplace, which bore on its mantelpiece a brass bell suspended from a wooden horseshoe and a calendar with a pair of kittens peeping from an old boot, Dunroaminers did not (and do not) mind. The significance lay in the messages conveyed by the individual objects, grouped in sets and suites if convenient, but easily violated if not. Complexes of associations rather then complex messages were important, , and if the objects spoke in identical or similar language systems this helped to harmonise the environment; if they failed to relate thematically, their significance individually was not reduced.

In semiological terms, symbol systems in Dunroamin could be defined more precisely, but such definition would disengage a particular characteristic (and one which may be aesthetically deplored), the confusion of the codes. Associational images are placed in illogical juxtapositions of period and content which defeats their clarity. It is at the meta-scale, where all are seen as constituents of one visual language – the language of Dunroamin where its symbols are related to its values – that they are best recognised and understood.

Many examples of symbolic motifs, from galleons to Dutch children, have been mentioned and they could be found in numerous contexts within the semi. Symbolic relationships, such as the three-piece suite round the fireplace, have also been noted, but the question arises whether these were consciously or sub-consciously chosen. It is doubtful that the fertility symbolism of the stained-glass window or the Alum Bay lighthouse would have been recognised or accepted by their purchasers. Much of their power lies in the fact that they *are* symbolic, and their meaning is recognised subliminally; the unreasoning attacks that such symbols have received are also an acknowledgement of their potency.

As has been shown, many domestic symbols operate at several levels and this helps to explain other apparent anomalies in Dunroamin's taste. It may appear strange that the suburbs chose – and still choose – to buy modern replicas of antique or period objects when authentic examples could be obtained relatively easily and, in the 1930s, at little extra cost. Fireside bellows of wood and leather affixed with shiny upholstery nails, imitation copper saucepans or unread sets of Dickens in tooled Morocco bindings proclaimed both an appreciation of the values of the past and a confident assertion of those of the present: the image was traditional but the manufacture was undeniably new, and had to be seen to be so. This duality also assists in explaining the tendency to miniaturisation, in the diminutive warming pan, the under-scaled brass cauldrons or half-size Dutch clogs on the mantelpiece. Not only was their novelty enjoyed, they were clearly non-functional even when they appeared to have some practical use. Often such ornaments were statements of appreciation of the rural and the historic but with a clear acknowledgement that they could be of no practical use in the suburb.

In the course of the Thirties the influence of Modern design was exposed in Dunroamin, often in ways which the advocates of the Modern Movement abhorred. They objected to the crudity, to the 'jazz-age' modernity which the shapes and patterns that the suburbs adopted represented. For the architects and designers, working for a cultural élite, it was enough to include the hints of Cubist or Purist aesthetics in their work. The shape preferences of Juan Gris or Amédée Ozenfant, the bare and unadorned lines of a Léger painting could be recognised by any follower of CIAM. Such cues were of little meaning in Dunroamin. The suburban resident who chose to modernise his home had to do so with shapes and forms that clearly expressed his decision to do so. Settees were streamlined, mirror corners clipped, linoleum patterns of triangles, circles and intersecting shapes (which owed quite a lot to Kandinsky, several times removed), declared unequivocally a taste for the new. Whether it was 'good taste' was not an issue.

Little attention hitherto has been paid to Dunroamin's symbols, and there have been few attempts to analyse them or consider the messages that they convey. In his *Theory of the Leisure Class*, Thorstein Veblen argued that the middle-class housewife is engaged in vicarious leisure for her husband.

> If beauty or comfort is achieved – and it is a more or less fortuitous circumstance if they are – they must be achieved by means and methods that commend themselves to the great economic law of wasted effort. The more reputable, 'presentable' portion of middle-class household paraphernalia are, on the one hand, items of conspicuous consumption, and on the other hand, apparatus for putting in evidence the vicarious leisure rendered by the housewife. [7]

Though it is true that Dunroamin expected the housewife to stay at home and not to be engaged in daily employment, this was because the woman's responsibility as home-maker and raiser of the family was specific. Part of her job was to keep the home 'nice and clean' but the mother who pounded the clothes or turned the mangle would have had little sympathy with the view that her labours corresponded to a law of wasted effort, though such an argument might have its supporters now.

Veblen's statement that middle-class paraphernalia comprised items of conspicuous consumption and provided evidence of the leisure of the housewife, might justifiably be claimed to apply in the latter instance, to the vacuum cleaner and other domestic appliances (taking apparatus in a literal sense). But the charge of conspicuous consumption needs his explanation:

goods are produced and consumed as a means to the fuller unfolding of human life; and their utility consists, in the first instance, in their efficiency as means to this end. . . . But the human proclivity to emulation has seized upon the consumption of goods as a means to an invidious comparison, and has thereby invested consumable goods with a secondary utility as evidence of relative ability to pay. [8]

In his shrewd and closely argued text he maintained that those who work aspire to a life of leisure, and that the symbols of that leisure in the form of expensive and largely superfluous goods, or embellishment of them, are imitated by those who strive to achieve the illusion of being within the leisured class, when in fact they cannot be a part of it. Here then, lies the key to the status symbol, by which one member of the class demonstrates his status on that ladder to others.

That the seeking of status through possessions was demonstrated in Dunroamin is not to be questioned: it exists in all strata of society. In the suburbs the acquisition of a 'better' semi in a 'better' district, the ownership of a garage and a car within it, the radiogram that succeeded the gramophone were all examples at different scales. Inhabitants of suburban semi-detatched homes did acquire objects which reflected some of the values of the monied and leisured aristocracy – but they also developed a taste that was their own. Jacobean dining-room suites might approximate the forms of genuine Jacobean antique furniture, but most of the objects on the shelves and in the gardens did not directly reflect expensive and authentic originals in the homes of the wealthy. 'Keeping up with the Joneses' became a cliché of comment on suburban life, though the phrase was 'keeping up with', not 'beating' the Joneses. Dunroamin had its own checks and balances against those who 'swanked' or were 'trying to be posh'; the margins for demonstrating status and success were extremely narrow, in that period of limited affluence, if one were to remain a member of the suburban community. Status-seeking in the suburbs was to become more of an obsession among the sociologists of the 1950s than it was within the suburbs themselves.

For the first generation in Dunroamin was a new breed, unknown to Veblen and unstudied by his successors. They were carving out a new kind of home and family-centred domestic life which was, in truth, 'neither town nor country', and hence not fitting into the stereotypes loved by planners and sociologists alike. An argument developed in the Victorian era may not be all that appropriate to the period between the wars when the suburbs were more intent on developing their own culture than on mimicking another. The theory which argues that the growth of mass-produced substitutes for leisured-class status symbols 'trickles down' to the lower social strata has a persuasive advocate in Peter Lloyd Jones. [9] But 'conspicuous consumption' and 'conspicuous waste' were less possible for Dunroamin's original inhabitants in the 1930s than for their children of the 1950s. In those meagre years houses were bought, windows selected, furniture chosen, ornaments acquired and gardens shaped less for the associations of status and wealth beyond their reach than for the values they expressed of the new, unprecedented, suburban, semi-detatched society of Dunroamin's drives and crescents.

=9=

LEARNING FROM DUNROAMIN

Values and the Houses We Live in

Paul Oliver

IN May 1939, a paper-covered publication *Houses We Live In* appeared on the bookstalls. Compiled by the Housing Advisory Committee at the request of Walter Elliot, Minister of Health, it gave good advice to builders on site layout and landscaping but was full of admonitions to the householder in his semi. Confident distinctions were made between the 'good house' and the 'ugly house' (goodness equated with beauty), and the owner was advised that 'to go one better than one's neighbour by needless change of style or colour is an invitation to some other neighbour to go one better still.'[1] As for doors, these should not look 'eccentric or pushful' the reader was warned; 'simple forms will always give better value than fancy shapes with stained-glass insets.'[2] Georgian and Modernist examples were used to compare with suburban ones.

Small though it was, there was a subtle difference in the attitude taken by *Houses We Live In* compared with previous writings: instead of attacking the suburban house and its occupant with the hope of dislodging him by derision, the Housing Advisory Committee had at last addressed him. Instead of pouring scorn upon his choice, it now sought to advise on his capacity to exercise choice. The advice, of course, was to make the Dunroamin semi as much like the council house as possible.

An interesting new trend might have developed had the war not intervened. Such hints of compromise were not encouraged. Instead, with the best of reasons – the war effort – front gardens were robbed of their boundary chains, moulded doors were replaced with flush ones and some of the distinguishing features of Dunroamin were reduced by controls on availability and design. The CC41 tag on the Utility furniture, that was virtually all that could be obtained new with precious coupon allocations, ensured that Scandinavian-derived chairs, tables, beds and curtains entered the home. If they looked and felt uncomfortable and undecorated to Dunroaminers, austerity was a virtue in governmental terminology equated with patriotism. So one of the values of Modernist aesthetics was made a symbol of national conscience.

With the end of the war the battle for suburban taste might have been won too. Roy Lewis and Angus Maude, historians of the middle class, writing in 1949, reviewed the post-war mood: 'the ideal of millions had become by 1945 something like the semi-detached, middle-class family of the late Twenties, but with greater security, less responsibility and the assurance of steady material advancement.'[3] If this was what they wanted it was not forthcoming. When, a couple of years after, the Festival of Britain was mounted as a 'tonic for the nation' the British version of Scandinavian and Bauhaus design gained further official endorsement. 'Director of Architecture' Hugh Casson gathered a team that included Maxwell Fry, Jane Drew, Ralph Tubbs, Basil Spence and the Architects' Co-Partnership who made distinguished contributions to the South Bank Exhibition, and who, naturally enough, did not miss the opportunity to advance the interests of Modernism.

Though the Modern Movement architects had effectively influenced national housing policies in their favour, the unthinking abuse of the suburbs had not abated after the war. As late as 1975, Shadrach Woods, a leading member of Team 10 – the offspring of CIAM (International Congress of Modern Architecture) – could seriously assert that 'the suburbs of Scandinavia, England or America are sources of concern, in a sense expressions of imminent atomic warfare, the latest development in the citizen's war against himself'.[4]

More considered arguments were advanced by the noted environmental historian Lewis Mumford, whose writings were published in both his native United States and in Britain, where they were widely read by architects and planners. They could find in his strictures much to confirm their views of Dunroamin when he wrote in 1961:

> [the] suburb served as an asylum for the preservation of illusion. Here domesticity could flourish, forgetful of the exploitation on which so much of it was based. Here individuality could prosper, oblivious of the pervasive regimentation beyond. This was not merely a child-centred environment; it was based on a childish view of the world, in which reality was sacrificed to the pleasure principle.

He deprecated the 'temptation . . . to shirk public duties, and to find the whole meaning of life in the most elemental social group, the family, or even in the still more isolated and self-centred individual. What was properly a beginning was treated as an end.'[5]

That the city was no less devoted to the pleasure principle, artificially promoted and stimulated; that the suburb defined its own priorities among public

LET HOUSE
AND GARDEN
Meet Outside
the Windows

Above, stone steps lead between masses of
Mossy Saxifrage and Arabis right up to the
house door.

In this plan the view
from the house is
through an arch to
the lawn and flower
borders.

An attractive formal
design for a small
garden, with lawn
surrounded by paved
paths. The paved paths
on the left lead to the
house; the space between
them might be filled with
Roses or other flowers.

'Crazy' paving, formal flower beds, sundial and sunray 'rustic' for the
suburban garden (from *Popular Gardening Book of Garden Plans*, 1934)

The original caption (1951) gave this pre-war-styled Streatham interior as an example of
Bad Taste and 'the hideous in architecture and design which photographer John
Chillingworth spotted on a tour of the British Isles. He found many signs of the insidious
creep of Subtopia . . .' (BBC Hulton Picture Library)

duties and neighbourly relationships; that the 'childish view' of life could be an alternative reality rather than illusion, was not accommodated in his critique.

Yet there were signs of some misgivings about the received opinions among a few writers. The late Nan Fairbrother, while she did not like the suburbs, considered that the very term was describing 'them unfairly in downgraded terms of something else'. She even compared the 'interwar suburban sprawl on the edge of London' with the 'Post-War New Town sprawl in the country' and came to the unpopular conclusion that 'of the two the early suburb wastes land less extravagantly, and has certainly come to better terms with its unbuilt areas'. [6]

A young generation of architects and designers who had been born in the suburbs also began to emerge in the Fifties and Sixties. They had to come to terms with the contempt of an older generation, as Ian Davis has narrated, and for many then, as now, feelings were mixed. Architect and propagandist for the Archigram group, Peter Cook, expressed their dilemma when he wrote that 'those of us (and we are in the vast majority) who were brought up in the suburbs, retain a love-hate relationship with them'. [7]

Cracks in the edifice of architectural criteria may be seen as stemming in part from the awareness of popular culture that the Pop Art movement provoked in the Sixties, and from increasing dissatisfaction with the failure of Modern Movement architecture which the Seventies witnessed. Both tendencies came together in the influential writings of, among others, Robert Venturi and Denise Scott Brown. *Learning from Las Vegas* [8] was, in 1972, a milestone on the route to a different architectural destination, which their own design work also exemplified. Venturi and Rauch organised and designed an important exhibition for the Smithsonian Institute in 1976, which wittily and graphically considered *Signs of Life: Symbols in the American City*. Attempting to 'survey the pluralist aesthetic of the American city and its suburbs' the exhibition gave abundant evidence of personalised symbolism in the domestic house. 'Winding roads, romantic roof lines, garden ornaments, colonial front doors and coach lanterns are decorative elements with symbolic overtones that residents use to communicate with others about themselves', Venturi wrote. In his view this communication was: 'mainly about social status, social aspirations, personal identity, individual freedom, and nostalgia for another time and place.' Suggesting that the 'symbolic subject matter' of domestic embellishment derives from historical, rural, patriotic and upper-class sources, Venturi concluded that suburban housing symbolism 'does not tell us why people live in Suburbia or much about the problems they experience in Suburbia; it merely tells us some of their aspirations while they are there'. [9]

Indeed, suburban symbolism is about personal identity and individual freedom; to some extent it is about social status and social aspirations. It is also true that many of the symbols used derive from historical and rural precedents, or from the 'estates of the rich'. But here Venturi is identifying the images of the suburb as sign rather than as symbol; he lists their subject matter, or denotative details, rather than their connotations, or the meanings that the motifs communicate through symbolism. By reading only their character as signs he finds no meanings that explain why people live in Suburbia. Though the suburbs of the United States are, in many ways, different from those of England, they are no less capable of expressing similar meanings through their symbolism. If Venturi has shown far greater respect for the suburbs than have the majority of architectural writers, even of his generation, he readily assumes that '*nostalgia* for another time and place' is the reason for historic and exotic imagery, rather than the *values* they express.

It is not too surprising that some recognition of the suburbs has been shown by one or two American architects; more surprising is the fact that it has taken so long. For studies of the suburbs commenced early in the United States, and sociologists were quicker to recognise the new patterns of living that were taking place on the edges of the city. 'Merely articulating the skeleton of the suburbs fails to reveal their heart', Harlan Paul Douglass observed in 1925. Though he found much to criticise in the suburb he was nevertheless aware that it was: 'more than the distant fringe of the city. It is a community developing according to a distinctive social pattern which it more or less distinctly realizes.' [10] Thirty years were to pass before British sociologists were prepared to share his view.

Though they gave the lead in suburban studies, American sociologists also fixed a number of stereotypes, and stereotypical methods of analysis. Class consciousness was embedded in their writings, and social status became the focus of F. Stuart Chapin and others. Chapin's Social Status Scale of 1933, though subsequently the subject of criticism by Louis Wirth, gave a picture of 'Material Equipment and Cultural Expression' [11] which had no counterpart in Britain until the mid Fifties. There were no corresponding analyses to his 'living-room scale' made in Dunroamin; sociologists in England appear to have been as far removed from the suburbs as were the architects. [12] So perhaps some excuse might be made for the architects who were unable to back up their abhorrence of the suburbs by sociological evidence, even if there can be no excuse for prejudice.

For ourselves, as authors of the present study, the dearth of reliable writing of any kind on the suburbs between the wars has been a serious handicap. In particular, the lack of either sociological or architectural studies has been acute,

With the passing of time Dunroamin's houses, gardens and streets have matured, and many have been sensitively adapted, with new porches, windows, and central heating; Ealing (Graham Paul Smith)

Dunroamin's latent responsiveness realised in the 1970s, near Hangar Lane, West London (Graham Paul Smith)

while the question of values and their expression in Dunroamin seems to have been totally overlooked. Consequently, much has had to be reconstructed from fragmentary data and much based on personal recollections, local experience and extensive interviews. The problems have been exacerbated by the processes of change that have taken place within the suburbs themselves; changes far more significant than any that may have occurred in the attitudes of architects and observers of the environment.

Dunroamin, though frustrated from further expansion by Town Planning Acts, the demarcation of the Green Belts and other measures which have much to commend them, did not disappear. Post-war Britain saw some housing of Dunroamin's type and character but the essential suburbs of the Twenties and Thirties have elements of form and detail that are special to the period. However, the buildings remain, and they have matured with the gardens and streets of the suburbscape. Decades have seen the weathering of woodwork, tiles, brick and pebble-dash. Walls have been resurfaced or painted, porches have been closed in or new ones built. New windows have replaced old ones, double-glazed and of 'picture' proportions; television aerials rise above the unused chimneys of centrally heated homes. Softening contours of trained and trimmed hedges, herbaceous borders and standard roses, luxuriating shrubs and flowering cherry trees, have removed the starkness from numberless streets.

In scores of ways – some subtle, like the delineation of mortar between rows of brickwork, some dramatic like the building of a garage with a 'granny flat' above – Dunroamin's houses have been modulated, adapted, altered. There was less need to do so when the houses were new, and no opportunity to do so during the war. But with increasing costs of building and labour and the burgeoning of Do-It-Yourself facilities for home-owners, suburban houses became the focus of home-improvement activities. The diversity of these adaptations to changing needs and tastes is evident from outside, but within the private domain walls have been demolished to make through rooms, kitchens have been modernised and living-rooms extended. In the process, the 'latent responsiveness', of which Ian Bentley has written, has been realised. The richness of form and detail, and the relative flexibility of the semi-detached house on its half-island site have proved to be remarkably appropriate to the demands made upon the houses by successive generations of occupiers. At the first plane of choice, the house as habitable shell has remained a constant, though it may have been added to. But the second and third planes, providing repertoires of alternative forms, details and fixtures, have been extended with comparative ease.

Though one may still meet people who have lived in one house for fifty years or more, their number is understandably dwindling. Many of Dunroamin's semis have seen two or three, even half a dozen changes of ownership, and each owner has made his mark upon the house. During this period the values of the times through which successive occupiers have lived have undergone more than one metamorphosis, while the values of the occupiers themselves, and the means by which they have expressed them in their homes, have also gone through processes of change.

Communications have had much to do with this. At the outbreak of war there was one private car to every 25 persons in Britain; by 1966 one in every two households had a car, while of those in the professional, managerial and intermediate non-manual classes (which presumably included a large proportion of households in the suburb), three-quarters owned one or more. [13] This increased mobility could take families away from the suburb to town or country, work or pleasure as they wished. On the other hand, television brought the world into their homes. Two years after the war, the proportion of the adult population with a TV in the home was around two in a thousand. As early as 1964, over nine out of every ten adults had television in their homes. [14] The effects on values and living patterns have been considerable, if much debated.

To Dennis Chapman, writing in 1955 on the results of work done some years earlier, the 'concentration of interest and energy of the parents in the cultivation of the home, which is reflected in its increased size and elaboration', conflicted with the responsibilities of the family in raising children. The problem may arise when the home 'may become dysfunctional for the society as a whole'. [15] But if the high-rise developments that were then on the drawing board were to display their 'dysfunction' in an alarmingly short space of time, the semis in Dunroamin did not.

On the contrary, in spite of increased private mobility and, through television, exposure to alluring facets of the larger world, Dunroamin continued to thrive as a focus for family life. Moreover, the drift to the South-East, the spiralling prices of houses and the persistent failure of any government to meet its housing targets, have seen the material value of inter-war semis increase. This, in turn, has promoted further concentration on the house as commodity as well as home – an inducement to adapt, extend or enhance the property, whilst meeting the changing needs of successive owners.

How this has happened and how it relates to other aspects of post-war housing is beyond the scope of the present work. Sufficient to note that the processes of maturation, adaptation and change have taken, and are taking, place and that the suburb's semis have proved remarkably capable of accommodating different needs. In view of the unremitting hostility which has been directed against Dunroamin, it is necessary, in conclusion, to summarise our findings. These are essentially concerned with the period of Dunroamin's growth, when the semis in the suburbs prepared the stage for the enactment of evolving living patterns which may persist, we believe, beyond the end of this century.

Criticisms of the suburb by architects, environmentalists and other writers have been sustained over many decades. Their opinions cannot be peremptorily dismissed, and many of their fears were undoubtedly justified. There is no question that immense areas of agricultural land were consumed, with little overall consideration to planning constraints and regulations. Once built, there were many suburbs where the houses were poorly made, inadequately equipped and finished, and dull in the environment that they created. But it is certainly wrong to assume that this applied to the majority of Dunroamin's suburbs; we would contend that the opposite is probably the case. Until some kind of inventory and overall evaluation of the suburbs of the time is undertaken, such a view cannot be substantiated or refuted. Our spot surveys in differing parts of the country suggest, however, that a high proportion of suburban houses were substantially built and, except where economic constraints were the tightest, created pleasant environments which were well appreciated by their residents.

Architects of the period, especially those committed to the new movement in design, found the pervasive semi-detached house in the growing suburbs unacceptable as a type. To quite an extent, the apparent non-employment of architects must have seemed as a conspiracy to rob qualified designers of the opportunity to exercise their skills and training in the interests of the community. They can indeed be forgiven their anger and frustration over this. However, to their discredit, they sought to engage in social engineering, assuming with no supporting evidence, that 'decent' (the term was much used) modern design was what the populace needed in the interests of the community rather than the individual. Architectural writers presumed to speak for the people, asserting in effect, that they knew what was best for them. When the development and sales of the new estates continued unabated they resorted to pleas, denigration or contempt.

In the view of these writers, often repeated, the move to the suburbs was an escape from the challenge of the city, from responsibility, from reality. They assumed moreover, that the Dunroaminer would not be happy in the environment in which he was 'trapped', but in turn would seek to escape from that too. There was much talk of the 'suburb from which there was no escape', as if some kind of Nemesis was pursuing the unfortunate victim of suburban living.

201

Though there was no sociological evidence to support it, and no indication of independent investigation to remedy the omission, architects and writers repeatedly stated that the suburb was isolating, that no sense of community could be engendered there, and that its occupants would withdraw into 'individualism'. This was, in itself, a crime against the community; communality was the ideal which architects believed was desirable (for others, if not for themselves). The opinions expressed were based on vaporous and, we are inclined to believe, hypocritical policies. Architects were to gain substantially by the adoption of the multi-storeyed flat blocks they advocated.

Refusing to admit that the semis of Dunroamin had any positive values, architectural writers considered the houses and their collective layout as mindless examples of non-design. Yet Dunroamin has great design consistency, which was unwittingly acknowledged by the fact that its *extreme* consistency was itself a source of criticism and of the frequent assertions of monotony. Non-design would have led to totally random and undisciplined layouts. The consistency of suburban forms and layouts was evidence of organisation according to a coherent system of values; ones which did not happen to be the same as those of the architects.

The conflict of values which is at the heart of the whole matter could never be resolved in debate on the floor of a council chamber, for there were no vocal advocates for Dunroamin. The architectural profession and its protagonists had things entirely their own way when it came to the media, especially radio, newspapers, journals and books. And, as has been shown, other mass media offered no support for Dunroamin but consistently ignored the suburban ethos. Evidence for the values of the suburb was therefore, only to be found within them, in the details, furnishings and articles of display in garden and home within the planes of choice outlined previously. Dismissed as a sham, the subject of ridicule, or curtly rejected as bad taste, these expressions of Dunroamin's values were never read, interpreted or respected. The meanings that they bore, which might have done much to bridge the gap between the trained designer's aesthetic and the qualities and standards by which suburban residents lived, were totally overlooked.

In their arguments for the new, 'clean-and-decent' design it seems that architects considered that the forms and plain, undecorated, white surfaces of Modern Movement buildings were value-free. That they were as controlled by concepts of style, as loaded with the imagery of boat-decks and machines as Dunroamin was of cottages and Jacobean details, was never admitted. Modern Movement imagery spoke of clinical efficiency as Dunroamin spoke of domesticity. Builders and developers were far closer to their prospective house purchasers than were the members of the design profession of the period. Though they drew from the designs of Voysey, Baillie Scott and Unwin they adapted them extensively to fit the needs of their middle-class clients. Perhaps it was this that led to the eclipse of the generation of Arts and Crafts architects for so many years.

Myths about the suburbs and suburban living abounded. From the old canard of 'keeping up with the Joneses' to the emphasis on status-seeking that was assumed to be characteristic of the Dunroamin milieu, prejudice was reinforced and justified by endlessly repeated, but unverified suppositions. Why were these beliefs and myths so prevalent among architects, and why were they so vigorously propagated? Was it because the alternative, perhaps the truth, was too unbearable to contemplate; that the semi in the suburb met precisely the physical, material, emotional and symbolic needs of its occupants? Did they fear that the speculative builders of the Twenties and Thirties, with grass-roots values, similar origins, modest building skills and little or no architectural expertise had somehow got it right? Was the tireless condemnation of them and the belittling of their occupants as childish or child-like, status-seeking, tasteless and ordinary in itself an escape from reality? Committed to a confused ideology, certain of the virtues of a concept of architecture that derived from the writings of Le Corbusier and the teachings of the Bauhaus; convinced of its capacity to design a bright new world of glass, steel and concrete that would provide a desirable environment for members of all classes – the architectural profession was obliged to take an arrogant and aggressive posture.

Professional designers found it impossible to accept the reality that Dunroamin represents, not escape but arrival, not status-seeking so much as achievement, not anomie but neighbourliness, not isolation but identification, not anonymity but individuality. They, and the majority of their successors today, have not been prepared to consider that the buildings in their original form, and the ways in which they were extended and modified, have been expressive of the changing values within Dunroamin – but seldom of dissatisfaction with it.

There are many questions concerning the inter-war suburbs, and some of these may never be satisfactorily answered. The extent that the builder's developments were a direct response to the needs of intending house-owners cannot be established with accuracy; the possibility, even probability, that the tastes of Dunroamin were shaped *by* speculative housing always remains. It could be argued that within the economic range there were few available alternatives to prospective buyers apart from those offered within the semi-detached houses of builders in a given locality. While the truth of this is not really in question, the success of housing of this type suggests that by a subtle alchemy the combination of Arts and Crafts domestic design, speculative development and house-purchasers' needs and desires, produced a model which had wide appeal to the newly suburbanised middle class.

It has been stated here that Dunroamin created a 'successful' environment, but it would be right to question the criteria by which it could be counted a success. From the position of the suburban family, it provided an environment where there was sufficient uniformity to feel a sense of identity with other houses in the street or district, and enough variety to provide interest while walking to the park, the shops or the station. For the average family the three-bedroomed model made adequate provision, while there was sufficient detachment, physical or symbolised, for it to retain its unity. These aspects were unrecognised by architects, writers and sociologists who were wholly committed to a single ideology and a single conception of architecture. The fact that their concepts largely failed when they assumed power and realised their housing projects holds many lessons for architects today.

There are signs that some architects, following the lead of Ralph Erskine in the Byker renewal project, Newcastle, have been consulting with prospective householders and providing greater opportunities for individualisation. Here though, the scale of the units is often mean, the gardens and yards shrunken, the materials often poor and crudely finished. Other architects, working under different financial constraints and for a different sector of the community, might well gain from both Erskine's example and that of Dunroamin. But it is not only a matter of using forms and materials, such as the designers of the Hillingdon Civic Centre, Robert Matthew, Johnson, Marshall and Partners, attempted to do. Situated within a suburban milieu it succeeded neither in relating to the local housing nor in communicating the messages of a civic centre. Individual-isation would be peremptorily dealt with here. Younger architects have recently viewed Dunroamin as a source of design details to be plundered and antho-logised, taking features of brickwork, bays, gables and porches for re-use in a sophisticated eclecticism. The process smacks of condescension; Dunroamin is not a bran-tub offering easy prizes for any designer who dips into it. The lessons that are to be found there are not so casually learned.

Nor it seems, is there much willingness to do so. On the threshold of the Eighties the joint resources of the Arts Council of Great Britain and the Victoria and Albert Museum were co-ordinated in a major exhibition at the Hayward Gallery, London. Entitled *Thirties: British Art and Design Before the War* it had many hundreds of exhibits. One category was devoted to 'Architecture: The Modern Movement', another to 'Architecture: a Spectrum of Styles'. In the latter, one sub-section (8.66) was called 'Speculative Housing' and comprised photographs

'Victims' of the housing boom as shown in the Thirties Exhibition,
Hayward Gallery, London, 1979–80 (Architectural Press)

of Rectory Gardens, Edgware and 'superior semi-detached homes, Becontree Estate'. Dunroamin was represented by a single photograph entitled *The Promise of Suburban Bliss*. Its caption read: 'Victims of the Thirties building boom. The Borders family outside their jerry-built house, aptly named *Insanity*'.[16] Fifty years after, the Establishment of architects and critics clings tenaciously to its clichés.

NOTES

Introduction

1 Thorns, David C., *Suburbia*, MacGibbon and Kee, 1972, p. 83.

2 Bonham, Reyner, *Los Angeles: The Architecture of Four Ecologies*, Allen Lane, the Penguin Press, 1971, p. 172.

3 Auden, W. H., and Isherwood, Christopher, *The Dog Beneath the Skin*, Faber, 1947, p. 117.

4 Freeman, T. W., *The Conurbations of Great Britain*, Manchester University Press, 1959, p. 139.

5 e.g. Briggs, Asa, *History of Birmingham, Vol. 11*, Oxford University Press, 1952, pp. 229–35.

6 *Census of England and Wales, 1931*, Preliminary Report, pp. 63–5, and Greater London Planning Committee, *Second Report*, pp. 23–4.

7 Mowat, Charles Loch, *Britain Between the Wars, 1918–1940*, Methuen, 1956; 1962, p. 227.

8 Bellman, Sir Harold, *Britain in Recovery*, 1945, pp. 397–437; 409–416.

9 Bowley, Marian, *Housing and the State, 1919–1944*, George Allen & Unwin, 1945, pp. 135–58; 271. Between the signing of the Armistice in November 1918 and April 1939, 4,309,425 houses of all kinds were built.

10 Bertram, Anthony, *Design*, Pelican Books, Harmondsworth, 1938, pp. 20–1.

11 Ibid., p. 35.

12 Fry, Maxwell, 'The New Britain Must be Planned', *Picture Post* Vol. 10. No. 1. 4 January 1941, p. 17.

13 Kelsall, Freda, and Longmate, Norman, *How We Used to Live*, Yorkshire Television Ltd, 1975, p. 39.

14 Anthony, Hugh, *Houses: Permanence and Prefabrication*, Pleiades Books, 1945, p. 61 and jacket notes.

15 Halsey, A. H. (ed.), *Trends in British Society since 1900*, Macmillan, 1972, p. 311, Table 10.24.

16 Howell, William, 'What's Wrong with Modern Architecture?' Interview with Nicholas Taylor, BBC Radio 4, 8 February 1972.

17 Ibid.

18 Taylor, Nicholas, *The Village in the City*, Temple Smith, 1973, pp. 107, 174, 208. See also, 'The Queer Bash Killers', *Sunday Times Magazine*, 7 February 1971.

19 The destruction of the Pruett-Igoe Housing Project, St Louis (built 1955, dynamited 1972) is considered by some

critics to have heralded the end of the Modern Movement.

20 Fry, Maxwell, loc. cit.

21 Webb, Michael, *Architecture in Britain Today*, Country Life, Feltham, 1969, p. 79.

22 Richards, J. M., *The Castles on the Ground*, illustrated by John Piper, Architectural Press, 1946.

23 Richards, J. M., *Memoirs of an Unjust Fella*, Weidenfeld and Nicolson, 1980, p. 188.

24 Jencks, Charles, *The Language of Post Modern Architecture*, Academy Editions, 1977. For the debate on Post-Modernism, see for example, *Architectural Design*, 4, 1977; 1, 1978; 8–9, 1979.

1 One of the Greatest Evils
Dunroamin and the Modern Movement

1 Morris, William, *Signs of Change*, Reeves and Turner, 1888, pp. 29–30.

2 Howard, Ebenezer, *Garden Cities of Tomorrow*, 1902, reprinted Faber, 1965, p. 145.

3 Baillie Scott, M. H., 'An Ideal Suburban House', *The Studio*, Vol. IV, 1894–5, pp. 127–32.

4 Simon, Alfred, 'Good and Cheap – A Reply', *Journal of the Design and Industries Association*, No. 9, 1918, pp. 31–4.

5 Baillie Scott, M. H., 'Good and Cheap – A Reply', *Journal of the Design and Industries Association*, No. 10, 1918, pp. 23–4.

6 Long, Lord, quoted in: Ward, Mary and Neville, *Home in the Twenties and Thirties*, Ian Allen, 1978, p. 8.

7 Lethaby, W. R., 'Housing and Furnishing', *The Aethenaeum*, 21 May 1920, reprinted in Lethaby, W. R., *Form in Civilization*, London, 1922, pp. 35–45.

8 Davidge, W. R., *London in the Future*, T. Fisher Unwin, 1921.

9 Davies, Crossley, 'Houses, but No Homes', *Architects Journal*, 7 February 1923.

10 Clarke, A., *The Story of Blackpool*, 1923, quoted in Barker, Theo (ed.), *The Long March of Everyman*, Penguin, 1975, p. 236.

11 Williams-Ellis, Clough and Amabel, *The Pleasures of Architecture*, Jonathan Cape, 1924, p. 17.

12 Priestley, J. B., 'Houses', *The Saturday Review*, 11 June 1927, pp. 897–9.

13 Williams-Ellis, Clough, *England and the Octopus*, Geoffrey Bles, 1928, pp. 12–16; 140–1.

14 Corbusier, Le (trans. Etchells, F.), *Towards a New Architecture (Vers Une Architecture)*, Architectural Press, 1927.

15 Corbusier, Le, quoted in Boudon, Philippe, *Lived-in Architecture, Le Corbusier's Pessac Revisited*, Lund Humphries, 1972, p. 29.

16 Boumphrey, Geoffrey and Coates, Wells, 'Modern Dwellings for Modern Needs', *The Listener*, 24 May 1933, pp. 819–22, reprinted in Benton, Charlotte (ed.), *Documents – A Collection of Source Material on the Modern Movement*, Open University, Milton Keynes, 1975, pp. 71–6.

17 Corbusier, Le, *Le Charte d'Athènes*, Librairie Plon, Paris, 1943; trans. *The Athens Charter*, Grossman, New York, 1973, pp. 59–61.

18 Bertram, Anthony, *Design in Daily Life*, Methuen, 1937, pp. 98–9.

19 Goldfinger, Ernö. Conversation with the author, 24 September 1980. Although the editor of the Athens Charter wrote (page 40, ref 17): ' . . . the text presented here is the result of debates among the assembled representatives

. . .', Ernö Goldfinger does not recall that the suburbs were even mentioned during the Congress. His explanation for the discrepancy is that when Le Corbusier wrote up the findings in 1943 (without notes, since minutes were not kept) he projected his views on to the delegates.

20 Corbusier, Le, *La Ville Radieuse*, Paris, 1933; trans. *The Radiant City*, Faber, 1964, pp. 11–12.

21 Boumphrey, Geoffrey, and Cadbury, John, 'Suburbs or Satellites?', *The Listener*, 27 February 1935, pp. 347–9.

22 Boumphrey, Geoffrey, *Town and Country Tomorrow*, Thomas Nelson, 1940, pp. 21–4.

23 Bradshaw, Harold, C., 'The Suburban House', Chapter 4 in Abercrombie, Patrick (ed.), *The Book of the Modern House*, Hodder and Stoughton, 1937, pp. 130–40.

24 Ramsay, Stanley, 'The Ready Built House', Chapter 5 ibid.

25 Lancaster, Osbert, *Pillar to Post*, 1938; reprinted *A Cartoon History of Architecture*, John Murray, 1958, p. 15.

26 Betjeman, John, 'Slough', *Continual Dew*, John Murray, 1937; reprinted in *The Best of Betjeman*, Penguin, 1978, p. 24.

27 Betjeman, John, 'An Approach to Oxford', in *An Oxford University Chest*, John Miles, 1938; reprinted Oxford University Press, 1979, p. 107.

28 Betjeman, John, *Ghastly Good Taste*, Chapman and Hall, 1933; reprinted Anthony Blond, 1970, p. 111.

29 Richards, J. M., *The Castles on the Ground, The Anatomy of Suburbia*, Architectural Press, 1946; reprinted John Murray, 1973.

30 Tubbs, Ralph, *Living in Cities*, Penguin, Harmondsworth, 1942, p. 33

31 Sharp, Thomas, *Town Planning*, Penguin, Harmondsworth, 1940, pp. 40–5.

32 Briggs, Martin S., *How to Plan your House*, English Universities Press, 1937, p. 31.

33 Richards, J. M., *A Miniature History of the English House*, Architectural Press, 1938, p. 65.

34 Gloag, John, *The Englishman's Castle*, Eyre and Spottiswoode, 1945, p. 163.

2 Arcadia Becomes Dunroamin
Suburban Growth and the Roots of Opposition

1 Dickens, C., *The Old Curiosity Shop*, Oxford University Press, 1973, p. 326.

2 Engels, F., *The Condition of the Working Class in England*, trans. and ed. Henderson, W. O., and Chaloner, W. H., Blackwell, Oxford, 1971, p. 55.

3 Cooke Taylor, W., *Notes of a Tour in the Manufacturing Districts of Lancashire: in a series of Letters to his Grace the Archbishop of Dublin* (2nd edn., 1842) p. 164.

4 Darwin, C. R., *On the Origin of Species by Means of Natural Selection, or the Preservation of Favoured Races in the Struggle for Life*. See, for instance, the discussion of the relationship between Darwinism and the ethics of Herbert Spencer in pp. 21–2 of Donald Macrae's introduction to Spencer, H., *The Man Versus the State*, Penguin, 1969.

5 Grossmith, G., and Grossmith, W., *The Diary of a Nobody*, Penguin, 1965, p. 19.

6 Radford, E., *A Collection of Poems*, 1906, p. 60., quoted in Dyos, H. J., and Wolff, M., *The Victorian City*, Routledge and Kegan Paul, 1973, Vol. I, p. 300.

7 Moyr Smith, J., *Ornamental Interiors Ancient and Modern*, London, 1887,

p. 68, quoted in Girouard, M., *Sweetness and Light: the 'Queen Anne' Movement 1860–1900*, Clarendon Press, Oxford, 1977, opp. p. 1.

8 Horsfall, T. C., *The Example of Germany* (Supplement to 'Report of Manchester and Salford Citizens' Association for the Improvement of Unwholesome Dwellings and Surroundings of the People'), Manchester, 1904.

9 Parliamentary Debates 1907, Vol. 170, col. 202, quoted in Minett, J., *'Community' as an Ideal in British Town Planning* (unpublished PhD thesis, Oxford University), 1975, p. 109.

10 Sitte, Camillo, *Der Stadtbau*, 1889; trans. *The Art of Building Cities*, Reinhold, New York, 1945.

11 For the influence of Kate Greenaway and other book illustrators on architecture, see Girouard, op. cit., pp. 139–51; and Ward, C., 'The House that Jack Built', *Bulletin of Environmental Education*, 88–9, Aug–Sept 1978, pp. 4–26.

12 Ashbee, C. R., *Should we Stop Teaching Art*, London, 1911, p. 23, quoted in Macleod, R., *Style and Society: Architectural Ideology in Britain 1835–1914*, RIBA, 1971, p. 128.

13 Sixty-nine architects and artists sent a 'memorial' protest regarding this matter to the RIBA in March 1891. This was followed in 1892 by the publication of a collection of thirteen essays by leading practitioners entitled *Architecture, A Profession or an Art?* For discussion, see Macleod, op. cit., Chapter 8.

14 The rise of the Liverpool Manner is discussed in Reilly, C. H., *Scaffolding in the Sky*, Routledge, 1938.

15 Macartney, M., 'The Practical Exemplar of Architecture', in *The Architectural Review*, Vol. XIX, April 1906, p. 155.

16 Ibid., p. 155.

17 Budden, L., 'The Standardisation of Elements of Design in Domestic Architecture', *Town Planning Review*, Vol. 6, 1916, p. 240.

18 Ibid., p. 240.

19 Adshead, S., 'The Standard Cottage', *Town Planning Review*, Vol. 6, 1916, p. 245. (Adshead was highly aware of Liverpool ideas, having been Professor of Civic Design there from 1909 to 1914.)

20 Ibid., p. 245.

21 Budden, op. cit., p. 240.

22 For discussion of munition workers' housing schemes, see Pepper, S., and Swenarton, M., 'Home Front: Garden Suburbs for Munition Workers', *Architectural Review*, Vol. CLXIII, No. 976, June 1978, pp. 366–76.

23 Extract from the King's Speech to Representatives of the Local Authorities and Societies at Buckingham Palace, *The Times*, 12 April 1919, quoted in Burnett, J., *A Social History of Housing 1815–1970*, David and Charles, Newton Abbot, 1978 (University Paperback edition 1980).

24 Adshead, op. cit., p. 244.

25 Heath, W. H., 'Town Planning and Density' (11), in Betham, E. (ed.), *House Building 1934–1936*, Federated Employers' Press, London, 1934.

26 Pawley, M., *Home Ownership*, Architectural Press, London, 1978, p. 68.

27 For a detailed description of the development of the Building Societies, see Cleary, E. J., *The Building Society Movement*, Elek, 1965.

28 Richards, J. M., *An Introduction to Modern Architecture*, Penguin, 1940, p. 106.

29 Gibberd, F., *The Architecture of England from Norman Times to the Present Day*, Architectural Press, 1938, p. 42.

30 Betham, E. (ed.), op. cit., particularly p. 112.

31 For a discussion of Hill's work, see Gradidge, R., 'The Architecture of Oliver Hill', *Architectural Design*, Vol. 49, No. 10/11, 1979, pp. 30–41.

32 Allen, G., 'Building to Sell', in Betham, E. (ed.), op. cit., p. 139.

33 For discussion of these and other early Modern Movement houses in Britain see Gould, J., *Modern Houses in Britain 1919–39*, Society of Architectural Historians of Great Britain (Architectural History Monograph No. 1), 1977.

34 Laing, J., 'Increased Mortages on Builders' Guarantees', in Betham, E. (ed.), op. cit., p. 86.

35 Lloyd, A., 'The Architect, and Housing by the Speculative Builder', in ibid., p. 120.

3 A Celebration of Ambiguity
The Synthesis of Contrasting Values held by Builders and House Purchasers

1 McAllister, Gilbert and Elizabeth, *Town and Country Planning*, Faber, London, 1941, p. 72.

2 Pevsner, Nikolaus, *The Englishness of English Art* (expanded version of 1955 Reith Lectures), BBC, 1956.

3 Brett, Lionel, *The Things we See No 2 – Houses*, Penguin, 1947, p. 15.

4 London Transport Advertisement 1924, quoted in Graves, Robert, and Hodge, Alan, *The Long Weekend: A Social History of Great Britain, 1918–1939*, 1950, p. 172.

5 *Evening News*, 'Homeseekers' Guide', 19 February 1926, pp. 3, 10.

6 Innes, Brenda, 'A Comparison of Three Houses in Two South London Suburbs – Bromley and Hayes', unpublished thesis for History of Architecture and Design 1890–1939 course, Open University, Milton Keynes, 1978, p. 10.

7 *Daily Telegraph*, 'Modern Homes', 20 September 1935, p. 23.

8 Baldwin, Stanley, quoted in 'The Village of New Ideas', *Daily Mail Ideal Home Exhibition Catalogue 1927*, London, 1927, p. 101.

9 Allen, G., 'Building to Sell', Chapter 14 in Betham, E. (ed.), op. cit., p. 149.

10 *Daily Mail Ideal Home Exhibition Catalogue 1927*, Advertisement for the Potters Bar Estate, London, 1927, p. 109.

11 Saleeby, C. W., *Daily Mail Ideal Home Exhibition Catalogue 1927*, 'Sunlight in the Ideal Home', London, 1927, pp. 103–4.

12 Unwin, Sir Raymond, 'Introduction', in Betham, E. (ed.), op. cit., p. 20.

13 *Evening News*, 22 February 1936, Advertisement for Parkwood Estates, p. 12.

14 Allen, Gordon, *The Cheap Cottage and Small House*, Batsford, 1929.

15 Allen, G., op. cit., 1934, p. 149.

16 *Daily Telegraph*, 5 July 1935, Advertisement for Callowbrook Estate, p. 27.

17 Laing, J., 'Houses for Sale', chapter 21 in Betham, E. (ed.), op. cit., p. 203. Interview with J. Laing (reprinted from *The Builder*).

18 Abercrombie, Patrick, *The Book of the Modern House*, 'Introduction', Hodder and Stoughton, 1939, p. xix.

19 Masterman, C. F. G., *The Condition of*

England, 1909, new edition 1960, pp. 57–8.

20 Orwell, George, *Coming up for Air*, Victor Gollancz, 1939; reprinted Penguin, 1962, p. 13.

21 Sinclair, Robert, *Metropolitan Man, The Future of the English*, George Allen and Unwin, 1937, p. 106.

22 Neal, Harold, 'Houses for Sale', chapter 21 in Betham, E. (ed.), op. cit., p. 207. Interview with Harold Neal.

23 Burnett, John, *A Social History of Housing 1815–1970*, Methuen, 1980, p. 244.

24 Ibid., p. 260.

25 Hughes, M. V., *A London Family between the Wars*, Oxford University Press, 1940; reprinted 1979, p. 46.

26 Way, Peter, 'Once it was all Fields', *Sunday Times Magazine*, 11 February 1968.

27 Daily Express Publications, *The Home of Today – Its Choice, Planning, Equipment and Organisation*, c. 1935, p. 8.

28 *Daily Mail Ideal Home Exhibition Catalogue 1927*, Advertisement for The Universal Housing Co. Ltd, p. 113.

29 Innes, Brenda, op. cit., p. 8.

30 Hobbs, G. Bryant, 'Buying an Estate House', *Good Housekeeping*, Vol. 24, 1933, p. 115.

31 Allen, Gordon, op. cit., p. 145.

32 Donner, Peter F. R., 'Treasure Hunt', *Architectural Review*, November 1942, p. 127.

33 *Evening News*, 19 February 1926, op. cit.

34 *Evening News*, 'Homeseekers' Guide', 22 February 1936, pp. 4, 12.

35 Cutler, Ben, *Ideal Homes in North Harrow* (sales brochure) c. 1930, quoted in Cooper, Elizabeth, *Pinner Streets Yesterday and Today*, Pinner and Hatch End Local Historical and Archaeological Society, Vol. V, 1976, p. 46.

36 *Daily Telegraph*, Advertisement for Geo. Wimpey and Co., 25 October 1935, p. 27.

37 Bundock, J. D., 'Speculative Housebuilding and some Aspects of the Activities of the Suburban Housebuilder within the Greater London Outer Suburban Area 1919–39', unpublished thesis for M.Phil, University of Kent, 1974, p. 248.

38 *Daily Telegraph*, 6 September 1935, Advertisement for Comben & Wakeling, p. 23.

39 Coad, Roy, *Laing, The Biography of Sir John W. Laing CBE*, Hodder and Stoughton, 1979, p. 97.

40 Laing, John, op. cit., p. 202.

4 Individualism or Community?
Private Enterprise Housing and the Council Estate

1 See Chapter 3 above.

2 For discussion of early LCC Cottage Estates see Beattie, S., *A Revolution in London Housing*, Architectural Press, 1980.

3 Unwin, R., *Town Planning in Practice: An Introduction to the Art of Designing Cities and Suburbs*, T. Fisher Unwin, 1909.

4 See, for example, the layout for cottages at Starbeck, Yorkshire, illustrated in Philpott, H. B., *Modern Cottages Villas and Bungalows*, John Dicks, 1914.

5 Hawkes, D., 'The Architectural Partnership of Barry Parker and Raymond Unwin', *Architectural Review*, Vol. CLXIII, No. 976, June 1978, pp. 327–32.

6 Tudor Walters Report, Parliamentary Papers 1918, Cd 9191, p. 49, para. 175.

7 Ibid. p. 4. para 4.

8 Ibid., p. 49, para 173.

9 Ibid., p. 49, para 174.

10 Ibid., p. 1.

11 Parker, B., 'Site Planning as Exemplified at New Earswick', *Town Planning Review*, Vol. XVII, No. 2, February 1937, p. 79.

12 Ibid., p. 180.

13 Tudor Walters Report, p. 36, para. 147.

14 Ibid., p. 12, para. 53.

15 Ibid., p. 12, para. 53.

16 Ibid. p. 46, para. 160.

17 Ibid., pp. 11–12, para. 53.

18 Ibid., p. 12, para. 53.

19 This idea is raised in Jones, G. S., *Outcast London: A Study in the Relationship Between Classes in Victorian Society*, Oxford University Press, 1972. It is developed in architectural terms by Tarn, J. N., *Five per Cent Philanthropy: An Account of Housing in Urban Areas 1840–1914*, Cambridge University Press, 1973; and shown to be an international phenomenon by Turkienicz, B., 'Utopia and Reality' (unpublished MA dissertation, Joint Centre for Urban Design, Oxford Polytechnic), 1979.

20 Tudor Walters Report, p. 18, para. 66.

21 Ibid., p. 18, para. 67 and illus. No. 11A, p. 19.

22 Ibid., p. 24, para. 83.

23 Ibid., p. 24, para. 83.

24 Ibid., p. 37, para. 149.

25 Ibid., p. 37, para. 150.

26 Ibid., p. 37, illus. 23.

27 Laing, J., 'Houses For Sale' (1), in Betham, E. (ed.), op. cit., p. 204.

28 Ibid., pp. 202–3.

29 Ibid., p. 203.

30 Tudor Walters Report, p. 18, para. 66.

31 Ibid., p. 18, para 66.

32 See Murphy, J., *The Semi-detached House: Its Place in Suburban Housing*, Housing Research Unit, Dublin, 1977, p. 57.

33 Tudor Walters Report, p. 25, para. 86.

34 Ibid., p. 18, para. 67.

35 Allen, G., 'Building to Sell', in Betham, E. (ed.), op. cit., p. 145.

36 Tudor Walters Report, p. 18, para. 67.

37 Unwin, R., 'The Value of Good Design in Dwellings', in Betham, E. (ed.), op. cit., p. 22.

38 Tudor Walters Report, p. 36, para. 147.

39 Lloyd, A., 'The Architect and Housing by the Speculative Builder', in Betham, E. (ed.), op. cit., p. 128.

40 See, for example, Collison, P., *The Cutteslowe Walls: A Study in Social Class*, Faber, 1963, p. 41; particularly Table 7: 'Superiority and Inferiority: Other Estate Compared with Self'.

41 Scott, L., 'Preservation of the Countryside' in Betham, E. (ed.), op. cit., p. 33.

42 When the local authorities turned to Modernism after the Second World War, Neo-Georgian began to lose its 'council house' connotations, and was taken over by the speculative builder because of its inherent cheapness. Even so, speculative Neo-Georgian differed from its local-authority forerunner in that it incorporated many of Dunroamin's 'individualising' characteristics. For example, terraces were often staggered on plan so as to express the individual houses; thus producing an effect which was alien to the spirit of both 'genuine' Georgian and its inter-war council house derivative.

43 Collison, op. cit., p. 76.

44 *Oxford Mail*, 20 May 1935, quoted in Collison, op. cit., pp. 67–8.

45 See Collison, op. cit., p. 36, Table 3.

5 Great Expectations
Suburban Values and the Rôle of the Media

1 The architect was the author's father, W. Norman Oliver, then employed in the Architects' Department of Gaumont-British. Further details in this chapter have been supplied by Mrs D. I. Oliver.
2 Young, Michael, and Willmott, Peter, *The Symmetrical Family: A Study of Work and Leisure in the London Region*, Routledge and Kegan Paul, 1973. The authors state that only 10 per cent of all women in Britain were in employment in 1931. See p. 101.
3 Hopkins, Harry, *The New Look*, Secker and Warburg, 1963, p. 328.
4 Anon., *The Home of Today*, Daily Express Publications, n.d. (c. 1935). See also Minter, Davide C., *The Complete Home Book*, Vols. 1 and 2, Gresham Publishing Company, 1937.
5 Radio Luxembourg on Long Wave 1300 M. Band might be considered an exception. A commercial station, it transmitted in English. This was also the period of radio hams, and amateur transmitting/receiving 'stations' proliferated in Dunroamin's back gardens.
6 Quoted in McCarthy, Albert, *The Dance Bands: The Dancing Decades from Ragtime to Swing, 1910–1950*, Spring Books, 1974, p. 77.
7 Halsey, A. H. (ed.), *Trends in British Society since 1900*, Macmillan, 1972, p. 558, Table 16.19.
8 See Sharp, Dennis, *The Picture Palace*, Hugh Evelyn, 1969, for a full account of the development of the cinema.
9 Halsey, op. cit., p. 559, Table 16.20.
10 Manvell, Roger, *Film*, Pelican.

11 For discussions of documentaries see Arts Enquiry Report, *The Factual Film*, Oxford University Press, 1947. For a wider discussion of films of the period seen in perspective see Rotha, Paul, *The Film Till Now*, Jonathan Cape, 1930, and the revised edition, Vision Press, 1949.
12 Mayer, J. P., *The Sociology of Film—Studies and Documents*, Faber, 1946, p. 258.
13 Exact figures relating incidence of crimes in suburban areas with those of the inner city have not been available. These conclusions are drawn from an examination of newspaper reports of the mid Thirties.

6 The Owner Makes his Mark
Choice and Adaptation

1 See, for instance, Allen, E. (ed.), *The Responsive House*, MIT Press, Cambridge, Mass., 1974; Habraken, N. J., *Supports: An Alternative to Mass Housing*, MIT Press, Cambridge, Mass., 1972; Lerup, L., *Building the Unfinished: Architecture and Human Action* (Library of Social Research Vol. 53), Sage, 1977.
2 Part-works which enabled the purchaser to build up volumes in instalments included the fortnightly *Harmsworth's Household Encyclopedia*, whose six volumes concluded in 1924. A decade later, *The Handyman's Practical Enquire Within* followed in a similar vein. Advice of a more permanent kind was available in books such as *How to Own and Equip a House*, Bateman, 1925; Minter, M., *The Book of the House*, London, 1925; and *The Complete House Book*, Gresham, 1937.

3 See, for example, Gibson, J. J., *The Senses considered as Perceptual Systems*, Houghton Mifflin, Boston Mass., 1966.

4 Halsey, A. H., *Trends in British Society Since 1900: A Guide to the Social Structure of Britain*, Macmillan, 1972, p. 310, Fig. 10.1.

5 Anon., *The Complete Illustrated Home Book*, Associated Newspapers, London, undated, p. 9.

6 Ibid., p. 111.

7 For discussion, see Cowan, P., 'Studies in the Growth, Change and Ageing of Buildings', in *Transactions of the Bartlett Society*, 1, Bartlett School of Architecture, London, 1964. See also Musgrove, J., and Doidge, C., 'Room Classification' in *Architectural Research and Teaching*, Vol. 1, No. 1, May 1970, pp. 31–6.

7 The Galleon on the Front Door
Imagery of the House and Garden

1 Annual Report of the Medical Officer of Health of the City of London, 1927. Quoted in Sinclair, Robert, *Metropolitan Man: the Future of the English*, George Allen and Unwin, 1937, p. 177.

2 Quennell, Marjorie, and Quennell, C. B. J., *A History of Everyday Things in England*, Part Four: 'The Age of Production, 1851–1948', B. T. Batsford, 1948 (4th edn), pp. 133–5.

3 Quennell, Marjorie, and Quennell, C. B. J., *The Good New Days*, B. T. Batsford, 1935. Photographs and captions, Figs 65, 68, 71, 80.

4 Pearson, S. Vere, *London's Overgrowth and the Causes of Swollen Towns*, C. W. Daniel, 1939, pp. 38–9.

5 *Economist*, 8 May 1937, supplement on London. Quoted in Pearson, op. cit., p. 40.

6 Ibid.

7 North Harrow Ratepayers Association, letter to the *Evening Standard*, May, 1932. Quoted in Sinclair, op. cit.

8 Pevsner, Nikolaus, *Middlesex*, 'Buildings of England', Penguin, 1951, p. 103.

9 Gloag, John, *Design in Modern Life*, George Allen and Unwin, 1934; reprinted 1946, pp. 19–20.

10 Bertram, Anthony, *Design*, Pelican, 1938, p. 58.

11 Bayley, Stephen, *The Garden City*, Unit 23, Open University Press, 1975, provides a good summary of influences on the style.

12 Simpson, Duncan, 'Beautiful Tudor', *History of Taste*, No. 3, *Architectural Review*, Vol. CLXII, No. 695, July 1977, pp. 29–36.

13 Paterson, Oscar, 'Modern Stained Glass' in *Modern British Architecture and Decoration* (ed. Charles Holme), *The Studio* Special Number, 1901, p. 26.

14 Ibid., illustrations, p. 144–6.

15 *Catalogue No. 66*, The Metal Agencies Co. Ltd, Bristol, September 1937, p. 990.

16 Ollett, F. A., *Alfred Stevens 1817–1875*, 'Dorset Worthies No. 7', Dorset Natural History and Archaeological Society, Dorchester, 1963, p. 4.

17 Walt Disney's full-length cartoon film *Snow White and the Seven Dwarfs*, 1938, depicted the dwarfs as animated garden gnomes.

18 Huygen, Will, and Poortvliet, Rien, *Gnomes*, English edn. New English Library, 1977.

8 A Lighthouse on the Mantelpiece
Symbolism in the Home

1 Young, Michael, and Willmott, Peter, *The Symmetrical Family – A Study of Work*

and Leisure in the London Region, Routledge and Kegan Paul, 1973.

2 The full range of 36 designs was illustrated in Handicrafts 1931 Annual, Odhams Press for Handicrafts, September 1930.

3 Several of these favourite paintings were on show at the National Gallery, the Tate Gallery and the Wallace Collection, from which large prints in colour or half-tone could be purchased.

4 Weightman, John, 'A View of the Côte d'Azur', Encounter 73, October 1959, pp. 8–11.

5 See for example illustration in Desroches-Noblecourt, C., Tutankhamen, Penguin, 1965, p. 98.

6 Other songs of the period are to be found, for comparison, in Spaeth, Sigmund, A History of Popular Music in America, Phoenix House, 1948.

7 Veblen, Thorstein, The Theory of the Leisure Class, 1899; first published UK, 1925; 3rd imp. George Allen and Unwin, 1957, pp. 82–3.

8 Ibid., p. 154.

9 Jones, Peter Lloyd, 'A Taste of Class', Architectural Review No. 984, February 1979, p. 77.

9 Learning from Dunroamin
Values and the Houses We Live in

1 Housing Advisory Committee, Houses We Live In, Ministry of Health, HMSO, May 1939, p. 28.

2 Ibid., pp. 34–5.

3 Lewis, Roy, and Maude, Angus, The English Middle Classes, Phoenix House, 1949, p. 85.

4 Woods, Shadrach, The Man in the Street: A Polemic on Urbanism, Penguin, 1975, p. 38.

5 Mumford, Lewis, The City in History: Its Origins, Its Transformations and Its Prospects, Secker and Warburg, 1961, p. 563.

6 Fairbrother, Nan, New Lives, New Landscapes, Architectural Press, 1970, p. 181.

7 Cook, Peter, 'The Suburban Ethic', Architectural Design, 9, 1974, p. 563.

8 Venturi, Robert; Scott-Brown, Denise; Izenour, Steven; Learning from Las Vegas, MIT Press, Cambridge, Mass., 1972.

9 Venturi and Rauch, Signs of Life: Symbols in the American City, Aperture for Smithsonian Institution, Washington DC, 1976, pp. 5–6.

10 Douglass, Harlan Paul, The Suburban Trend, Century Press, New York, 1925, p. 33.

11 Chapin, F. Stuart, Contemporary American Institutions, Harper, New York, 1935. See Chapter XIX, 'A Measurement of Social Status'; also discussion by Louis Wirth, 'Social Stratification and Social Mobility in the United States', Current Sociology, 11, No. 4, 1953–4, p. 293.

12 See Chapman, Dennis, The Home and Social Status, Routledge and Kegan Paul, 1955. Chapman applied Chapin's scale. See Chapter 7, 'The Measurement of Social Status'.

13 Halsey, op. cit., p. 541; p. 551, Table 16.9; p. 552, Table 16.11.

14 See Spraos, John, The Decline of the Cinema, George Allen and Unwin, 1962.

15 Chapman, loc. cit.

16 See Hayward Gallery Catalogue, Thirties: British Art and Design Before the War, Arts Council of Great Britain, October 1979, p. 184. The photograph of the 'Victims' is not illustrated.

SELECTED BIBLIOGRAPHY

Few books give more than a passing comment on the suburbs in Britain between the wars, and a list of recommended reading is necessarily brief. The following works are valuable for the reasons stated. Other references are cited in the Notes.

Background

BURNETT, J., *A Social History of Housing, 1815–1970*, David and Charles, Newton Abbot, 1978: Methuen (University Paperback), 1980. An important summary of all kinds of housing in Britain during the stated period, with good material on suburban growth.

DOBRINER, WILLIAM (ed.), *The Suburban Community*, Putnam, New York, 1958. Broad collection of American writing on 'theory and research in the sociology of the suburbs'.

JACKSON, ALAN A., *Semi-Detached London*, George Allen and Unwin, 1973. Excellent survey of 'suburban development, life and transport' in Greater London, from 1900–1939.

THORNS, DAVID C., *Suburbia*, MacGibbon and Kee, 1972. Considers the British suburbs as part of a world-wide phenomenon of suburban growth, and differentiates between the types.

Suburbs and Values

CHAPMAN, DENNIS, *The Home and Social Status*, Routledge and Kegan Paul, 1955. Evaluates by sociological methods, expressed in many charts, the 'making of the home' in, to a large extent, the suburbs.

LEWIS, ROY and MAUDE, ANGUS, *The English Middle Classes*, Phoenix House, 1949. Values of the middle classes, principally post-war but with many references to the Thirties.

MOWAT, CHARLES, LOCH, *Britain Between the Wars, 1918–1940*, Methuen, 1956, 1962. Wide-ranging analysis of the history, policies, mores and values of the Dunroamin period.

RICHARDS, J. M., *Castles on the Ground*, Architectural Press, 1946; reprinted John Murray, 1973. The first book to give serious consideration to the suburban environment in Britain.

TAYLOR, NICHOLAS, *The Village in the City*, Temple Smith, with *New Society*, 1973. Lively, unreferenced discussion of the suburbs and critique of post-war architecture and housing.

INDEX

Page numbers in italics refer to illustrations
(*n*) indicates note